Predictions for 2015

Revised Edition

Kurt B. Bakley

authorHOUSE®

AuthorHouse™
1663 Liberty Drive
Bloomington, IN 47403
www.authorhouse.com
Phone: 1-800-839-8640

Published by AuthorHouse   12/23/2014

ISBN: 978-1-4969-6138-9 (sc)
ISBN: 978-1-4969-6137-2 (e)

Dedication:
In memory of The Bakley Family?
If they don't heed the warnings of Billy Graham is
dead, someone on the roof, angels visitation in spirit
or physical and dreams and visions warning of these
impending disasters of a tidal wave and volcano
eruptions and to leave the area at a certain time and
go to a certain place. If you don't the mourning
is going on for you as Isaiah 61:1-3 predicts.

Contents

Acknowledgements.. ix

Introduction.. xi

Chapter One: Predictions for 2015 1

Chapter Two: The end... 25

Chapter Three: Chinese Yearly Cycles 34

Chapter Four: The Narrative of the carving.................... 36

Chapter Five: Final Notes.. 41

Chapter Six: The Carving... 157

Chapter Seven: Come to Christ...................................... 169

Appendix A: Recent prophecies fulfilled...................... 179

About the Author.. 245

Acknowledgements

Also a thank you to HarperCollins for their permission to use one of their drawings modified with arrows and letters from their book "Secrets of the great pyramid" by Peter Tompkins page 173. Used by permission. See drawing one.

Drawings 2-6 were drawn by me.

Every Bible quote in this book is from the Old King James Version which is in public domain.

Scripture quotations marked KJV are from the Holy Bible, King James Version (Authorized Version). First published in 1611. Quoted from the KJV Classic Reference Bible, Copyright © 1983 by The Zondervan Corporation.

Introduction

In this book I will show how coded messages in the Bible predict earthquakes and/or volcano eruptions for 2015. I also will show other predicted events using those codes for the year 2015. Chapter 7 of my book *Predictions for 2013-2014* shows how and where I get these codes for the predictions of the year 2015.

The predictions made in this book are sometimes based on Chinese astrology. In Chinese astrology there are 12 signs that rule one year every 12 years. Unlike our astrology that rules one month every year. The cycle of every 12 years means that predictions can be based on those yearly cycles. In another words the year 2015 minus cycles of 12 years backwards can tell us what will happen in 2015. Ecclesiastes 1:9 states that things that now happen happened in the past the same as the ancient Egyptians and Mayans believed.

Another difference of Chinese astrology is that it rules two hour time periods each day. Since there are 12 signs this covers a 24 hour time period of a day that each sign rules. The signs in our astrology don't do that. And in Chinese astrology the 12 signs also rule our 12 signs and 12 months. The polar opposites of these signs Chinese, or ours, are connected to the same date and time and event. If an event in July-August of 2015 is predicted, then in January-February of 2015 or 2018- 2019, the polar opposite, is when the same event or another event may happen.

Chinese astrology begins it New Year of its certain signs on the second new moon after the winter solstice. This means New Years Day is different each year and begins sometime in January or February each year. This makes our past year go into January-February by Chinese New Year's settings.

I also use in this book year/chapter codes of the Bible told of in Chapter 7: The Codes of my book *Predictions for 2013-2014*. This is where a chapter in the Bible means a certain modern day year plus or minus the Chinese 12 year cycle.

The Chinese Snake rules our Taurus sign and month of May. The city of Los Angeles is in the Taurus zone as told in chapter 7 of my other book *Predictions for 2013-2014* and is ruled by Leo. The Leo sign (lion) runs from July 21-23 to August 21-23 and with its cusp of seven goes to August 28-30. Does the term "Babylon the great is fallen, is fallen," in the book of Revelation 14:8 and 18:2 mean two times Los Angeles is hit by an earthquake? Are those two earthquakes the one on January 17, 1994 that hit Northridge and the other "one hour" away as Revelation 18:17 predicts? Change the hour to a day of 24 hours and then change to years added to 1994 and it equals 2018 into 2019 when the second earthquake happens in Los Angeles. See also Revelation chapter 6. Or is Babylon, a spiritual name for the U.S. and especially Los Angeles, fallen twice once in 1994 and then again in 2018-2019 right when the sun goes into a supernova and causes the earth to shake and be utterly destroyed just like Revelation 6:12-17 predicted? The "one hour" Babylon the great is fallen, is fallen that the book of Revelation 18:2-3, 6, 10 predicts in one hour or 60 minutes changed to six years added to 2013, counting each year or not, equals the years 2018-2019. The "wine of the wrath of her fornication" in (verse 3), could mean the wine harvest, which is July-August of 2015 and 2018-2019. Those months are in the fifth month (July-August) of the Bible's calendar as Zechariah 7:3, 5, 8:19 predicts for a fast to help stop very bad events from happening.

Revelation chapter 14 predicts in verse 8 that "Babylon is fallen, is fallen" by the middle angel of three. Could that be the half hour (=middle) of Revelation 8:1? Or is it three years as three angels trouble occurs for the U.S. (Babylon) on August 10, 2013, August 10, 2014, August 10, 2015? Or is Revelation six angels three more angels from August 10, 2016, August 10, 2017 and August 10, 2018, plus or minus three days or July-August of 2013-2018 as the first three angels then three more angels as years in the vine or grape harvest (=July- August) or wrath of God's winepress for those times and years that Revelation chapter 14 predicts? In Revelation chapter 14 predicts three angels then three more angels to make six angels or years. That equals six angels translated as six years plus the half a year as a half an hour (Revelation 8:1) from August 10, 2013 equals January 2019. It also could mean the three angels are the three woes on August 10, 2013, August 10, 2014, August 10, 2015 plus three and a half years from August 10, 2015 to January 21, 2019. That equals the three angels, plus three and a half angels as Revelation chapter 14 predicted. They all could mean trouble for Babylon (=U.S.) on all those exact dates, or on August 10, 2015 then on January 21, 2019. The second angel of three in Revelation chapter 14 is two or half of three added to three equals three and a half angels, or years, plus three more angels to make three more years. When you divide you always divide by two making two the half a year. Will the U.S. as Babylon is fallen, is fallen happen in Los Angeles in one of those years then in the end is again fallen totally just as Revelation 6:12-17 predicts on a lunar eclipse in January of 2019 to make two times Babylon (U.S.) is fallen? Is one of those two fallen the great tidal wave of July-August of 2015, then add three and a half years later it falls again totally in a supernova in January 21, 2019 on a full moon? The moon is given the number 2 as the second angel and the two fallen that Revelation 14:8 predicts. The second angel of Revelation chapter 14 when Babylon is fallen for the second time could mean the two great earthquakes that hit the U.S. (=Babylon) on August 10, 2013 and August 10, 2014, plus or minus three days. The year 2014 could mean the chapter number of Revelation chapter 14 as the year when the second great earthquake happens. Those two earthquakes would make Babylon (=U.S.) fall twice in two years from 2013-2014. Verse 8 of Revelation chapter 14 where Babylon (=U.S.) falls twice might mean our eighth month when it falls twice or August of 2013 and August of 2014. The smoke that rises up from her for ever as predicted in the book of Revelation would be the sun's smoke from its supernova at that time of January of 2019 six angels and a half hour, or half a year, from the first earthquake in Babylon (=U.S.) in 2013? Three angels from July-August of 2013-2015 and three angels from 2016-2018 and a half to January 21, 2019, when the seventh angel sounds its trumpet, which is the last of the three angels or three woes Revelation chapters 8, 10, 11 predicts as the last woe and last trumpet to sound at the very end.

Note: The exact hour and/or minutes of solar and lunar eclipses and full and new moons in this book and my other books may be off by several minutes or hours plus or minus because different books give different times. Why this is I don't know.

If this book fascinates you then read my other books titled *Predictions for 2016-2018, The Divine Code 3 and Predictions for 2013-2014.* Also read *About the Author* at the end of this book for all my other books you may want to read. It tells you where you can buy them because they are only available at a web site given. It will also tell you which ones to read first and how to read them, which is very important.

November 11, 2011

Kurt B. Bakley

Note: The introduction and first three chapters and the seventh chapter were written by the date above and has not been changed. This book is the Revised Edition of that book with three new chapters and six drawings added. I am the withholding power of the antichrist and false prophet and satan just as II Thessalonians chapter 2 predicts. That power is in wisdom of all my books if satan succeeds in destroying the U.S. and my publisher then the books of mine may disappear. But if God takes me and I die that power may be gone and the antichrist and false prophet and satan may prevail. But those who read all my books and remembers them will not be deceived by those three spirits. Those books will take the edge off of satan plans for a strong delusion by God revealing them before hand and in advance of these three spirits that come in UFO's and deceive with science. It may stop those three or take the sting or edge off their deception. And if the Lord establish these works of my hands (=books) as Psalms chapter 90 predicts and the Lord delayeth or tarries His Coming for about a 1000 years then my books will help the Saints to be faithful and righteous for those delays. See the book "The end of the days" by Arthur E. Bloomfield pages 258-261. This note and three new chapters are written by the date of February 14, 2015. The ancient Egyptian carving shows a lion looking backwards at its tail under Libra and near Virgo with his two front paws on a box with two or three wavy lines in it near a small ox and bird and ox horns on top of a man and the grime reaper with a sickle in his hand gives the dates of September 27, 2014 and September 24-27, 3005 A.D. which is the Chinese Year of the Ox when the end comes and the Second Coming of Christ happens to take His Saints who die or are alive who kept the faith and righteousness with great patience. Was this a prediction of an earthquake as the wavy lines on a Richter Scale, wavy lines of a stormy sea and wavy lines of a volcano eruption and tidal wave and a war or terrorist attacks on September 24-27, 2014-2015 and 3005 A.D.? Those dates are the end of Leo cusp star time, the beginning of Virgo star time and the beginning of Libra by old reckoning. If the Lord tarries from the first dates to the second dates don't become alarmed for this was prophesied in the Bible, Nostradamus and ancient Egyptian art like the carving seen in chapter Six. Don't be left behind or fall away under satan's plans of UFO's and Science because the Lord delayeth or tarries His Second coming for 1000 years just as Billy Graham taught long ago and Jesus predict people would laugh at end time prophecies when the antichrist, false prophet and satan deceives the world with his strong delusion. See Matthew chapter 24, Mark chapter 13, Luke chapters 17 and 21 and II Peter 3:1-18. Those prophecies predict not to be caught up in a holyday or Holiday (=Rosh Hashanah) or feast days and the last trump that Corinthians and Revelation predicted. One preacher claims an old tradition of blowing seven trumpets at the "feast of trumpets" or Rosh Hashanah, which is the Jewish New Year by their Civil calendar. Revelation chapters 10-11 predict the last of seven trumpets would be the very end of the world and Second Coming of Jesus. This is the faith and patience of the Saints who ready themselves and wait like Isaiah chapters 40-41 and 48 and Luke 21:19, 34-38 predicts. Please forgive me for the typo's in this part of the introduction and chapters 4-6. I was sick certain days plus my computer was getting bad and I didn't have much time to fix them or did I have the money to have it edited. Thus, typo's, spelling errors and bad grammar and English are in them, but I still think you can get the powerful message from them. It maybe what Ecclesiastes 5:6 means by you saying to the angel it is in error not only for the many typo's but also for the dates nothing happened on. You also must remember that when I give dates and years of 2014-2015 to predicted events it can mean some happen on those dates in 2014 and others in 2015. The "psycho" movie started filming on November 11, 1959. Is November 11, 2015 a date when these events happen? Tony Perkins who played in that movie was born April 4, 1932, which polar opposite is September 27, 2014 or 2015. Also the carving from ancient Egypt shows

Sagittarius the archer and horse (=Chinese Year 2014) shows the date of the JFK assassination on November 22, 1963. Is that a date of these events of this book predicted by some ancient prophecies for 2014 and/or 2015? See my books entitled "The boy who could predict earthquakes" and read this entire book for details of these predicted events. Other dates like March 20-21, 2015 a solar eclipse, April 4, 2015 a blood moon or lunar eclipse and September 27-28, 2015 another blood moon and the feast of tabernacles are all possible dates of the fulfillment's of these ancient prophecies recorded in this book. Jeremiah 51:46, Obadiah 1-6, Luke chapter 21, Deuteronomy chapter 32 and Amos chapters 1-2 all may be all giving the date of 32 years from 1981-1982 which equals 2013-2014 plus two years or 2014 and 2015 a double trouble years for earthquakes as those verses predict. They come to 2012-2013-2014+2=2014-2015-2016. Both Amos chapters 1- 2 and Luke chapter 21 predicts two years before an earthquake. Add two years top these dates and it equals 2014-2015-2016. That is the "by and by" or two years. And my writing in this book predicts war between Israel and Iran, but doesn't happen but is a rumor to happen then. And as Jeremiah 51:46 predicts a rumor one year (=September 24-28, 2014 or December 21-25, 28-29, 2014-2015) and nothing of a war with Iran, then the next year another rumor in this book and war or ruler against ruler as Zechariah chapter 14 predicts possibly on the feast of tabernacles on September 27-28, 2015 a blood moon. That chapter predicts not only a war, but also a earthquake.

The dream I had about showing many people my grand parents back woods along with the movie "Psycho" may both give the dates November 22, 2014 and November 11,

2015. My Grandfather being born February 12, 1893 would have a polar opposite that or August 12, 2014. The polar opposite that year he was born equals 2014 and the year he died was 1976 the Dragon Year (=2012). Add Shania Twain and one person next to her to make three or three months/years added on to August 12, 2012 equals November 10-11, 2015. The movie "Psycho" began filming on November 11, 1959 which polar opposite is 2013 adding three years to that date counting each year or starting by the Jewish Civil calendar equals November 11, 2015 when very great wars start, great earthquakes, great storms, great tidal waves, great volcano eruptions and any other man made or natural disasters happens. The exact date of my angel visitation with Bates Street or avenue was in August and may have been August 12, or 25, 1995 plus 12 equals August 12, 2007+2 years=August 12, 2015-2016, with two years added to the Dragon Year the year he died equals 2012+2=2014, which adding three or four months to that equals November 10-11, December 21-25, 28-29, 2014-2016 starting by the Jewish Civil calendar in 2015 in September- October equals 2016 from their calendar to ours. And as for November 22, 2014 we seen the Sagittarius sign of half horse and archer on the new moon equals that exact date. The "double" predicted in the Bible in Isaiah 61:7 and Zechariah 9:10-14 would make the date of November 11 be doubled or November 22, 2014 when some or all these events happen. Many people don't know it but November is the first month and New Year's Day in it by the old Anglo-Saxon calendar. Old Halloween is November 10-11. In that time we get the word "Hallow be thy name, thy kingdom come…." Was that a clue to these events happening in November of 2014 and 2015? See my book "End Time Signs II" for my dream and some other details about these things. Remember Jesus predicting pray that your flight be not in winter nor on the Sabbath Day (=Saturday to the Jewish people). See Matthew 24:19-20 and Colossians 2:16-17. To the Jewish calendar November is winter season and not fall or autumn as we believe. November 22, 2014 is a Saturday, new moon and when celebration of Halloween and New Years Eve and Day happen on October 31 and November 1 or November 10-12 by the old calendar. Isaiah chapter 18 predicts as a time of fire on the mountains, the blowing of the trumpet on the new moon and the holy day of the Jewish Sabbath (=Saturday). I read once how the ancients set fire on the mountain tops to get rid of evil spirits and the Jews do it to start a new moons by that same way or blowing a trumpet.

Final note: What to look for as signs to flee or move before hand so your life and possessions are spared. When you hear Billy Graham and/or Erich Von Daniken has died then flee from the U.S. East Coast and San Francisco-Seattle. Also look for dreams, visions, angel visitations and some one on the roof top as signs to flee these areas. Isaiah chapter 6 is our year of 2014 and it predicts a "tenth" which could not only mean December Latin for "ten", but also 10 years from date to date of December 21-25, 2024. It also could mean a Trinity of trouble and predicted events of this book for December 24-25, 28-29, 2014, 2015 and 2024 when the end comes for the America's. If these events of a San Francisco or Seattle earthquake comes true shortly after the death of Billy Graham and/or Erich Von Daniken and you see someone on the roof top and had dreams and visions about these events and a angel appears to you as a sparkling bluish-white light that makes you smile ear to ear then listen to what he says along with the dreams and visions. See Ecclesiastes that predicts to say not to the angel my books are false and in error or God may destroy you and all the works of thy hands.

Ten years later on December 21-25, 2024 move to New Zealand or Australia a year before hand if the events of December 24- 25, 28-29, 2014-2015 come true. This will save your life and that of your family and hold on to your possessions. If nothing happens on December 21-25, 28-29, 2014 and 2015 then don't worry about it. The Maya's may have predicted this date. But people calculated it wrong starting at a wrong date. December 21-25, 2012 nothing happened! But what about 12 years later a Chinese cycle to December 21-25, 2024? December 21, 2024 is a Saturday or the Jewish Sabbath Day, in winter and on a birthday of John the Baptist (December 24-25). Remember Jesus predicting in Matthew 24:19-20 and 11:12 to pray that your flight be not in winter or the Sabbath Day (=Saturday) or on John the Baptist birthday of December 24-25, 2024 when God shakes the heavens and earth with the eruptions of the super volcano in the midst of the U.S. destroying all of the U.S. and parts of the world. John the Baptist was born December 24-25, 5 B.C., which was the Chinese Year of the Dragon the same as December 21-25, 2024 is.

There are at least six predictions of these events and dates when Billy Graham dies or Erich Von Daniken dies till when people give gifts to one another as we all do around the world on those dates. See Luke 21:34-37, Haggai chapter 2, Revelation chapter 11, Jeremiah chapter 30 and two verses in Ecclesiastes which predicts the day of prosperity (=Christmas Day) is the same date as when the date of adversity (=trouble) happens and the other is a day of death is better then a day of birth according to John the Baptist birthday is on December 21- 25, 2014, 2015, 2024. Jeremiah chapter 30 mentions "merry" (=Merry Christmas) and "Thanksgiving" as times of trouble, which was cover earlier in this introduction the November dates and predicts near "Thanksgiving" in the U.S. Jeremiah chapter 30 is in Chapter/Year codes our year of 2014 the Chinese Year of the Horse. If on December 21-25, 2014 there is San Francisco or Seattle earthquake beware of a tidal wave in 2015 on those same dates. Then go thy way as Ecclesiastes 9:7 and Daniel 12:13 meaning leave the U.S. East Coast and Florida and the areas of San Francisco, Seattle and New Madrid before December 21-25, 28-29, 2015 comes. Thus, saving your family and possessions. The same holds true for you to move to New Zealand or Australia by December 21-25, 2024. Haggai chapter 2 ninth month and 24th day equals our calendar of December 24-25, 2014-2015 and 2024. And Song of Solomon chapters 2-3 equal our years of 2002-2003. The chapter 2 of that book predicts a man to travel up North after winter ends and spring time begins in 2015. Then chapter 3 of that book has people asking and wondering where their beloved is for he is gone.

If the tidal wave, earthquake, storm and Israeli Iran war doesn't happen on December 21-25, 2014 it may happen on December 21-25, 2015. In my book entitled "Predictions for 2013-2014" first chapter called Coded Earthquakes tells how to predict certain earthquakes by a one year anniversary with the second on a full moon. Some of these events may happen on December 21-25, 2014 and others in

December 21-25, 2015. December 25, 2015 is a full moon meaning in coded earthquakes a year before that date the first earthquake hits on December 21- 25, 2014. These dates could be the midst of the week Daniel 9:27 predicts. I often wondered how the antichrist could make peace between Israel and the world. It just seems impossible at least for satan, not God. That answer is he can't! He is not that clever or powerful. God is though. The 70th week of Daniel 9:27 happens 1000s of years ago according to The Ryrie Study Bible page 1235. The Ryrie Study Bible states that the antichrist was Antiochus Epiphanes who started a war with Israel for 2300 days predicted in Daniel chapter 8. The 2300 number of days is seven years or the 70th week by little less then 360 days of seven years or 250 days less. And just as the Bible predicted he stopped the daily sacrifice, offered a pig in the Jewish temple and place a statue of his god Jupiter in the Holy or Holies. It lasted for exactly three and a half years or midst of the week, till the Jewish people took back the Temple to its true worship on Christmas Day December 25, 165 B.C. They found some oil for their lamps they thought would last a coupe days, but miraculously lasted for eight days. Thus, the Holiday Hanukkah was born in the Chinese Year of the Rat the polar opposite of the Horse or December 24-25, 28-29, 2014 when again trouble happens for Israel on that year or next on the same date. Will Israel fight its enemies again like Haggai and Zechariah predicts? The four beasts and 24 elders of Revelation might be a clue to these same dates as the fourth month and 24th day translated from the Jewish Civil calendar to ours equals December 24-25, 2014 and 2015.

Amos 5:7-8 predicts a time when Orion, the seven stars (=Taurus), Gemini and Auriga The Charioteer are over head at midnight and seen till morning that we would see these events happen as predicted in this book. See Psalms 68:17, which predicts 20,000 Chariots (=Auriga The Charioteer) to come with angels as Revelation 3:22 predicts speaks to the saints warning them as I am about these events. They may even tell them of these books of mine. Amos 5:8 predicts to "turn the shadow of death into the morning and maketh the day dark with night that calleth for the waters of the sea and poureth them out upon the face of the earth." The day dark as night can mean the stopping of time making some places dark as night even in the day and at noon for three days. The shadow of death as the morning could mean a morning earthquakes and storms at these times of December 21-25, 28-29, 2014 and 2015. The waters of the sea pour out upon the face of the earth could mean the tidal wave that hits the U.S. East Coast at this time and dates by an earthquake and volcano eruption on a Island in the Canary Islands off the West Coast of Africa that has half the island split into or a crack in it from a 1949 great eruption and earthquakes. The volcano eruptions on these dates of December 21-25, 28-29, 2014 or 2015 would slide have the island into the sea causing a great tidal wave that heads across the Atlantic Ocean towards the East Coast of the U.S. See Revelation chapter 8 for details of this event.

The Wisdom of Solomon in the book The Apocrypha pages 190- 191 chapter 7:17-21 predicts the alterations of the solstices which if time is stopped on December 21-25, 2014 or 2015 for three days it would change the dates of the solstices and equinoxes. And places where time stops at night will make the day dark with night for three full days. Was this what Jesus meant by "shorten the days" in Matthew chapter 24 and Daniel 2:21-22 meant by changing times and seasons and removeth kings and set up kings. Are they the three kings or Presidents of Russia, U.S. and Iran who God soul loath or hateth? They are the three shepherds (=leaders) who God hatheth their souls and they are cut off (die in the first or one month) as Zechariah 11:8 predicts.

Chapter One

𝔓redictions for 2015

Does Revelation 8:1-13, 9:1-5 and chapters 11-12 predict three woes (troubles) to happen in August 10, 2013, August 10, 2014 and August 10, 2015, plus or minus three days? The one woe could cause smoke to come upon the earth covering a third of the stars, along with a very great earthquake and volcano eruption. Those events would cause a great mountain to be thrown into the sea causing a 100 or 2500-3000 feet high or more tidal waves to hit the Eastern Coast of Florida and the U.S. Read what the Bible predicts:

"And the second angel sounded, and as it were a great mountain burning with fire was cast into the sea: and the third part of the sea became blood;" Revelation 8:8. (Old King James Version).

"And the fifth angel sounded, and I saw a star fall from heaven unto the earth: and to him was given the key of the bottomless pit.

And he opened the bottomless pit; and there arose a smoke out of the pit, as the smoke of a great furnace; and the sun and the air were darkened by reason of the smoke of the pit."

Revelation 9:1-2 (Old King James Version).

"And the fourth angel sounded, and the third part of the sun was smitten, and the third part of the moon, and the third part of the stars; so as the third part of them was darkened, and the day shone not for the third part of it, and the night likewise.

And I beheld, and heard an angels flying through the midst of heaven, saying with a loud voice, Woe, woe, woe, to the inhabiters of the earth by reason of the other voices of the trumpet of the three angels, which are yet to sound!"

Revelation 8:12-13 (Old King James Version).

Is this describing a volcano eruption that smoke and ash covers over the third part of the U.S.? Is the fifth angel to sound that releases this smoke the fifth sign of our Zodiac, which is Leo the lion sign on August 10-11, 2015? Leo is ruled by the sun and fire where lava comes up from hell and causes volcanoes to erupt with smoke and ash. The smoke and ash then destroys trees, grass and crops causing a great famine, which locust are known to eat the crops causing crop failure from them and the smoke from the bottomless pit, which is where fire and brimstone from hell comes up out of volcanoes. See in the Bible Deuteronomy 32:22-23. Also Revelation 16:10 predicts the beast's kingdom will be full of darkness. The beast is the son of satan the dragon and as I will show was born in Florida or off its coast in the Bahamas. Does the whole U.S. become dark from this volcano eruption or a third of the south where the beast was born?

One cable station called *The History Channel* aired in 2011 a program called *Countdown to Armageddon* that told of a great crack that was open on a island with a volcano off the West Coast of Africa in the Canary Islands. They said if the volcano erupted with an earthquake half the island where the crack is will slide into the Atlantic Ocean and cause 2,500-3000 feet high or more tidal waves to race across the Atlantic Ocean right towards Florida and the Eastern U.S. Coast and totally or partially destroy it for at least 20 miles inland. Is this what the book of Revelation chapters 8-9 and 12 meant? Is that what Revelation 8:8 mountain with fire falling into the sea meant as this event of a volcano in the Canary Islands erupting and sending part of the island into the sea causing this great tidal wave and destruction? Is chapter 8 verse 8 of Revelation a clue to the eighth month of August in 2015-2016 when this drastic event happens? Is Revelation verse 8 of chapter 8, along with the second (number two) angel to sound, that of August the eighth month (=chapter 8) and the eighth day (=verse 8), plus two (angel=8+2=10) equal August 10, 2015 when this event happens? Will the earth on the Eastern sea board of the U.S. and in Florida swallowed up the flood so it doesn't go inland more than 20 miles saving the one woman born May 19 and other women and men just as the book of Revelation 12:15-17 predicted? It also predicted that when that event happens and the serpent or satan sees he didn't kill the one woman or women and men and the one child of the woman, now a grown man, by this flood (tidal wave) he will set out to make war with her seed the Jews and Christians and God's two witnesses living in North Carolina and Virginia Beach by this tidal wave or some other means. Is that war the serpent makes with her seed a attack or war in Israel and war with Christians as the tidal wave that hits the Eastern Coast of Florida and the U.S., or by other means over a space of three and a half years later? The book of Revelation 12:15-17 predicts this:

"And the serpent cast out of his mouth water as a flood after the woman, that he might cause her to be carried away of the flood.

And the earth helped the woman, and the earth opened her mouth, and swallowed up the flood which the dragon cast out of his mouth.

And the dragon was wroth with the woman, and went to make war with the remnant of her seed which keep the commandments of God, and have the testimony of Jesus Christ." Revelation 12:15-17 (Old King James Version).

Does Revelation 12:14 predict this one woman born May 19 to flee into the wilderness (South) and stay there for three and a half years protected from the serpent's wrath. Naples, Florida is South West of Central Florida and may protect her from these tidal waves and hurricanes because of all the land in between it and the Eastern Coast of Florida. How it will protect from other storms, attacks and ash and smoke from the volcano is not clear. There's to the East of Naples, Florida a place called The Great Cypress Swamp and the Everglades towards the South as great places that the Bible calls "wilderness" as Revelation 12:14 predicted. Whether the one woman is to flee there or North and inland is not clear at this time.

Chapter 12 of Revelation tells of time, times and a half or 1260 days when satan is cast out heaven and comes down to the earth. At this time he knows he has a short time (three and a half years) and goes to destroy God's people the Jews (Israel) and Christians (U.S.=God's two witnesses?) with a flood (tidal wave) caused by an volcano eruption cause by the dragon in hell at the time of the old serpent called the devil or satan when he first fell. In my book *The experiment at Philadelphia* I tell how satan first fell from heaven in August and was born in Florida or the Bahamas off the coast of Florida known as the city of Atlantis. Was Revelation chapter 12 predicting trouble for Florida in August of 2015 or 2016 by this great tidal wave (flood=Revelation 12:16)? Then three and a half years later (time, times and a half or 1260 days) will come the end? Counting backwards from the end in January 21, 2019, the exact 1260 days, equals August 10, 2015, plus or minus three days. The end is when satan or the dragon brings a third of the stars from heaven down on earth to completely destroy it. Was this referring to a sun supernova that II Peter in chapter 3 predicts for the end of the world? Are the third of the stars and the great hail the weight of a talent (88-100 pounds each) be parts of the outer sun exploding and coming down upon the earth to cause a great earthquake and destroy every island, mountain and the whole earth just as Revelation 6:12-17 and 16:21 predicts? Or do these events happen three and a half years, or three years from July-August of 2015, which equals July-August or January-February of 2018-2019? At that time there will be a great the roaring of the seas (=waves=tidal waves) and the sun, moon and stars darkened by an earthquake and volcano eruption and/or a solar and lunar eclipses. The solar and lunar eclipses happens in January of 2019 right before and when the sun supernovas and shakes the heavens (planets and moons)? Luke 21:25-27 predicts this:

"And there shall be signs in the sun, and in the moon and in the stars; and upon the earth distress of nations, with perplexity; the sea and the waves roaring;

Men's hearts failing them for fear, and for looking after those things which are coming on the earth: for the powers of heaven shall be shaken.

And then shall they see the Son of man coming in a cloud with power and great glory." Luke 21:25-27 (Old King James Version)

That prophecy could mean both volcano eruptions, tidal waves, attacks, wars and/or storms at these times given that cause the sun, moon and stars to be darkened by those events and/or by solar and lunar eclipses. Will there be at these times strange lights by the sun and the sun giving more light as the light of seven days and/or for about seven days before it goes into a supernova scaring men with heart attacks and greatly disturbs the nations with great perplexity? A sun supernova would shake not only the earth, but all the planets and moons in our whole solar system along with shaking the sun very violently. The son (Jesus) coming with great glory is the strange light by the sun and is the sun giving off great light (glory) at that time in a supernova when Jesus comes back right before to take all people to heaven. See II Peter chapter 3 and Mark 13:13. The glory of His Coming could literally mean the great light coming from the sun when it supernovas. The "cloud" could be smoke and ash from the volcano, a storm, angels, mushroom clouds from a nuclear war or attacks and/or smoke from the sun supernova that ascends up forever as Babylon is fallen for the last time and as her smoke arises up forever just as

Revelation predicted. The great heat of Revelation 16:8-9 and Isaiah 30:26, 24:23 might be shortly before these times when the sun goes into a great supernova. At that time the sun becomes much stronger in light and causes the moons and planets to increase in light as the sign of His coming in great glory. Then immediately after tribulation in those days the stars from heaven fall and the heavens shake after these signs in the sun, moon and stars and the seas and waves roaring in tidal waves or storms.

"For then shall be great tribulation, such as was not since the beginning of the world to this time, no, nor ever shall be." Matthew 24:21 (Old King James Version)

"Immediately after the tribulation of those days shall the sun be darkened, and the moon shall not give her light, and the stars shall fall from heaven, and the powers of the heavens shall be shaken:

And then shall appear the sign of the Son of man in heaven: and then shall all the tribes of the earth mourn, and they shall see the Son of man coming in the clouds of heaven with power and great glory." Matthew 24:29-30 (Old King James Version)

"Immediately after tribulation in those days" could mean immediately after the earthquakes, volcano eruption with tidal waves and smoke to darkened the sun, moon and stars, war or attacks by nuclear bombs, then will the stars fall and then another great tribulation happens when the sun goes into a supernova. I looked up meteor showers for August and January and there are two sets that appear shortly after or before the dates given on August 10, 2013-2018 and January 21, 2019. They are the Perseids meteor shower of August 11-13, 2013-2018 and the Quadrantids January 3, 2019, plus or minus three days each. Is this what the above verses meant by stars falling from the sky (heaven) immediately after tribulation? It all makes sense this way because you have the smoke, heat, light and the great troubles on earth at this time due to those events. Then a day or two or seven days later the stars fall from the sky in these meteor showers. After that pieces of the sun as stars start hitting the whole earth destroying all islands and mountains and the earth and solar system shaking the heavens with great violence.

During these times a strange light may be seen near the sun, which is the Son of man coming with great glory to take all people off the earth before it's destroyed and taking them to heaven. Comets, asteroid impacts on earth or other moons or planets, and also strange lights and darkness, with solar and lunar eclipses may also occur at this time along with other supernovas and strange lights in other stars way out in space seen at night and day. Revelation 16:8-9 and verse 10 predicts great heat possibly from volcanoes and/or the sun followed by great darkness in the kingdom of the beast (U.S.). It fits perfectly with these old prophecies of tribulation from a volcano with its lava having great fire and heat followed by smoke and ash from it causing darkness in the U.S. and making the sun, moon and stars grow dark.

Will the sun flaring up to seven times mean solar flares and possible disruption or stopping of our TV's, radios, E-mails, internet, phones and electricity? It's no wonder Luke 21:25-26 predicts men's hearts failing them for fear of the things coming upon the earth after these signs from heaven, storms, volcanoes and tidal waves.

These events of volcano eruptions, tidal waves, hurricanes, attacks or wars and earthquakes for July-August of 2014-2015- 2016-2017-2017-2018-2019 are all recorded in these scriptures:

"The burden of the desert of the sea. As whirlwinds in the south pass through; so it cometh from the desert, from a terrible land.

A grievous vision is declared unto me; the treacherous dealer dealeth treacherously, and the spoiler spoileth. Go up, O Elam: besiege, O Media; all the sighing thereof have I made to cease." Isaiah 21:1-2 (Old King James Version).

"Behold, a whirlwind of the Lord is gone forth in fury, even a grievous whirlwind: it shall fall grievously upon the head of the wicked.

The anger of the Lord shall not return, until he has executed, and till he have performed the thoughts of his heart: in the latter days ye shall consider it perfectly."

Jeremiah 23:19-20. (Old King James Version).

"And the Lord shall be seen over them, and his arrow shall go forth as the lightning: and the Lord God shall blow the trumpet, and shall go with whirlwinds of the south."

Zechariah 9:14 (Old King James Version).

In these prophecies Isaiah 21:1-2 predicts "whirlwinds" would happen, which is the plural of that word the same as Zechariah 9:14. Isaiah 21:1-2 also predicts the "desert" twice and a "terrible land" the same as Isaiah chapter 18 does, which describes the United States. Are the "deserts" that of Africa where those terrible whirlwinds come from? The Canary Islands are off the Coast of West Africa and Africa has one on the greatest deserts of the world. Also the desert mentioned twice and the south mentioned twice in Isaiah 21:1-2 and Zechariah 9:14 all mean wilderness and the south where Florida is. And Jeremiah 23:19-20 predicts that these whirlwinds fall upon the head of the wicked. The wicked is satan's son born long ago in Florida or off its coast near the Bahamas. It also says we will know this prophecy perfectly in the latter days when the thoughts of His (God's) heart is known. The thoughts of His (God's) heart may mean these books I written and the heart sign of Leo ruled by the sun and fire that causes volcano eruptions and tidal waves from Africa to this terrible land (=great land) of the U.S. in the south (Florida, which is the home of the first wicked and first antichrist). If the prophecies of this book come true on August 10, 2015, plus or minus three days, then we will know perfectly what that prophecy meant. The places of Elam and Media Isaiah 21:1-2 predicts are modern day Iran and the "arrow" of Zechariah 9:14 could be Israel and Iran attack each other at the time of these great tidal waves and/or hurricanes. They may all happen around the same time or in July-August 2013-2014-2015-2016-2017-2018 or January of 2019.

The words "whirlwinds" or "whirlwind" in those Bible verses above are after the Hebrew words of 5492, 5486 and 5488 in the Hebrew dictionary of the *Strong's Concordance of the Bible*. The Hebrew word 5492 means this: "hurricane, storm, Red Sea, tempest." The word 5486 means this: "to snatch away…i.e. terminate: consume, have an end, perish, x be utterly." The Hebrew word 5488 means this: "a reed, the papyrus:- flag, Red {sea], weed." The Red Sea is where Moses and the Israelites cross over where Mount Sinai is near on the other side which Moses got the law from in May-June. In May-June of 2014 is when we seen in my books that the sun is near Auriga, The Charioteer, when 20,000 people read this book and my others because of angel visitations just as Psalms 68:17 predicts. Then the next year after that in July-August we see the earthquakes, volcano eruptions and tidal waves (whirlwind). The papyrus and Mount Sinai predicted in Psalms 68:8, 17, along with Jeremiah 23:19-20's "whirlwind" might mean in the Hebrew dictionary these books of mine. The ancients made books from the papyrus weed. The books (papyrus=books) could be this book and my others that 20,000 read by these months of May-June 2014 when an earthquakes and volcano eruption (Mount Sinai) causes great tidal waves (=whirlwinds) then in July-August of 2014 or 2015-2016. Psalms 68:8 predicts God shakes the earth, brings down the heavens (comet impact?; hurricane?; missiles?; smoke and ash?) and mentions mount Sinai, which could represent a volcano off the African West Coast in the Canary Islands. The flag mentioned in one of those words for whirlwinds is what we read in my book *Predictions for 2013-2014* as "banners" of Song of Solomon 6:10. That word "banners" is connected to the word "anniversary," which is that of a great earthquake or events a year earlier on August 10, 2014, plus or minus three days, which is the Leo sign that rules the heart (thoughts of His heart=Jeremiah 23:19-20) and is ruled by the sun (=volcanoes). The flag and trumpet is that of wars, coming disasters and new moons which comes in July-August of 2014-2015-2016 possibly in the Leo sign of those months, which rules the heart and God's heart when he shows his wisdom through these books of mine and you know without a doubt he is right.

Other Hebrew words for whirlwinds are the Hebrew words 5591 that is connected to 5590, which means: "to rush upon" meaning very fast as tidal waves travel very fast where as hurricanes don't travel very fast. We could of along have been misreading and miss-interpreting the word "whirlwinds". The Bible may have meant, at least in some places, tidal waves for the word "whirlwind" and for the word "flood." The Hebrew word for whirlwind being Hebrew 5590 means: "be sore troubled, come out as a (drive with the, scatter with a) whirlwind." The English Dictionary definition for whirlwind means this: "any circling rush or violent onward course." The circling rush (=fast) could be what the Bible calls tidal waves that happen at these times when people read about in this book along with the date and exactly what happens making the very prophecy perfectly clear just as Jeremiah 23:19-20 predicted on the head (place evil was born) of the wicked in the south (Florida) and/or the White House.

Will a volcano eruption cause these tidal waves and the third of the stars to be darkened as Revelation chapters 8-9 predicts? Or will a comet or asteroid impact in the Atlantic Ocean and/or Africa? Will it be like a fiery mountain falling into the sea and causes smoke and dust if it hits on land or if it impacts in the Ocean and causes great tidal waves? If it hits on land than it will kick up dust that covers and darkens a third of the stars just as Revelation chapters 8:10-11 predicts.

"And the third angel sounded, and there fell a great star from heaven, burning as it were a lamp, and it fell upon the third part of the rivers, and upon the fountains of waters;

And the name of the star is called Wormwood: and the third part of the waters became wormwood; and many men died of the waters, because they were made bitter." Revelation 8:10-11 (Old King James Version).

The darkened sun, either by volcano ash and smoke or dust by a comet or asteroid, would cause the crops to fail causing a great famine as the book of Revelation in the Bible predicts for August 10, 2015, plus or minus three days, or July-August of 2014-2015-2016. If you see someone on the rooftop in the summer of 2015 and you live in Florida or the East Coast of the United States than drive away from Florida and the East Coast and go inland as far as you can. In Florida get on I-75 and go north through Georgia then pick up Road 24 and then Road 65 into Indiana and stay there till the trouble is over. Read my book *The Divine Code 3* for more details of these events. If these events happen in the summer (July-August) of 2014-2016 and you see a person on the rooftop then do the same thing just mentioned. If an angel appears to you at one of these times and tells you to flee the area then listen to him and not say the author is insane or in error as Ecclesiastes 5:6 predicts. This angel will be bluish-white and sparkling that makes you smile ear to ear.

The "head of the wicked" that the "whirlwind" falls upon grievously as Jeremiah 23:19-20 predicts could be the comet or asteroid from the planet Wormwood that satan was the head of long ago. That planet was between

Mars and Jupiter and the asteroid belt there now along with comets are the remains of that planet. Satan blew that planet up when he fell from heaven to the earth to have his son (fourth beast-antichrist) born in Florida or off the Coast of Florida long ago. See Revelation chapters 8-9 and Amos 5:7-8. If a comet or asteroid hits the earth or ocean it would be from Wormwood and be as a fiery mountain falling into the sea that causes a whirlwind (tidal wave or hurricane or nuclear bomb?) to fall grievously upon the head of the wicked (antichrist or President Obama-Cain White House?) in Florida or the East Coast of the U.S. just as Revelation chapters 8:10-11 and Amos 5:7-8 predicted. And as Revelation chapters 8:10-11 predicts that star would cause the waters to become bitter and people and the wild life die because of the bitter waters (=red tide? Or gases or poison form the comet, asteroid or volcano?).

Update: On September 18, 2011 *The Discovery Channel* ran a documentary called *How will the world end?* In that show it told of a volcano off the West Coast of Africa that has a great crack in it. If the volcano should erupt with an earthquake then part of the island it is on would fall into the sea causing a great tidal wave to head towards Florida and the East Coast of the U.S. It would travel 550 miles an hour and be 100 feet tall and destroy everything inland for 40 miles from Miami to New York according to that show. This volcano and island maybe the same one mentioned above seen on *The History Channel* in the Canary Islands off the West Coast of Africa with a crack in it. Why the differing heights of the tidal wave and miles in land it destroys is different is not known at this time.

These events of earthquakes, volcano eruptions, hurricanes, tidal waves, attacks, wars and comet or asteroid impacts could be for July-August or March-April of 2014-2018, or August 28-29 or September 26-27 of those years, but also in January of 2019 and are times when to flee Florida and the East Coast of the U.S. and to flee from Jerusalem, Israel to the mountains in the East or Petra, Jordan. These ancient prophecies may mean massive destruction for the U.S. by tidal waves (=rivers, streams and waters) and massive destruction of Israel by nuclear fire from Iran (=Elam-Media). See Isaiah 30:25-26. The "towers" in Isaiah 30:25 could mean skyscrapers in New York and other East Coast cities of the U.S. destroyed by these great tidal waves at a time of nuclear fire in Israel and/or the U.S. with nuclear power plants melt down because of an earthquake and/or tidal waves. Isaiah 30:25-26 predicts:

"And there shall be upon every high mountain, and upon every high hill, rivers and streams of waters in the day of the great slaughter, when the towers fall.

Moreover the light of the moon shall be as the light of the sun, and the light of the sun shall be sevenfold, as the light of seven days, in the day that the Lord bindeth up the breach of his people, and healeth the stroke of their wound."

Isaiah 30:25-26 (Old King James Version)

Revelation 8:1-7 predicted the half hour in heaven and a golden censer filled much incense (spices) for the prayers of the saints (Billy Graham and Pat Robertson?) when hail falls from the heavens and sets on fire the trees and grass.

"And when he had opened the seventh seal, there was silence in heaven about the space of half an hour.

And I saw the seven angels which stood before God; and to them were given seven trumpets.

And another angel came and stood at the altar, having a golden censer: and there was given unto him much incense, that he should offer it with the prayers of all saints upon the golden altar which was before the throne.

And the smoke of the incense, which come with the prayers of the saints, ascended up before God out of the angel's hand.

And the angel took the censer, and filled it with fire of the altar, and cast it into the earth: and there were, voices, and thunderings, and an earthquake.

And the seven angels which had the seven trumpets prepared themselves to sound.

The first angel sounded, and there followed hail and fire mingled with blood, and they were cast upon the earth: and the third part of trees was burnt up, and all green grass was burnt up." Revelation 8:1-7 (Old King James Version).

Were these prediction predicting the volcano eruption and earthquake in August of 2015? The "incense" of the prayers of the saints could be myrrh and frankincense, which are ruled by Aquarius and the Sun that rules Leo. August 10, 2015 is the Leo sign, which polar opposite is the Aquarius sign. And the saints killed at this time or by this time would be praying and their prayers in heaven reaches down to earth along with a meteor shower we see or will see happens shortly after August 10, 2015. This time though they reach the earth in fire and blood (death of people hit by them or burned up by them) and burn up trees and grass. Those verses tell of two or three angels, but are not the last two or three angels or the three angels of Revelation chapter 14. Add two or three days and years to verse 7 of Revelation chapter 8 and it equals 8:7+2- 3=8:10, or our August 9-10, 2015, which is the Leo sign, plus or minus two or three years from 2015 equals 2013-2014 and 2016-2017-2018-2019 when these events may happen. And three years and a half an hour or year of six months to that date and it equals January 20-21, 2019, which is a lunar eclipse or blood moon when pieces of the sun fall to earth as stars mingled with fire and blood in a sun supernova that burns up trees and all, read closely "all" grass is destroyed. To have that happen that would have to mean a sun supernova causing it. The voices, thunderings and earthquakes, along with the hail are meteor shower or missiles. The hail could mean missiles raining down fire from their tails and once on ground nuclear explosions destroying the trees and grass with fire on Israel and Iran in one of those dates. The one date above is August 9, which in 1945 the U.S. dropped the second atomic bomb on Japan. Will on August 9-10, 2015, plus or minus three days or one year Iran attacks Israel with two or three nuclear missiles launched with fire (=blood) from their tails and landing and exploding with fire burning up the trees and grass. This is the fire mingled with the hail (missiles) that Revelation 8:1-7 predicts. And near this same time a earthquake off the West Coast of Africa from a volcano causing a tidal to hit Florida and the U.S. East coast. The "voices" of Revelation 8:1-7 might mean the sun supernova as II Peter chapter 3 predicts when the sun supernova's it makes a great noise and will shake the earth very violently with hail (missiles) or pieces of the sun destroying the trees and grass. The "lightnings" might mean a storm or hurricane hitting the U.S. at one of these dates.

Isaiah 48:1 predicts Jacob (U.S.) to come out of the waters of Judah. Juda or Judah Revelation chapter 5 states is a lion or our Leo sign (Judah) when August 10, 2015, plus or minus three days equals when a tidal wave (waters) hit the East Coast of the U.S.

"Hear ye this: O house of Jacob, which are called by the name of Israel, and are come forth out of the waters of Judah..." Isaiah 48:1 (Old King James Version).

Isaiah chapter 29 predicts:

"Woe to Ariel, to Ariel, the city where David dwelt! Add ye year to year; let them kill sacrifices.

Yet I will distress Ariel, and there shall be heaviness and sorrow; and it shall be unto me as Ariel.

And I will camp against thee round about, and will lay siege against thee with a mount, and I will raise forts against thee.

And thou shalt be brought down, and shalt speak out of the ground, and thy speech shall be low out of the dust, and thy voice shall be, as of one that hath a familiar spirit, out of the ground, and thy speech shall whisper out of the dust.

Moreover the multitudes of thy strangers shall be like small dust, and the multitudes of the terrible ones shall be as chaff that passeth away; yea, it shall be at an instant suddenly.

Thou shalt be visited of the Lord or hosts with thunder, and with earthquake, and great noise, with storm and tempest, and the flame of devouring fire.

And their multitudes of all the nations that fight against Ariel, even all that fight against her and her muntion, and that distress her, shall be as a dream of a night vision.

It shall even be as when an hungry man dreameth, and, behold, he eateth; but he awaketh, and his soul is empty: or as when a thirsty man dreameth, and behold, he drinketh; but he awaketh, and, behold, he is faint, and his soul hath appetite: so shall the multitude of all the nations be, that fight against mount Zion.

Stay yourselves, and wonder; cry ye out, and cry: they are drunken, but not with wine; they stagger, but not with strong drink.

For the Lord hath poured out upon you the spirit of deep sleep, and hath closed your eyes: the prophets and your rulers, the seers hath he covered.

And the vision of all is become into you as the words of a book that is sealed, which men delivered to one that is learned, saying, Read this, I pray thee: and he saith, I cannot; for it is sealed:

And the book is delivered to him that is not learned, saying, Read thus, I pray thee: and he saith, I am not learned.

Wherefore the Lord said, Forasmuch as this people draw near me with their mouth, and with their lips do honour me, but have removed their heart far from me, and their fear toward me is taught by the precept of men:

Therefore, behold, I will proceed to do a marvelous work among this people, even a marvelous work and a wonder: for the wisdom of their wise men shall perish and the understanding of their prudent men shall be hid." Isaiah 29:1-14 (Old King James Version).

In Bible chapter/year codes Isaiah chapter 29 is our year 1929 when the Stock Market crashed and there was a great depression during prohibition and no food for the dust bowl in those years and no money to buy food. The prohibition act was made on January 16, 1919 and went into effect on January 16, 1920. The five Ariel's of Isaiah chapter 29 added as five days to January 16, 1919 equals January 21, 1919, which was the Chinese Year of the Sheep or Goat. The year 2015 is the Chinese Year of the Sheep or Goat, which marks the time of three and a half years from August 10, 2015 to exactly January 21, 2019 as 360 day years or 1260 days. And in the year 1920, when prohibition went into effect, just as Isaiah chapter 29 predicted, a man staggers, but is not drunk, dreameth of drinking and awakes and is thirsty and dreams of eating, but awakes faint all could mean these times of the great depression and lack of money for food and famine and no alcohol. Will this happen again in 2013 like in 1929, which was the Chinese Year of the Snake the same as 2013 is? The five Ariel's of Isaiah chapter 29 could be five years added to 2013 or 2018- 2019 when these events happen. Or will its polar opposite of 2013 or 2019 be when the stock markets crashes and economic troubles happens in 2019? The years 1919-1920 when prohibition was voted on and put into effect is the Chinese Years of the Sheep or Goat in 1919 and the Chinese Year of the Monkey in 1920, which to us nowadays are the years 2015-2016 when the stock markets may crash literally? Will it be the New York stock market and/or the Pacific stock market, which is in the city of San Francisco when a great earthquake, great tidal waves and/or attack occurs as Isaiah chapter 29 predicts? Do both suffer crashes in 2013 or 2015-2016 or 2019? The lack of alcohol could be from hops and barley in the great plains of the U.S. that have great drought and heat causing the lack of beer and other alcoholic beverages. Is this due to the volcano eruption and darkness?

Isaiah 29:11-12 predicts a book given to someone learned and they say they cannot understand it because it is sealed. Then it is delivered to someone unlearned and they say I am not learned. In 1985 I advertised my book and got two responses for it from one that sounded like a unbeliever and unlearned and from another who sound they were learned. The year 1985 is the Chinese Year of the Ox, which polar opposite is the Chinese Year of the Sheep or Goat, which is 2015 when the great trouble happens causing death, economic troubles and famines the same Chinese Year as 1985 and 1919. Then three and a half years later the end comes in January 21, 2019 the same month when prohibition was put forth in January 16, 1919 and enforced on January 16, 1920.

There could be wars, earthquakes, volcano eruptions, storms and tidal waves in both August 10, 2015 and January 20-21, 2019 according to these prophecies. Ariel by the way means "lion of God" or the Leo sign of the lion, which August 10, 2015 is. January 20-21, 2019 is the cusp of the Capricorn sign, which is a sea goat. The ancient Jewish people sacrificed one goat for a sin offering. Could the add year to year and kill sacrifices be that of two years (add year to year=1+1=2), plus one year (sacrifice one goat=one year) equals three years from a lion (=Ariel) to a goat (=sacrifice)?

That time period being August 10, 2015 the Leo sign of the lion (=Ariel) and the Chinese Year of the Sheep or Goat, plus three and a half years to January 20-21, 2019 as the cusp of the Capricorn sign that is a sea goat (sacrifice). The lion is the fifth sign (=August 10) the fifth year of 2015 and the Goat as Aries the ram family is given the number 9 after the year 2019. Proverbs 30:30-31 predicts this:

"A lion which is strongest among beasts, and turneth not away for any.

A greyhound; and he goat also; and as king, against whom there is no rising up." Proverbs 30:30-31 (Old King James Version).

The lion is August 10, 2015 in the Leo the lion sign and the he goat is the cusp of the Capricorn sign on January 20- 21, 2019, which is the Chinese year of the Dog (=greyhound). The Lord's prayer states: Our Father that art in heaven hallow be thy name, thy kingdom come…, might have been a clue to these times as well because God's hollowed named spelled backwards equals dog and January 20-21, 2019 is the Chinese Year of the Dog when God's kingdom comes through the doors of heaven.

The "noise" predicted in Isaiah 29:1-14 might be nuclear missiles (devouring flame, noise and earthquake and tempest or great wind) and/or a sun supernova as II Peter chapter 3 predicts for the end. Isaiah 29:1-14 prediction of a great fire, earthquake, noise, storm or whirlwind (tidal wave) could be the war of August 10, 2015 and those same events in the end time in January of 2019. The add year unto year and let them kill sacrifices in Isaiah 29:1 might mean two years added unto the seventh year of 2017 when a peace treaty comes and people say peace, peace and peace and safety then two years later (the add year to year or two years) the end comes in January of 2019 as two added to 2017 equals 2019 in January the month of when prohibition started.

January 20-21, 2019 at midnight has Leo the lion seen over head. On those same dates at noon the polar opposite of midnight has Pegasus the flying horse behind or near the sun. Was this what Revelation chapter 19 predicted in the stars for Jesus Christ return on a white flying horse shining as bright as the sun or more because the sun is in a supernova phase? And Leo has a star named Regulus known as the "prince" or king and Revelation chapter 19 predicts Jesus comes back riding on the white flying horse with the name King or Kings and Lord of Lords. Revelation 22:20 predicts Jesus comes quickly which a supernova of our sun would be a great light and noise with hail or pieces of it flying towards our earth at tremendous speeds (=quickly). Revelation chapters 14 and 19 puts these events at the grape harvest of July-August from 2013-2018 and/or a half year later in January 2019.

The "arrows"-"arrow" of Dueteronomy 32:22-23 and Zechariah 9:14 might mean many missiles or bombs shot at the White House (=Scorpio) and/or Israel (=Taurus=born May 14=Taurus sign) from Iran or Pakistan. In the stars we see at night the Milky Way runs from Scorpio to Sagittarius to Taurus. See drawing 25 in my book *The Experiment at Philadelphia* page 441. Iran is in the Scorpio zone and Israel is Taurus in which the stars of the Milky Way predicts arrows flying at one another in missiles and bombs in a war in July-August-September-October of 2015-2016 or 2013-2014.

Pakistan is in the Sagittarius zone and Washington, D.C. is ruled by Scorpio. Sagittarius is an archer of arrows or missiles and bombs shot at each other in a war between the two places and as is shown in the stars and Milky Way.

President Obama and Mitt Romney birthdays are August 4 (Obama) and March 12 (Romney). And as Ecclesiastics 7:14 predicts the day of prosperity or happiness is the same day as trouble (adversity). Will on August 4 or March 12, 2013-2019 we see this happen on one or both of their birthdays? Or will Herman Cain's birthday be the time of these events?

Chapter Two

The end

Revelation 6:12-13 predicts a solar and lunar eclipse and then many stars falling to the ground. January 5-6, 2019 has a solar eclipse or darkened sun (sackcloth) happen on that day. Then on January 21, 2019 there is a lunar eclipse (blood) moon at exactly 12:12 a.m. eastern standard time give or take a few minutes and its duration. That's very close to 12:18 a.m. when I had the vision of lights in my bed room starting at that exact time and lasting for six hours on August 28-29, 1982, which was the Chinese Year of the Dog the same as January 21, 2019 is. Revelation chapters 9 and 11 predict five-six months of trouble and/ or three and a half years of trouble. The lights I saw for six hours in August 28-29, 1982 is six months of trouble when the devil comes down to earth knowing he has but a short time as Revelation 12:12 predicts, as well as three and a half years (See Revelation 12:6). Is that "short time" five or six months starting in August 28-29, 2018 to January of 2019? Or is it three and a half years (42 months; 1260 days; or time, times and half) from the ninth of AV or July 16-17 or August 28-29, 2015 or in July-August, 2015 to January of 2019? Jesus predicted in Matthew 25:1-13 predicts a time of the bridegroom to come is a little after midnight in which I showed in my other books to be 12:18 a.m. the same time I saw the vision of lights in August 28-29, 1982 the Chinese year of the Dog. The stars falling to the ground at that time could be pieces of the sun exploding in a supernova as Revelation 6:12- 13 predicts happens when there is a lunar eclipse (blood moon). That will cause every mountain and island to be moved out of its place exactly as Revelation chapter 6 predicted.

The Billy Graham dream I had of him being insane and then sane and I am playing cards may have the following meaning. The deck of cards is 52. The moon rules insane in which we get the word loony from. The moon is given the numbers two and seven in numerology. Multiply two (=moon) times 52 (=cards) equals 104 minus seven (=moon) equals 97 added to Billy Graham's birth year till the time he dies is 97+1918=2015 in July-August of 2015. That is when he and Pat Robertson die taking away God's two witnesses as Revelation chapter 11 predicted. Thus, leaving satan unchecked and thrown out of heaven at that time to cause great earthquakes, storms, wars, terrorist attacks, volcano eruptions and tidal waves, flooding, hail, red tide or oil spills, strange lights in the sky, plane crashes or meteor or comet impacts on earth or other planets or moons, on the ninth of Av or July 16-17, August 28-29, or July- August or September 26-27 of 2015. At that time floods or storms may strike Florida and/or the U.S. as Revelation chapter 12 predicts when satan is cast out of heaven and causes a flood in the south (Florida) and all kinds of trouble for three and a half years or 1260 days. Is that flood another Hurricane like Andrew that hit in southern Florida in August of 1992? The second Iraq war started in the Chinese Year of the Sheep or Goat in 2003. The Chinese Yearly cycle is 12 years from then when in July-August of 2015 there is war again with the U.S. (=spiritual Babylon) which is the Chinese Year of the

Sheep or Goat. From then to January of 2019 is when God withdraws the Holy Spirit from the earth by the deaths of Billy Graham and Pat Robertson (by the tidal waves?) and throws out satan from heaven and he comes down to earth having great wrath for a short time of three and a half years. Israel, the U.S. and/or the world at this same time in July-August of 2015 till January 21, 2019 may also witness great earthquakes, tidal waves, wars, attacks, a great falling away to sins, apostasy with much violence, record river flooding and flooding, red tides, hail, drought, heat, cold, blizzards, wild fires, religious fighting and disagreements, economic disasters and very high inflation, strange darkness, strange lights, twisters, great famines, pestilence's, bugs and insect over populated, great man made invention failures, fearful and great signs from heaven (the sky) and other man made and natural disasters. See the Bible's II Thessalonians chapter 2, Haggai, Revelation chapters 8-9, Isaiah chapters 18 and 42, Matthew 24:7-8, both Joel and Acts chapters 2, Luke 21:19-11, 26, Revelation chapter 6 and Psalms 99:8.

Billy Graham and Pat Robertson might die before the tidal wave or the end happens as Isaiah 57:1 predicts the taking away of them from the evil to come. This means both could die between now (August 11, 2011) and August 10-13, 2013-2018 or January 21, 2019 having them taken away from the evil to come as Isaiah 57:1 predicted. Or do they die in the tidal wave or of natural causes or shooting or by the antichrist shortly before (three and a half days) the end on January 21, 2019?

II Thessalonians 2:8 predicts the antichrist is killed by "the brightness of his coming:.... Does this mean when Jesus comes back there's a supernova that shines very bright and destroys the antichrist and the earth with its glory as other Bible prophecies predict? And if that time is a Sunday-Monday then it's like in creation and the creation of Adam and Eve, which equals the one becoming two and the two becomes one. Sunday has the word sun in it, which is given the number one. Monday has the word moon in it and is given the number two. January 20-21, 2019 is a Sunday-Monday when the two become one like in creation and how Adam and Eve started children. In creation the very first particle was one. It then broke in two and made two. The two then collided (big-bang) and made one and all particles in the Universes. With Adam and Eve God made first Adam as one. He then took a rib out of Adam when he was asleep (=outer space=nothing) and it made two. Adam and Eve then had sex, or became one, to make all people on earth just like creation. The sun is male and the moon is female as the days of Sunday-Monday can mean when they join as one as the bride and bridegroom at midnight that the U.S. has as joining of the two days. In the end satan stands inside the core of the sun to bring the end just as the beginning when the two become one.

Is the fifth angel sounding his trumpet and the half an hour of Revelation 9:1-2 and 8:1 five-six months and years from August 2013 to August 2018, plus five or six months to January 21, 2019? The half an hour in Revelation 8:1 would be a half a year from July-August of 2018 when smoke from a great volcano erupts and causes the tidal waves and smoke darkening the sun, moon and stars for the third part of the U.S. and the third part of the day and night as we read earlier in the book of Revelation chapters 8-9. Is the "fifth" angel the fifth month to the Bible's calendar, which is

July-August when in 2015 or 2018 these events happen? Five months from August is January. Is the fifth also the fifth year of 2015? Will something happen in July-August of 2018, then some things else in December 24-25, 2018 and then other events and the end in January of 2019? The Bible does give those exact dates and scenarios. Are the earthquakes, volcano eruptions, tidal waves, smoke darkening the sun, moon and stars and all other events predicted in this book happen in January of 2019?

The Mayan's started their calendar in August 11 or 12 or 13 by some different authors. See *The Mayan Prophecies* by Adrian G. Gilbert and Maurice M. Cotterell page 184; *The Orion Prophecy* by Patrick Geryl and Gino Ratinckx page 154; and *The Mayan Factor* by Jose Arguelles page 72. That's awful close to August 10, 2015 or 2018 when this earthquake and/or volcano eruption and tidal waves could hit. Maybe time differences could put it August 11 or 12 or even the 13, or plus or minus three days. Is the exact date August 10-11?

If the volcano erupts and causes a great tidal wave that hits Charlotte, North Carolina and Virginia Beach, Virginia and kills Billy Graham (=if he lives there in Charlotte, North Carolina?) and Pat Robertson if he lives in Virginia Beach, Virginia, then that ancient prophecy will be fulfilled as Revelation chapter 11:7 and 14:13 predicted long ago. It predicted that the beast (=satan) that ascended out of the bottomless pit (hell=volcanoes) causes tidal waves (flood) and what kills (=satan is hell and fire where volcanoes come from) God's two witnesses (=Billy Graham and Pat Robertson). UFOs (beast-satan-antichrist) have been reported to appear near volcanoes near or during when they erupt. This was reported on the cable show *The History Channel* on a show called *Ancient Aliens* in 2011. So the prophecy could literally be true as hell causes volcano eruptions just as the book Deuteronomy 32:22-23 predicted. The "arrows" on those verses could mean bullets or missiles. And Revelation 14:13 predicts those who die at this time in Babylon (U.S.) will rest in heaven from their labors and their works of the gospel do follow them.

Revelation chapter 12 predicts satan tried to kill a child by a flood (storm=hurricane) at his birth from a woman who was born September 27 and fled into the south in 1981 some 27 years (hand=27 bones) after his birth. Revelation chapter one in chapter/year codes is our 1981 A.D. And Revelation 1:10 states John wrote or experience the book of Revelation on the Lord's Day, which is Sunday. Through my other books I state that the book of Revelation happened on June 12, 96 A.D. by the old Julian calendar, which was a Sunday (Lord's Day). Add three and a half months instead of years as time, times and a half or 1260 days as Revelation chapter 12 predicts a woman to travel to the south in that time to June 12, 1981 and it equals September 27, 1981, which was a Sunday (Lord's Day) and when me and my mom and dad traveled from the North East to Florida arriving in Ocala almost exactly at noon to 1 p.m. three and a half days from when we started counting each day. That day was my mother's birthday who gave birth to me in a storm or flood.

Add 35 years counting each year and it equals a time that satan (red dragon=12 month=August=red lava flow from erupting volcano) again tries to kill this same child, now a grown man, again with a flood (tidal waves and/or hurricanes) at this time in July-October (August 28-29?; September 26-27?; October 15?) of 2015 or 2016. That man could be called God's two witnesses and killed by these same great tidal waves (floods-hurricanes) that Revelation chapter 12 predicts caused by the volcano eruption. The "red dragon" of Revelation 12:3 is satan who is king of volcano eruptions that gives off red lava that are caused by him in hell. The sun, moon and 12 stars of the woman in Revelation chapter 12 could mean a Sunday-Monday on August 9-10-11, 2015-2016 when this flood happens. The "sun" is Sunday and the "moon" is Monday. The 12 stars could be August 12, 2013-2014-2015-2016-2018, or the Pisces zones that rule Florida where this man lives. Florida is also where the dragon's son was born there or off the coast in the Bahamas, which was part of the ancient city of Atlantis.

The red dragon, woman with the sun and moon and 12 stars could also have another meaning. That meaning is that the red dragon is a full moon lunar eclipse known as a blood (red) moon in the Chinese Year of the Dog polar opposite of the Dragon. And Revelation chapter 12 that predicts this red dragon, sun, moon and 12 stars has 17 verses in it. Could the chapter number 12 and the 12 stars along with 17 verses mean 12:17 a.m. in the morning on Sunday into Monday January 21, 2019, which is the start of a full moon and/or a lunar eclipse (blood moon)? The full moon then according to the book *Astronomical Tables of the Sun, Moon and Planets* by Jean Meeus page 197 states it happens at exactly 12:17 a.m. on January 21, 2019. It could be off a couple of minutes plus or minus, but is awful close to the exact dates and times given here and in my other books. See my book *The Divine Code 3* available by December of 2012. And both Revelation chapter 12 and 12 stars mentioned in it equals 21 reverse, which would be January 21, 2019 in the Chinese Dog Year in its 12th month (=12 stars and chapter 12) of the Chinese calendar, which would be January.

God saves this woman mentioned above in 2006 (=12 years= 2018-2019) who flees like an eagle into the south. The eagle is a bird or air sign of Libra. And September 25-27, 1981, when she flees into the south took three and a half days and is the Libra sign of the air and she arrives on her birthday of September 27, 1981 a Sunday just as August 10, 2015 is some 35 years later. She flees by car into the south with her son for exactly 3.5 days/years (1260 days, time, times and a half of time or 1260 Revelation 12:6, 14) till a flood tries to kill her son again on that date or in July-September. Delete the decimal point of the 3.5 days/years and it equals 35 years from 1981+35=2015, counting each year, or the year 2016. The "time, times and a half" or 1260 days or 42 months could also mean "time" as one decade, "times" as two decades and a "half" as five years (=half a decade). Add them together and it equals 35 years. See Revelation chapter 12, which predicts when satan, or that old serpent and dragon tries again to kill her son.

Is September 26-27 near her birthday and on her birthday when we see another predicted event happen 12 years later like what was suppose to happen on that date in 2003? Twelve years added to September 26-27, 2003=September 26-27, 2015. The book in the Bible, Colossians 2:16-17, predicts that future events happen on older dates as signs of the future dates. Are these exact dates September 7-8, 19, 26-27, 2015-2016?

Song of Solomon chapters 2 and 6:10, 13 predicts travel in the year 2002 (=Chapter 2), plus 12 years in 2014. Then in chapter 6 of Song of Solomon equals 2006 the Chinese

Year of the Dog Year in 2018-2019 when four returns or four years more added to 2014, which equals 2018-2019, which is when the end comes.

Daniel 12:11-13 predicts the end in 2625 years from the time the abomination of desolation occurs. The "abomination of desolation" is when the king of Babylon came to Jerusalem and stood in the Holy of Holies in the Jewish Temple there or placed a pagan statue there in 606-607 B.C. Subtract 2625 years from then and it equals 2019-2020, or counting each year 2018-2019 A.D. Is that when satan or the antichrist stands in the core of the sun where the Holy of Holies is in heaven causing it to go into a supernova making it very bright and killing him (satan and the antichrist and all demons) and is not only a very great abomination, but what causes desolation (=destruction) of the whole solar system. See Matthew 24:15.

Chapter Three

Chinese Yearly Cycles

In the introduction of this book I told you how Chinese astrology has 12 yearly cycles instead of our astrology of 12 monthly cycles. I also show how going back in time by 12 yearly cycles can show us what will happen in the future by 12 yearly cycles.

The year 2015 counting backwards by 12 yearly cycles equals 2003, 1991, 1979 and 1967. Those years in history has some important dates and events. In 2003 on March 19-20 near a full moon came the second Iraq war. The year 1991 on January 16-17, near a new moon came the first Iraq (Babylon) war. Then in 1979 on January 31 and February 1 and November 4 came the over throw of Iran's leader and for the religious leader to return from France to take control on January 31-February 1, 1979. On November 4, 1979 Iranians stormed the U.S. embassy and took U.S. hostages for 444 days. Three Mile Island nuclear power plant had a melt down on March 28, 1979. Will in March of 2015 (=1979) we see another nuclear power plant disaster and/ or be attacked like in Iran by Israel then Iran attacks Israel? And finally on June 5-10, 1967 was the Israeli six day war. Will Israel see some war or attack in June or July-August of 2015?

Martin Luther King, Jr., was assassinated on April 4, 1968 and RFK was assassinated on June 4-5, 1968. Will another political leader be assassinated in the White House or in the south, or by tidal wave or by plane crash in 2015 or 2016? The year 1968 is not exactly in the Chinese Yearly cycles of 12. It is one year off, but the prophecies can happen in that year plus or minus one year. Does these prophecies predict trouble with Iraq known as Babylon, or a spiritual Babylon of Turkey, Rome, Italy, the U.S. and Los Angeles in 2015-2016? And/or will Iran and Israel face trouble then? Is the third of the stars we saw in the first chapter of this book that which Revelation predicts be missiles or bombs at these times of July-August or some other month (March? June?) in 2015 on these nations of Babylon? Does Isaiah 40:1-2 predict double trouble for Jerusalem at these times. Was the word double predicting another war in Israel in June like in 1967, or some other months in 2015-2016? Are the "arrows" of Deuteronomy 32:22-23 and Zechariah 9:14 that of bullets that kills the U.S. or Israeli President or God's two witnesses or someone famous.

Chapter Four

The Narrative of the carving

The following letters A-H explains the JFK assassination predicted by an ancient Egyptian carving from the Temple Hathor in Denderah, Egypt. See Chapter Seven for the drawing of the carving and the letters A-H explaining the details of these ancient prophecies. See drawing One in chapter 6 after you read below what that drawing means.

A. Carving dated 100-300 B.C. or 1800 B.C. or an earlier copy from 5000 B.C.
B. Two candlesticks or lamps.
C. Sagittarius half Horse half archer.
D. Man on top of Libra has the numbers 3, 6, 7, 12, 3-1 or 12:31 p.m. local time when three shots from a Libra man from the sixth story of a seven story building (=Texas School Book Depository) rang out causing the wounds to both JFK and Governor Connally.
E. Gemini's head (=JFK) hit from behind.
F. Governor Connally's wounds were to the back, chest, right wrist and left thigh as seen on the carving with the imaginary line going through Gemini's head and into the back of a man in front

of him holding a staff with his right hand, which equals political power (=Governor Connally.)

G. The duck of goose not seen on this drawings but is on the actual full drawing by Sagittarius equals the family of Roosters or the Chinese Rooster sign who's polar opposite is that of the Rabbit which rules the Year 1963 when the JFK assassination happened.

H. Sagittarius is shooting arrows (bullets, missiles or planes) at the exact spot where Libra ends and Scorpio begins, which is November 22, 1963 that exact date of the JFK assassination. If you add a generation as one preacher teaches is 51.4 to that date it equals November 22, 2014, which is a new moon. Will something major happen then? If you add the .4 to that date it equals March 20-21, April 4, 20-22, 2015 and between the November 22, 2014 and April 4, 20-22, 2015 equals December 21-25, 26, 28-29, 2014. Is that when some majors events happens?

Putting this all together equals you having a Libra man (Oswald=October 18=Libra) on top of a seven story (seven mountains) building (=the Texas School Book depository) from the sixth story (=Libra is the seventh sign and is given the number six shooting at the back of the head three shots that rule Libra or Jupiter the number 3. The third shot hits JFK in the back of the head and comes out his right front of the head and goes through governor Connally back, out his front chest hitting his right wrist and going into his left thigh as the carvings shows with an imaginary line through these signs from the two candlesticks or lamps. Two candlesticks or lamps equals two shooters with one on the grassy knoll or behind the picket fence who shoots almost the exact time as Oswald fatal third shot. Sagittarius is ruled by Uranus that is given the number 4 as four shots of arrows and maybe three or four nuclear missiles shot at both Israel and the U.S. in 2014 or 2015. Gemini, JFK's birth sign, and being the first Catholic U.S. President, equals the hours of 11 a.m. to 1 p.m. when the assassination took place on seven hills or mountains as the Pope in Italy rules from the same mountains or stories of the Texas School Book Depository. All are fulfilled at this time except for the resurrection of JFK from a fatal head wound as Ezekiel chapter 30, Daniel chapter 11 and Revelation 13, and 17 as the eight king or U.S. President to die in office.

In the temple where this carving is are carvings on the walls or hallway showing a giant light bulb, a apache helicopter and a modern day jet fights 1000s of years before they ever were invented.

The ancient carving also shows Gemini not as twins boy's, but as a king or President with his wife, which is exactly the way JFK and his wife were sitting in the car. And Daniel 11:24 predicts Oswald in the 11th month (=Chapter 11) of our November on the 24th day (=24 day=24 verse) which was a Sunday in 1963 when Jack Ruby shot Oswald and killed him on live TV and on that date and left RFK to stop his warfare with the Mob who over ran all of the U.S. with gang violence and much riches exactly as predicted by Nostradamus as a man in the "misty woods" was the guilty party. Read the book "The man on the grassy knoll". Also see my books "The Seven Thunders," "The Antichrist," "The

Divine Code 2," "End Time Signs II" and all my other books as well documenting these events.

H. See drawings 1-6 in Chapter 6 for the drawings of the ancient Egyptian carving and stars that revealed ancient prophecies. The U.S. White House is in the zones of Pisces which constellation is two fishes tied together by the tails by a rope. This could have the prediction of two subs by Russia firing one to three nuclear ballistic missiles at Israel and the U.S. Pisces is the number 12th sign and is given the numbers 1 (=first sign and sun=1) and 3 (=ruled by Jupiter the number 3) and are as subs by Russia under the sea launched on those two nations by a leader in the Libra zone (=Moscow) and born on the seventh day of Libra or October 7, 1952 the Chinese Year of the Great Red Dragon that the President of Russia now (=June 30, 2014) is born in as President Putin shoots at the double zones of Pisces that the White House is in or near it. Why Russian leader Putin does this is for Israeli attacks on Iran that is its ally in which they attack Iran at that time and Israel and the U.S. counters its attack on Iran and Russia. the leader or President of Iran at this time of late June 2014 was born in the Taurus sign that Iran is ruled by and in the Scorpio sign Iran is also ruled by, along with Sagittarius the archer of arrows or missiles flown by Israeli jets at Iran. See drawings 1-6 in chapter 6 for these predictions on an ancient Egyptian carving and stars shown in the sky or heavens. See Revelation chapter 12 for details of this great red dragon that predicted these events by the red communist state of Russia who draws down a third of the stars by his tail. The Draco constellation is named as the Dragon whose tail goes by the Milky Way and the many stars that are many missiles by Israel on Iran

Russia's ally. See Revelation 6:12-13 and chapter 12 of that book in the Bible. These are the three shepherds or leaders that God hates as Zechariah 11:8 and verse 16 predicts as leaders of Iran, Russia and the U.S. are all killed in the first (=one) month of September-October or December-January or March-April or June-July of 2014-2015. Those leaders are President Putin, Iran's leader and President Obama.

Chapter Five

Final Notes

In the book "The Philadelphia Experiment" it tells of a man which was an eyewitness to the event said when it was going on that he saw things or figures on the docks that don't seem to be there. Did he see God Almighty with Jesus Christ and the Holy Ghost and satan, the antichrist and false prophet making Einstein to have discovered God? Read my book "The Experiment at Philadelphia: Did Einstein discover God? It is available at this web site WWW. Authorhouse.Com.

The two candlesticks or lamps seen on the ancient Egyptian carving on the ceiling of the temple Hathor that shows a imaginary lines through them and through a man on top of Libra and the back of the head of Gemini means "fire" in Greek or Hebrew. The Gemini sign that JFK was born under rules the arms. Put the two together and you have firearms or rifles and guns shot at the back of Gemini's head and right front from the grassy knoll or behind the picketed fence. Those two people are Oswald and Rogers that show four billets at JFK (=Gemini) hired by the king (=leader) of the South as two nuts he wanted to hire to kill JFK in the South in one of the largest or fattest (=largest state=Texas) province and known for oil (fattest).

My Grandmother was born on August 4, the same as President Obama. My grandfather died March 21, 1976. Are those dates important for predicted events in 2014-2015?

The Malaysian airliner flight 370 went missing maybe what Nostradamus C10:Q75 predicts as "he will never return in Europe" (EU) or Asia because he was on that plane that went missing and his body never found. Even the time is near in polar opposite of 11 a.m.-1 p.m. or 11 p.m. to 1-2 a.m. on March 6-7-8, 2014.

In the hallway or in the temple itself of the temple Hathor are carvings of a giant light bulb, an apache helicopter and a modern day jet fighter carved 1000s of years ago before the were ever invented. See Daniel 11:19-21 for prophecy of this Malaysian flight 370 that went missing and my book "The Seven Thunders" pages 60, 72-73 and 87. The antichrist may have been on that flight and will never return, not in Europe as Daniel predicted nor in Asia as Nostradamus C10:Q75 predicted. Another may well appear in Asia in our future and maybe just be a well known writer of Science that deceives the world with his or her's books or by an UFO or UFO's landing with those same books.

The book of Ezekiel in the Bible predicted a king with two arms (=Gemini=JFK) are broken and one is healed. Was this a prediction of the antichrist's head wound and then comes back to life like JFK later on in our future or someone else? JFK right hand man was RFK his brother as the other arm. Both JFK and RFK were born and died in polar opposites of the signs of Gemini and Sagittarius (=cusp of Sagittarius=RFK).

The reason Governor Connally was pictured on the ancient carving in front of JFK (=Gemini) was because he was most likely conceived in the Gemini sign being born in February 25- 28 a year before or on JFK's birthday or after it.

The ancient Egyptian carving from the temple Hathor shows a man in a circle on top of Libra. The circle can mean a new or full moon and Libra means Oswald's birth sign in the years 2014-2017. Libra, in numerology, is given the numbers six and is the seventh sign. And the two trays of Libra equals two times six or twelve. And Jupiter rules Libra and is the number three. The Jewish Civil calendar starts near Libra as the first (=one) month in our September. Put them all these numbers all together and you have 12:31 p.m. the exact minute of the JFK assassination.

The 51.4 years of a generation one preacher said to added to November 22, 1963 equals November 22, 2014 when events may happen on, which is a new moon. Add the .4 to that date and it equals March-April of 2015 when some or all these predicted events happen on. You have a solar eclipse (=darkened sun) on March 20-21, 2015 and April 4, 2015 is a lunar eclipse or blood moon, which begins Passover and near to Easter. And as the movie "Psycho" and my angel visitation in August 1995 with three birds on his neck and crosses over to Bates Street or Avenue as Norman Bates the "Psycho" played by Tony Perkins makes the prophecies for April 4, 2015 meaningful. Mr. Perkins was born April 4, 1932. Was this angel visitation a sign for that date of April 4, 2015? April 4 is 95 days into the year and 270 days left in the year. Polar opposite that is September 27, 2014-2015 when it's 95 days left in the year and 270 days into the end of the year.

Iran's new President was born November 11 or 12 making him, a Scorpio. Washington D.C. is ruled by Scorpio with two Scorpio's fighting each other. And Sagittarius is an archer of arrows shooting at the end of Libra and the beginning of Scorpio on November 22, 1963 and 2014 or 2015. Iran also is in both the Scorpio and Sagittarius zones. See drawings 1-6 in Chapter 6 of this book. November 22, 2014 is a new moon will something happen then.

My book "The boy who could predict earthquakes" on the rear cover has the dates of May 19-20, 2013 when a great storm hits the U.S. A great tornado hit the U.S. on that very date. A code within a code.

Is the polar opposite of the Bates actor in the movie "Psycho" that of the dates September 26-27, 2014-2015 as his birthday mentioned above? Daniel chapter 10 predicts an Israeli attack on Iran (=Persia) on the fourth day of their first month on their civil calendar or September 27-28, 2014- 2015. Add 21 days to that date and it equals a date or time span when Israeli attack on Iran and Iran and/ or Russia fights back and Israel attacks again Iran just as Daniel chapter 10 predicted! Colossians 2:16-17 predicts events happening on or near a new moon (September 24-27, 2014), on a Sabbath Day of Friday evening into Saturday September 26-27, 2014 or 2015 and a holyday or Rosh Hashanah on September 24-27, 2014 or 2015, which is September to December of 2014 equals 2015 translated to our calendar from the Jewish civil calendar.

The dates of October 7-8, 15, 17-18 or on September 13-16, 27-28, 2014-2015 could be dates for predicted events such as hurricanes to hit the South or Florida as are holidays of the feasts of Trumpets and feast of tabernacles. See Jeremiah 20:14-18. In those verses are dates of those just mentioned when God overthrew the cities in those verses just mentioned. There could be two or three predicted events on those dates just mentioned. They could be one for one for one year or two for one year or two years predicted events such as hurricanes, tidal waves, volcano eruptions and a limited nuclear war. The volcano eruption could be off the West Coasts of Africa that causes a island to slip into the sea and caused a great tidal wave to rush across the Atlantic Ocean towards the U.S. Eastern Coast line. The third could be a limited nuclear war between Iran and Israel and/or Russia and the U.S. Read my books entitled "Predictions for 2015 Revised Edition", "Predictions for 2013-2014", "The Seven Thunders", and "End Time Signs II at this web site where you can order them: Authorhouse.Com.

These events are signs that the kingdom of God is at hand. Jesus started His ministry saying "the kingdom of God is at hand" along with John the Baptist. The "Strong's Concordance of the Bible" has three full pages of the word "hand or hands" mentioned in the Bible. The human hand has 27 bones in it which corresponds to the 27th day of September in 2014-2015. Is this a clue to that phrase and date? Both the Books of Daniel and Revelation are the 27th books of the New and Old Testaments in the Old King James Bible. The book of Revelation in the Bible is the last book of the Bible. Was that a clue of end time signs on the date September 27, 2014-2015? Daniel chapter 10 was written in 537-536 B.C., which in Chinese astrology is the Years of the Pig and Rat. The polar opposite of the Rat is the Chinese Year of the Horse, which September 27, 2014-2015 are. Remember that the Jewish Civil Calendar begins its new year in September-October in 2014, to our 2015. So that 2014 past those dates equals 2015 till that time in our next year.

The book of Jasper mentioned in the Bible, but not found in the Bible was found by one preacher who said that it told of Judges or Courts in the time of Sodom and Gomorrah passed laws legalizing sex in open streets. This is just as Judges and Courts are doing now in the U.S. making legal same sex and rights, right before those cities were destroyed. The "days of Lot and Noah" as the Bible predicts will be like that in the end times we are now in. The "days of Noah" happened when UFOs and alien encounters were happening in the open just as Revelation 13:13 predicts for our future now or near or far future. "The days of Lot and Noah" as the Bible predicts the end time signs are like, can not only mean like what I just said, but certain dates or months those two people are associated by. For example, "The days of Noah" is connected to Noah's flood and the dates May 19-20 or November 10-11 or the months of May-June and November-December 2014-2015, 2024, 2026- 2027, 2060-2061 and 3005 A.D. See II Peter chapter 3, Matthew chapter 24, Luke chapters 17, 21, Mark chapter 13 and Genesis chapter 6. The creation, flood and end may all fall on those dates or months and years. The "flood" can also mean tidal waves and hurricanes at those times of months and years that hit the U.S. or on September 27, 2014-2015.

The Book of Revelation was written by John the Disciple on the island of Patmos near the Western part of Turkey where the seven churches are exactly below and across the sea is the great pyramids and Sphinx at Giza, Egypt. All these places are in the Virgo-Libra zones which is ruled buy in Latin the days of the week of Wednesday-Thursday, which are ruled by Mercury and Jupiter. In Latin those planets are given the names of Wednesday-Thursday. The sphinx in Egypt is the body of a lion (=Leo) and head of Virgo (=virgin woman). Revelation 5:5, 22:16 predicts the end as the Root and Offspring of David. The Root of David is Jesse his father born June 27, His offspring is Solomon born October 15 and David and Daniel born September 19 some 280 days to June 25. Was June 27 a clue to these prophecies to happen on the 27th day of September 2014-2015 and/or September 27, 3005 A.D.? The latter date is a Thursday when the end (=Omega) comes and the Revelation and Mystery of God is revealed as Revelation chapter 10 predicts. That date is not only the end of Virgo and the beginning of Libra, but is also the time of Leo's end and the beginning of Virgo (=Sphinx) due to the precession of the equinoxes. It is also the cusps of Virgo-Libra signs.

The angel visitation I had connected to the movie "Psycho" gives three dates of predicted events with two dates are the same many years apart. One of those dates already happened with the Japan earthquake and tidal wave, which the movie pointed to an omen (=bird) happening on the Friday 11th of March 2011 A.D. at 2:43 p.m. That date and time is shown in that movie's beginning on December 11 a Friday at 2:43 p.m. The exact minute was only off by three minutes at 2:46 p.m. local time on Friday March 11, 2011. The day 11 can be three like when the movie "Psycho" began on November 11 and is the 11th month and year is 2011 and 11th month late or the cusp on March 11, 2011 by the Biblical calendar. See my book "The boy who could predict earthquakes." The three birds seen around the angel's neck was predicting three events which fall on the same dates. Those same three dates are December 21-25, 28-29, 2014,

2015 and 2024. September 26-27, 3005 A.D. is the final date. The middle bird on the angel's neck had two red tip wings on it showing the same bad Omen's on the same dates just given. That along with the Japan earthquake and tidal wave make three omens or birds. "Psycho" the movie has the lady driving out of the city where you can see in the streets Christmas decorations, which are for Christmas Eve and Day of three bird and bad omens we just read the dates of on December 24-25, 28-29, 2014, 2015 and 2024. The "Psycho" movie was release in June of 1960, which is when the true Christmas Eve and Day are on June 24-25, with 12 Chinese Yearly cycles added to 1960 and its polar opposite both in years and months equals December 24-25, 2014.

As for the exact minute of the end on September 26-27, 3005 A.D. Matthew 25:1-13 may give a clue to what it is. As my book "End Time Signs II" predicts the 10 virgins in those verses mean 12:18 a.m. on a Wednesday-Thursday September 26-27, 3005 A.D. at 1:18 a.m. due to Daylight Savings Time in the Eastern U.S. Those dates of 1995, 2014-2015 and 3005 A.D. are all about the same moon phase. The movie "Psycho" came out in June of 1960, which was the polar opposite year of our year 2014 as the date predicted above on December 24-25, 2014, 2015 and 2024. When you count in Chinese 12 yearly cycles from 1960 it equals 2014 as the polar opposite. Count backwards from 3005 A.D. equals 2009 A.D. the polar opposite of 2009 A.D. is September 26-27, or December 21-25, 28-29, 2014-2015 A.D. Norman Bates (=Bates street or avenue plus the birds as omens) in the movie "Psycho" was Tony Perkins born April 4, 1932, which we read earlier as the polar opposite of

September 27, 2014-2015 or the polar opposite we just read as December 24-25, 2014.

The circle with a man in it on top of Libra seen on the carving equals a new moon at the end of Libra and beginning of Scorpio. The star time of that is no other than November 22, 2014 the anniversary of the JFK assassination in November 22, 1963 with the duck or Goose near it which rules in Chinese astrology the year of Rabbit the polar opposite of the Rooster which is in the bird family that rule Virgo that is when these events happen on star time of Virgo on September 27, 2014 or 3005 A.D.

The box that the three wavy lines are in on the carving in or near Libra-Virgo and Pisces equals three different events all connected to three wavy lines or stormy seas (=wavy lines), earthquakes (wavy lines=Richter scale) and war or attacks of a nuclear bombs (wavy line) shot at Libra, which is Israel and Russian. The U.S. and Iran on September 24-28, October 8-9, 15, 17-18-19, 2014-2015. Pisces (=U.S.) where one of the boxes (coffins) see on the ancient Egyptian carving is the Eastern U.S. and Libra (U.S. and Russian and Israel) and Leo (President Obama) seen. See drawings 1-6 in Chapter 6 in this book. All three wavy lines in the ancient carving in Eastern U.S. and on September 27-October, 2014-2015 equals wavy lines of the sea wavy, wavy lines on the Richter scale and wavy line in the sky and heaven and earth as nuclear missiles and bombs hit Israel, Iran, Russia and the U.S. This is the shaking of the heavens and earth that many Bible verses predicted. These events could also mean 2 subs (=Pisces two fishes which run below the waters as a sub does of Russia and the U.S. that shoot three nuclear tip warheads at Israel for Israel's attack on Iran and one sub launching nuclear tip missile of the White House making the landscape darkened or destroyed as Zechariah 11:8, 17 and chapter 14 predicted.

Revelation 6:12-13, Joel and Acts chapters 2 all predict these events as happening on a sackcloth and darkened sun on a solar eclipse when the moon is a new moon or dark and on a blood moon when there is a lunar eclipse on March 20-21, 2015 and April 4, 2015. But if those dates are earlier it would put them in September-October of 2014 just as Psalms chapter 90 and Nostradamus C1:Q56 predicted as a date changed to sooner when terrible vengeance's happen on these places. See drawings 1-6 in Chapter 6 of this book. These date of September 24-28, 2014 and March 20-21 and April 4, 2015 means God's right hand (=September 24-28, 2014-2015) and God left hand (=March 20-21). Those dates are when or near when Jesus Christ was conceived and born nine months later on June 24-25 and when John the Baptist was conceived on March 20-21 and born on December 24-25. They are polar opposites of each other as left and right hands are. And December 25, 2015 is a full moon, but is not a lunar eclipse or blood moon.

Isaiah chapter 21 predicts as well as the ancient Egyptian carving does with a 12 year period from, when a dog President (=President Bush born 1946 the Chinese Year of the Dog) was who fighting a Taurus woman (Saddam Hussein) in the circle between Pisces (=12 Years from the first Bush) to launch an attack on Iraq and Saddam Hussein (=Taurus) near a full moon and end of Pisces as the second Bush did. The 12 years added to 1991 and 2003 in the first months by the Julian and Gregorian calendars are when a Dog (=President Bush senior) attack Iran in January 16-17,

1991 near a new moon. And the second war happened 12 years later by another U.S. President born in the Chinese Dog Year of 1946 who attacks Saddam Hussein (=Taurus=Saddam=the Destroyer=Abaddon or Apollyon for five months August to January of 1990-1991=Revelation 9:10 in their attack helicopters as Irvin Baxter says) on a new moon in 1991 or near a full moon and the end of Pisces in March 19-20, 2003 just as the carving shows. See drawings 1-6 in chapter 6 of this book. When adding 12 years to that near a new moon(=new moon and full moon both equals a circle), which the woman or Taurus (Saddam Hussein) was born and when both Iraq wars started 12 years apart on new moon and full moons. But Nostradamus predicted in his quatrain C1:Q56 that the changes in time from sooner (=March 20-21 and April 4, 2015) are changed like the later dates of June 24-25, 3005 A.D. Add 12 years to 2003 and it equals March 20-21, April 4, 2015 on solar and lunar eclipses to near a new moon on September 24-28, 2014. Isaiah chapter 21 also predicts "watch of the night and inquire twice then return, come and whirlwind of the south past through" Could this has mean two times are night troubles comes and to watch those nights and inquire, inquire, return, come. The return could be that of the Rapture in September 24-28, or December 21-25, 28-29, 2014-2015 some dates earlier then when 12 years are added to 2003=+12=2015 on a solar or lunar eclipse. That would mean March 20-21 and April 4, 2015 changed in dates to September-October 2014. The earlier can also mean later then June 24-25, 3005 A.D. changed to September 27, 3005 A.D. instead of June of 3005 A.D. or changes year on that date making it a year early and months after June 24-25,

3005 when the full end of the earth comes with Christ's Second Coming if you don't count the Rapture or it doesn't happen then as the (inquire, inquire) return, come as the Second Coming and Rapture. Isaiah chapter 21 and Zechariah 9:14 predicts whirlwinds of the South past through. The word "whirlwinds" is plural meaning more than one. Could this mean two or more great storms (=Whirlwinds= hurricanes or tornadoes?) hitting The U.S. South at one of these times when arrows fly and stars from the heaven fall with many missiles shot by Israeli jets on Iran followed by a Russian subs by Israel shoot (arrows) three nuclear tip bombs on Israel and one Russian sub off the coast of the White house fires on it. The many missiles and planes are that of the drawings 1-6 in chapter 6 in this book. With the many stars of the Milky Way fired from a Libra man (=President Putin=Libra zone) and born on the seventh day of Libra to our calendar or October 7, 1952 shoots three nuclear bombs at Israel by a fish under the sea as a Russian sub. Israel's many jets and bombs (=Milky Way) attack on Iran (=Taurus=Milky way goes through not seen on the drawing,) but a man on top of Libra is seen at the tail of the Dragon (=Draco) in a circle (new moon or full moon) on Libra (=Israel and the U.S. that Libra rules democracy two nations of the U.S. and Israel symbol of Libra two trays or two parts of governments. Washington, D.C. is ruled by not only double Pisces, but also Scorpio. And Moscow, Russia and its Leader President Putin are Libra's and Iran President is Scorpio born and is now (July 1, 2014) in office and President Obama was born in the Leo sign all match the stars and ancient prophecies. See drawings 2-6 in chapter 6 of this book. Iran also rules the Scorpio and Sagittarius zones which Sagittarius is half Horse and have man as a archer of arrows. This would make the prophecies of the stars come true along with Aquila (=eagle jet fighter) and Sagitta the arrow (=smart bombs) in the Milky Way near Scorpio, Sagittarius and Libra to all line up with predictions told about in the heavens. See drawings 1-6 in chapter 6 of this book. If Billy Graham dies at this time then it leaves the withholding power of the Holy Ghost so that the antichrist and false prophet could be revealed and the Rapture comes at this time. But another Holy Ghost man may come at this time and reveal all of satan's plans beforehand taking the sting out of them or stopping them all together. See "The End of the Days" by Author E. Bloomfield pages 258-261. The "sooner and later changes are made" predicted by Nostradamus C1:Q56 may mean thee sooner dates of these great vengeance's doesn't come early (=sooner) in June of 2014 and September 2014 nor does they come later in March 20-21, 2015 and April 4, 2015, but they come in December 21-25, 28-29, 2014. As for the blood moons and solar eclipses and just new moons and full moons may be separate prophecies them the sun and moon grows dark because of a super volcano eruption and ash, smoke and gases go around the earth darkening the sun, moon and stars for days, months or years causing many very bad famines and chaos. Along with that pieces of rock will fall down upon the earth just as Revelation 6:12-17 predicts as stars falling from heaven and people hide in caves from the great wrath of God for the hail. Luke 21:9- 11, 24-25-26 predicts scary signs from heaven and this is at least one of them. Another maybe the earth's rotation stopping causing dark at noon and noon at midnight which would literally scare the nations and people into a heart attack exactly as Luke chapter 21 predicts. They don't know it will only last three days and that it is done for very good reason. That is long life and peaceful earth of animals, growing things with no more cures on people or the earth and animals. And with the witholding of the tree of life changed to positive or taken away all diseases are cured and eternal physical life. But no more pain of babies or periods for women will be sterile. This is because we couldn't keep multiplying for 1000 years plus the tree of life is Lithium which causes pregnant women to give birth to babies with heart defects. And speaking of women Obadiah 1-6 may predict a U.S. woman President elected in 2016 and again in 2020 whose alive to see these great wars and there is a war or super volcano eruption of Yellowstone at this which is warned by angels (=ambassadors) and rumors at these times. The woman maybe Hillary Clinton who is from Little Rock, Arkansas and sees these wars and disasters in <u>four</u> berries and <u>five</u> berries on the vine, which are 201<u>4</u> and 201<u>5</u> and 202<u>4</u>. And as Obadiah 1-6 predicts a leader from a place called "Little" (="small) and "Edom" (=Rock) would be the next leader of the U.S. and a woman who sees the country be destroyed like George Washington angel told him as well as a preacher Perry Stone told of predicted these same things long ago. Then there will be small and greatly despised just as Obadiah 1-6 predicted on the dates of this book or in the grape harvest in July-August-September as Obadiah 1-6 and Zechariah chapter 14 predicts, along with a nuclear war or solar storm hitting the earth. Jacob and Esau were born September 19. Edom represents Jacob the twin (=two) brother of his named Esau. Are these prophecies of two years or by and by or two years before the earthquake in Amos 1:1-2-3-4 that of two years added to the end date everyone thought was December 21, 2012? Add two years to that and come to December 21-25, 28-29, 2014 or 2015. And will in 2024 the U.S. is destroyed and the Americans die and few or small numbers survive with them being greatly despised by many Muslims and other people around the world for their wickedness and blame for these events.

On one of the drawings of the ancient carving from the temple Hathor in Egypt shows the monkey's tail going down to Libra and near or next to the dragon (=Draco) is a jackal or dog, Monkey or baboon and a bird with a box with three wavy lines in it near Pisces which I just describe. Pisces is the two fishes that goes under the sea as a sub does and shoots from under the sea three or one nuclear tip ballistic missiles at Israel (Libra) and the U.S. (Pisces) in the Libra sign of September 24-28, October 8-9, 17-18, or December 21-25, 28-29, 2014-2015. This is the symbolism of Pisces and the box with three wavy line sin it the same as Libra with a lion below it as shown on drawings 1-6 in chapter 6 of this book. On the carving is that of Leo the lion's front feet on a box with three wavy lines in it just as Pisces has. Thus, the jackal or dog means Libra sign of September 22-October 23, 2014 is when a bird (=Virgo cosign of Gemini=bird) drawing down a star on a Leo leader who is President Obama, along with one missile drawn down to Moscow and President Putin (Libra=Dog=jackal in Chinese astrology) and Libra can mean Washington, D.C. who shoots many stars or missiles on Iran along with Israel as the three wavy lines in two boxes (coffins) in Pisces (D.C.) and on Russian (Libra and Israel) when two or three or more storms, hit the South

U.S., two great earthquakes hit the U.S. and war or attacks hit the U.S. The preacher Perry Stone said in his show in late June early July 2014 that the ancient letters of Hebrew meant the first letter as the Ox and the last letter a cross. Could that have meant the OX year when the cross is finished at the end and brings people to heaven? September 25-27, 3005 is the Chinese year of the Ox. When the end comes as the same mark that marked the death of Jesus Christ.

The star chart in chapter 6 of this book in drawings 1-6 shows Taurus not seen with the Milky Way of many stars coming across heaven to Sagittarius, Sagitta (the arrow) and Aquila the eagle as archer of many arrows (=Sagitta) missiles) shot by Israeli jet planes (eagle=planes) at Iran with many bombs and missiles fall from Israel on Iran. The Sagittarius is half man and half archer of arrows. That could mean the Chinese Year of the Horse in 2014 shoots many stars (Milky Way) or missiles or bombs on Iran as the Milky Way see of drawings 1-6 shows. Taurus where the Milky way stars comes from rules Persia or Iran and Scorpio where it goes to next to Sagittarius and Libra could have meant Iran's ally Russia shooting three nuclear tip ballistic missiles at Israel for their attack on Iran and then Iran, Russia and the U.S. are attack by one missile on the U.S. and Russia and many on Iran. See drawings 1-6 in chapter 6 of this book for the star chart and parts of this carving that predicts these events.

Jeremiah chapter 6 predicts trouble out of the North for Benjamin (=Netenyahu President of Israel now July 1, 2014) in the last days according to the Bible. The "Out of the North" to Israel is Russia which may attack Israel if Israel attacks Iran.

The Book of Revelation also in the Bible was written down on June 12, 96 A.D., which was a Sunday or "Lord's Day" as Revelation chapter one predicts that day. September 27, 2014 is the Sabbath day to Israel and Isaiah Chapter 49 verse 15 predicts a woman forgetting her son born on October 15 (=October 15), but God doesn't forget him. My Mother was born September 27, 1922 and died of Alzheimer's on July 30, 2006 which was a Sunday and when the woman clothes with the sun is seen in heaven. Just as revelation predicted in chapter 12 long ago. Alzheimer's disease is a forgetting sickness. Isaiah chapter 49 in chapter/year codes equals our year 1949 when on October 21, 1949 Benjamin Netanyahu was born on a new moon or near it just as September 24-28, 2014-2015 are on or near a new moon or full moon. Will the events predicted in this book happen then or September 27-28, 2014-20015? The other dates are Saturday-Sunday in 2014 and are Jewish-Christians Sabbath Days. August 10, 2014 (Song of Solomon 6:10) is also a Sunday (=Sabbath) and August 4-5, 2014 (Song of Solomon 6:13) are the ninth of Av when predicted events are expose to happen, along with one on my mother's birthday on September 27, 2014 which is a Jewish Sabbath starting at 6 p.m. the evening before that date or Friday September 26, 2014.

With the Book of Revelation in the Bible being written down on June 12, 96 A.D. on our Julian calendar and the Disciple John who wrote it makes a lot of connections to these ancient prophecies. One, is John's birthday of June 20 a symbol date of God's two witnesses who reveal the little book (=small book) of Revelation chapter 10. Which in Chapter Year codes equals our Chinese Year of the Horse in 2014. The Chinese Year of the Horse rules our Gemini sign, which is June 20 that is the end of that sign. My friend Bob and brother Lon also fits the two witnesses who come up from hell (=dunghill) to preach and prophesied to the world for three and a half years now or near the end in 3005 A.D. Bob was born December 24-25 the birthdays of Elijah, John the Baptist and Moses.

The date of June 12, 96 A.D. to the Gregorian calendar is June 24-25, 2014-2015 A.D. With 13 days added to the Julian calendar of June 12 equals those dates. June 12, 2014 plus three and half months or time, times and as half or 1260 or 42 months can represent add to June 12, 2014 equals September 26- 27-28, 2014 when the little book is revealed by God's two witnesses as Revelation chapters 10-11 predict. Will one of those witnesses die on June 12, 2014 then three and half months later the end time events happen on September 26-27-28, 2014? Billy Graham and Pat Robertson are two of the two witnesses of God predicted in the Bible. Both of whom were born in the Chinese Year of the Horse in 1918 and 1930 and is the year 2014 (=Chinese Year of the Horse). The Chinese Year of the Horse rules are Gemini the sign of the twins or God's two witnesses. Or will Billy Graham die on September 2, 2014 plus three and a half weeks equals September 26-27, 2014 when Billy Graham and Pat Robertson both die on one of these date of June 12, 24-25, 27, 29, September 2, 24-28, December 21-25, 28-29, 2014=2015?

Isaiah chapter 6 in Chapter 6 in Chapter/year codes is also the Chinese year of the Horse as well as is 2014. Isaiah 6:11- 12-13 predicts great trouble in the midst of the land meaning Yellowstone Park super Volcano erupting on the "tenth" in Latin" or December 24-25, 2024

(=2014+10=2024). That volcano is in the midst (=middle-mid west) of America just as Isaiah 6:11-12-13 predicts. See also Matthew 11:12. John the Baptist was born December 24-25 as that verse in Matthew 11:12 predicts as a time of great violence in the sky or heavens from this super volcano eruption causes. The seed born when the leaves begin to fall from the tree are Solomon's and my birthdays of October 15, which in 2014 in the midst of the month or October 8-9, 15, 2014. The violence in the heavens that Matthew 11:12 predicts at this time could mean one of these events: nuclear war, Venus and earth stop rotating for three hours/days/weeks/months/years, a comet or asteroid hits the earth or seas and Yellow stone Park super volcano erupts. Isaiah 9:10 we heard a lot about in the Harbinger book, but one thing they left was the next verse equals 9-11 which the Harbinger book is all about. Jesus' death on the cross preceded by three hours of darkness which could be a solar or lunar eclipse, but could be a solar eclipse in our future. This could also happen by a new moon or rotation stopping by the earth and Venus at dark on the Eastern U.S. time zone. See Matthew 27:45 and 11:12.

Isaiah 6:12-13 predicted men of a far off (=U.S.) to be removed or run for your lives on December 24, 2024. At that time or shortly after shall be a great forsaking in the midst (=mid-west) of the land as Yellowstone Park's super volcano erupts and men fleeing or removed can mean the 20,000 people who read this book and my other books. The term Isaiah uses as "a people a far off" or men removed "a far off" predicted as the men and people of the U.S. which is "a far off" from Israel. Isaiah chapter 18 predicted as a people meted (=measured) out into states or United States of America.

Proverbs 27:1, 10, 15 predicts a woman from a flood or tidal wave or hurricane or both at that time of that woman's birthday on September 27 and her son's birthday of October 15 (=verse 15). The Chapter number 27 of Proverbs can mean September 27 my mother's birthday. Verse I of that chapter claims it will fail as prophecy in the year 2003 on September 26-27, which was Rosh Hashanah the Jewish Civil new Year's days as Colossians 2:16-17 predicted a failing prophecies comes true in the future as September 26-27, 2014 and 3005 A.D. they come true on. These dates were in 2003 A.D. as a foreshadow of things to come as Colossians 2:16-17 predicted the same or near the same moon phases and a day of the week as 2003 as is in 2014. The friend's house that verse 10 of Proverbs chapter 27 predicts who was born on December 24 Christmas Eve, the end of the day and beginning of a new one as the Jewish civil calendar works on days. Thus, his birthday is on December 24-25, in which we read equals 2024 A.D. on those dates. In 2003 I did hear people judge for meat and drink as Colossians 2:16-17 predicted, but it may have meant high blood sugar and throat closing up as I had in May-June 2014 I had and continue to have in May-July of 2014. Does this mean I will be healed of those problems? Will it be on September 26-27, 2014 when I am healed? Isaiah 17:44 and 40:28-31 also predicts me as having weak legs and faint or fall along with loosing weight. All those things are happening to me in 2014 before September 26- 27, 2014 when I waited on the Lord at his right hand. See Matthew 26:64. The human hand as we read has 27 bones in it and is the symbol of the fall equinox on a new moon of September 24-26, 2014. Those dates are the right hand of God on the fall equinox and fall on a new moon, holyday (=Rosh Hashanah) and the Jewish Sabbath on September 26-27, 2014, which starts on evening time Friday September 26 and ends Saturday evening on September 27, 2014 or those dates and a holiday to the September-October of 2015 according to a lunar calendar. During this same time period from 2003 to September 24-28, 2014 I often said "help me mother" even though she was dead since Sunday July 30, 2006 not knowing it meant her birthday of September 27 when I would receive help. See Ecclesiastes 9:7. That date is in the month the ancient Israel had their wine harvest in as Ecclesiastes 9:7 predicted as well as other verses in the Bible like Revelation chapters 14 and 19 predicts. The ninth chapter of Ecclesiastes can mean on our Gregorian calendar the month of September-our ninth month. The seventh verse can mean September, which is also September in Latin for seven and Libra is the seventh sign that starts September 22-23 to October 19-22, of 2014 when these events may happen in.

The two candlesticks or lamps seen on the ancient Egyptian carving are the two candlesticks and two olive trees or branches are God's two witnesses. They are pictured on the ancient Egyptian carving from the Hathor as two candlesticks or lamps going thorough the end of Taurus the bull and the beginning of Gemini (=two witnesses) today that time is June 20, 24-25, 27, 29, 2014-2015. See drawings 1-6 in chapter 6 of this book for that ancient Egyptian carving and star symbolism that shows these times and events. Also see the carving in Chapter 7 and

Zechariah 4:11-12 and Revelation Chapter 11. The olive trees or branches are ruled by the Cancer sign from June 21-July 22-23, 2014. The two candlesticks or lamps shown on that ancient Egyptian carving goes through that same times of June 20, 24-25, 27, 29, 2014. Will all these events happen then or three months later on September 24-28, 2014-2015 or by the Lunar calendar on those dates in 2015? Three and a half months from June 12, 2014 is September 27, 2014-2015 when these events predicted happen plus or minus three days.

My book entitled "The boy who could predict earthquakes" in the introduction of that book pages vii-xiii and xix predicts a plane missing at 1:18 a.m. and 2:43 p.m. when an earthquake and trouble with a nuclear power plant. One was a minute off of flight 370 that went missing on March 8, 2014 at 1:19 a.m. local time and the other was March 11, 2011 as a great earthquake and tidal wave hit Japan at 2:46 p.m. According to my book "The Boy who could predict earthquakes" the Japan earthquake of March 11, 2011 a Friday at 2:46 p.m. was off by three minutes. The missing Flight 370 went off air 1:19 a.m. on March 8, 2014 a minute off as that book predicted along with a nuclear power plant being knock out and melt down by the tidal wave. See also the exact date and year in my book entitled "The Seven Thunders".

I am writing this at evening time on June 9, 2014 after being sick for a certain time. Daniel 8:26-27 predicts the evening and the morning. Add three and a half days to that date and hours from morning to evening and it equals June 11- 12, 2014 in the seventh hour or morning when Israel attacks Iran. I plan to watch the evening and morning news on those dates. Daniel 12:7 time (=day), times (= two days) and a half 6-12 hours equals three and a half months from those dates of September 26-27, 2014 when these events happen. The 12 hours or years Daniel chapter 8 predicts can mean June 24-25, 2014- 2015. When you add three months and three days to that date of June 24-25, 2014 it equals September 26-27, 2014 when all these prophecies come true. Twelve days added to June 11-12, 2014 equals June 23-24-25, 2014 when all these or at least some of these prophecies come true now or in the future possibly the far future. If they don't happen on June 12, 2014 they may strike Iran 12 days later as the vision of Daniel 8:26-27 predicts on June 24-25, 27, 29, 2014 or 2015 plus three months and three days or September 24-30, 2014-2015. The "double' warfare in June of 1967 and June of 2014 could be changed to September-October of 2014-2015. Isaiah 40:2 and Daniel 10:19, 2021. The 21 days and 12 days come from Daniel 8:26-27 and 10:4, 19 changed from hours of 12 to 12 days and three weeks changed to three months and three days to June 24-25, 2014 which is June 12 when Revelation was written down plus 12-13 days to June 24-25 plus three months to September 24 plus three days to September 27-28, 2014-2015.

Maybe what the last paragraph was what Nostradamus meant by changes (plural) made by sooner and later dates for great horrors and vengeance's happen when approaching the Balances (=Scales=Libra) in C1:Q56? Did it mean two dates in the months of September, one in 2014 on September 27 and the other in 3005 A.D. in the month of September both on September 27? The moon on that date of June 12-13, 2014 might be not a lunar eclipse but a full moon known as the "full strawberry moon" which is red with three and a half months (time, times and half months) equals September 27-28, 2014-2015 when these very ancient prophecies happen. See Revelation chapter 12. My mother died of Alzheimer's on July 30, 2006 a Sunday morning at 5 a.m. We read in this book how the Book of Revelation was written down on June 12, 96 A.D. That day was a Sunday and was sent to seven churches in the western Turkey time zones that rule Virgo-Libra. The exact planets they rule are Mercury and Jupiter are names in Latin for Wednesday-Thursday. Those days was on June 11-12, 2014. We read in this book how Revelation was written down on June 12, 96 A.D. on a Sunday (=Lord's Day) in the Julian calendar, which is 13 days behind our Gregorian calendar making June 24-25, 2014 A.D. be our June 11-12, 2014. A.D. See the books off Haggai 2:18-23. Both the books of Haggai and Revelation tell of the same months and day of the four beasts and 24 elders as the fourth months and 24th day as the calendars of the Bible and the Jewish Civil calendars, which gives the dates of June 24 and December 24, 2014-2015 A.D. or the Julian calendar of June 12, 2014-2015 A.D. Were these dates what Psalms chapter 90 meant by predicting an earlier date? In chapter/Year codes Psalms chapter 90 equals our year 2014 A.D. That same year equals September 27, 2014 as Revelation chapter 10 equals our year 2014. In chapter 10 of Revelation it predicts a small book paperback 5x8 with 175-200 pages with seven chapters revealed early or satisfy early as Psalms chapter 90 predicts. That chapter number is the year of 1990 A.D. plus 24=2014 when these events happen the same year as Revelation chapter 10 when a little books (5x8=175-200 pages with seven chapters). In that chapter 10 of Revelation in that chapter it predicts a small book written on the front and back pages sealed with seven seals or seven chapters. The angel in that same chapter is standing on the earth (=Gemini) and the sea (=Cancer) and lifts his right hand up to heaven. The right hand is the summer solstice on June 20-21 and the fall equinox on September 22-23, plus four as the beast are four after these four season equals September 26-27, 2014 when these prophecies come true. The earth and sea that the angel stands on and lifts it right hand to heaven are that of June 12 by the Julian calendar or June 24-25 by the new Gregorian calendar with three and a half hours/days/weeks/months/years to these events. Adding three and a half months to June 12 equals September 27, 2014-2015-2016-2017 when these events all happen on. Gemini, Orion, Taurus and Auriga are all seen in heaven at midnight over head on December 21-25, 28-29, 2014-2015. Was these dates what the angel lifted his hand up to heaven with a little book in it to be revealed and read when travel (=to and fro) for the Christmas Holidays happens as Daniel 12:4 predicts? John is told by the angel or God to eat the book and he did and its was sweet in his mouth and once swallowed was sour or bitter in his stomach. Sugar is sweet and Lithium give nauseous or bitter stomach, which is the tree of life for sugar has hydrogen in it the number one on our atomic elements chart and Lithium is number three as the Trinity of God with the middle equaling nothing or neutral.

A watchman of the house that in the middle of the night is when a thief cometh that predicts the Greek word for an earthquakes in the Bible means commotion's, air, gale and tempest, which means an air attack by Israel on

Iran. The words mean that word in Greek are "second", Moon, Brilliancy or full moon. The word second can mean the number 2, which is given to the moon and Cancer sign on a full moon or brilliancy on June 12-13, 2014 plus three and half months equals September 27, 2014-2015. The word from the Lord I received early in May 2014 might not be for June of 2014, but September 27, 2014. I became sick on May 29, 2014 when I saw a doctor. Twelve days (=12 hours from evening to morning as the book of Daniel chapter 8 predicts) later I was healed on June 8-9, 2014. These are certain days of Daniel 8:26-27 when I was sick and was healed. I then was raised up and did the king's business. Sunday June 8, 2014 is ruled by the Sun that rules kings. This could also be found in Revelation Chapter 12 as 12 stars or days ending on Sunday June 8-9, 2014. The great red dragon could mean Sunday as the time of when Adam and Eve ate of the fig tree that rules Libra the sign when her son (me) was born. Sundays seem so depressing and this is why. The tail of the dragon pulls down two or three stars of Libra and then a flood time (one day), times (=two days) and a half (=six to 12 hours) on a full Strawberry (Red) moon is on June 12-13, 2014 plus three and a half months equals September 23-28, 2014 or 2015 near or on a new moon and on or near a full moon that has a lunar eclipse or blood Moon starting from Sunday June 8, 2014. Or are these events December 21-25, 28-29, 2014 and 2015 when there is a full moon on Christmas Day in 2015?

These things are also the time of my birth when a flood or storm Hurricane Hazel came and tried to destroy me at birth hitting the Hospital and knocking out the electricity when my mother was in labor and being wheeled up to the room up stairs to be delivered in which the storm knock out the electricity to the elevator, but the nurse knew of another way up there. That Hurricane was named Hurricane Hazel the same color of my eyes. I was born October 15, 1954 at 8:11 p.m. on a Friday, which is Latin for Venus the bright and morning star that ruled Libra or October 15 and the year is the Chinese Year of the Horse the same as 2014.

The two became one as is then and now Sunday (=sun=one) and Monday (=two-and as the June Bride when Jesus started his ministry on June 26 A.D. Israel became a nation in 1948 A.D. which is the Chinese Year of the Rat the polar opposite of the Horse in 2014. One sign of Gemini rules by the Chinese Horse and is the sign of the twins or two into one as Jacob came out holding his brother's heel on September 19-20 the same as my dad's birthday and his grandfather was Jacob Bakley and his father was named Jesse Bakley born June 27 the same as David's father. My mother, as explained earlier came from strict Christian home, but later in life rebel and betrayed Christ and Christianity and became secular. She was full of Satan. I was full of the antichrist and the false prophet and grew up in a secular home. I then became a born again Christian. I then became secular again to know all of satans' plans and knowledge in advance. Such knowledge as UFOs, science, psychics. MYSTERY BABYLON and all things. Then I betrayed satan and said no to being the antichrist and false prophet. And I turned again to Christ for salvation in which he gave me in early May 2007 A.D. when I was born again the second time being dead twice as Jude in the Bible predicts of me. I then wrote down all satan's knowledge and plans for the future in all my books and plan to reveal them in

September or December of 2014. This is what the author of the book entitled "The End Of the Days" by Arthur E. Bloomfield meant on pages 258-261 by learning satan's plans in advance of UFOs and science you can take the sting out of them and might just prevent them. Isaiah chapter 48 also predicts these things. My mother is the one who hears not nor knows not because she died in 2006 and is in heaven. And as Isaiah chapter 49 predicts she was dyeing of a forgetting diseases (Alzheimer's) at the walls or four walls and eighth number of the word "continuing" on a Sunday July 30, 2006 the Chinese Year of the Dog the same she was born in and died at 84 years old which is the 8 and 4 put together as Isaiah chapter 48 predicted. That same chapter predicts her as a transgressor from the womb, but God would spare her, her life by not cutting her off and taking her to heaven on a Sunday. One week before her death as was told by the Holy Ghost to pray for her and God to take her to heaven and he did. The same for my dad I prayed at his death and God took him form hell's pits to heaven. He was born in the Chinese year of the Sheep or Goat and he died in the year of the sheep or goat or its polar opposite. See Job and Isaiah chapters 48-49, Revelation chapter 12, Psalms 68:17 and Amos 5:7-87 which predicts 20,000 chariots (angels) of God and seven Taurus (seven stars), Orion (=pyramids and sphinx) and Gemini (June 20) near them and the Charioteer (=chariots). The "charioteer" are 20,000 angels that are sent to tell others (see Revelation 3:22) of these books of mine near those constellations when car travel (Charioteer) people travel by to and fro when knowledge increases of times, dates and events. See Daniel 12:4. The "sea" in Amos 5:8 could be Cancer that begins of June 20-21, 2014 or 2015 and is the first day of summer. June 12, 2014 or 2015 is still spring. Remember Jesus predicted all these events happening then on June 12, 2014-2015 then know that summer is nigh or 9 days away till the end. Three and a half months from then in September 27, 2014-2015 when the predictions come true as a change for June to September as Nostradmus predicted. Those four constellations are near or behind the sun on June 12-25, 2014 or 2015 so you can't see them at this time. But with three and a half months added to them equals September 27 and October of 2014 or 2015 you can seen them in early morning or evening. The sphinx and great pyramids at Giza, Egypt are the symbols of this time span and four constellations as the four corners of the pyramids.

It just maybe that Nostradamus' C1:Q56 changes in dates is polar opposites making several changes on dates. Could he have meant earlier (=sooner) then March 20-21 and April 4, 2015 changed to September 27, 2014 and the "latter" as June of 3005 changed to September 27, 3005 A.D.? Or from June 12, 24-25, 2014 or 2015 to September 27, 2014. Or December 21-25, 28-29, 2014. Any of these dates are important to prophecies happening.

In that dream I had about my grand mother's and grand father's woods behind their house could have several meanings. They are the days of death of both plus 3 days/ year to each. We read in my other books how these dates equals three years after the Chinese Dragon Year of 1976 and 2012+3=2015. The year of the dragon is also our years of 2024 when the end of the U.S. happens and 2060 when the end happens on December 24-25 the day John the Baptist was born. See the book of Matthew 11:12 prediction of God shaking the heavens and earth on John the Baptist birthday and year which was 5 B.C. the Chinese Year of the Dragon the same as 2024 A.D. and 2060 A.D. Is that what the ancient Mayans meant by the end in the dragon year not on 2012 A.D. but in 2024 A.D. or 2060 A.D.? Did they start at a wrong date? Also the ninth of Av in all these years came be when these events happen on August 4-5, 2014 and July 25-26, 2015. The year of 1981 when me and my mother and father moved from to Florida form the North East (see Isaiah and Song of Solomon chapter 8) was the year/ chapter codes of Revelation chapter 1 as 1981 the Chinese Year of the Rooster. We arrive in Florida at 12-1 p.m. at McDonald's restaurant in Ocala, Florida on September 27, 1981 my mother's birthday. Three years and days added to my grand father's death on March 21, 1976, the Chinese Dragon year as is also is 2012 equals 2012+3=2015 March 20-21 a solar eclipse or the polar opposite that date of March 21 equals September 21+3=September 24, 2014 the date of the start of the new moon and Rosh Hashanah. If Billy Graham dies September 24, 2014 or 2015 plus three and a half days to September 27-28, 2014 is when these events happen. Shania Twain with one person next to her equals three or 3 or 30 days added or subtracted from August 28 her birthday. Thirty days added to her birthday equals September 27, 2014- 2015 when these events happened. Thirty days subtract from August 28 equals July 30, 2006 when my mom died. June 12, 24- 25, 27, 29 2015 and March 20-21, April 4 are also dates of these events even though Nostradamus predicts their change. Song of Solomon 6:10 predicts a fair moon (=full moon) clear Sun (=Sunday) in the morning and as terrible as an army with banners (=anniversary). Could that army mean the Babylonians and

Roman when the 9th of Av fell on in 587-585 B.C. and 70 A.D. The Roman king Augusts was born September 23, 63 B.C. and we get our month of August from his name and his year of birth in the Chinese year of the Horse the same as August 10, 2014 on a full moon, a Sunday, August and the Chinese Year of the Horse when predicted events happen on? Or dos it mean September 23- 24 plus three and a half days to September 26-27, 2014 when these events happen on or near Augustus' birthday? Or is it December 21+3.5 days till December 25, 2014 and 2015, which the latter is a full moon day and anniversary of an earthquake a year before on Christmas days as Coded Earthquakes my book entitled "Predictions for 2013-2014" that predicted a Hanukah school shooting during Hanukah at a school in 2012 and early 2013 in January there was already several school shootings. That same book predicted flu or sickness to be worry full in those years into 2015.

During world war II and the Vietnam war medics and nurses notice all the same thing that dying soldiers would call for their mothers. Was this the meaning of me calling "help me mom" all the time for decades? Were they and I all calling for help on September 27, 2014-2015 my mother's birthday? That date as Nostradamus C1:Q56 predicts as a time of terrible vengeance in 2014, 2015 and 3005 A.D.

If an earthquake strikes on September 27, 2014 then a year later another great earthquake hits on that same date on a full moon and lunar eclipse (=blood moon) just as Joel and acts chapters 2 predicted. Please read my book "Predictions for 2013-2014" first chapter named "Coded Earthquakes" for details. It's possible the first earthquake on September 27, 2014 strikes San Francisco or Seattle with a tidal wave as double trouble for the U.S. as Isaiah 40:1-2, 61:7 and Zechariah 9:10- 14 predicts. The year 2014 is ruled by the Horse in Chinese astrology which rules our Gemini sign which rules San Francisco and Seattle longitude zone. See my book "The Experiment at Philadelphia" Appendix G for all these codes I use. Isaiah 6:12-13 predicts this shaking or forsaking in the land and is in Year/Chapter codes our year 1906 when on April 18-19 the great San Francisco earthquake and fire happened. Then on the anniversary of that quake will another happen on September 27- 28, 2015 in New Madrid, Missouri? The first earthquake to hit New Madrid, Missouri came in 1811 A.D. when the Chinese Year of the Sheep or goat was as it is in September 27, 2015 or December 21-25, 28-29, 2014 and 2015. And as Isaiah 61:7 and chapter 49 I will mourn the death of another being my brother like I did my mother in 2006. My brother moved to a new house near the sea and I warned him of these dates in September 24- 27, 2014 to be on the look out for a tidal wave. If nothing happens then they may stop listening to me even less then before and they die in the tidal and I move to another place before that happens as a wise man foresees the danger and hides from it as the Bible predicts.

The death of Billy Graham on June 24-25 or 12, 2014 or 2015 or September 21-24, 2014 or 2015 plus three an a half days later equals September 24-25, or 27-28, 2014 or 2015 as too when all these events happen. Daniel 10:4 predicts these horrible events or vengeance's to happen on the first month and 24th day which from the Jewish Civil calendar to our equals September 24, 2014 or 2015. Daniel chapter 12 predicts when a righteous man leads 100's of millions of people to Christ as born again Christians then the end will come. Billy Graham has done that. September 24, 2014 equals Rosh Hashanah on the evening of that day. Three and a half days from then or before then or on that exact date are dates of September 21, 24, 27-28 or December 21-25, 28-29, 2014-2015 when Billy Graham dies and these events happen.

On June 16, 2014 two great tornadoes form side by side in Nebraska-the mid-West and not the South as predicted in the book of Zechariah 9:14. Was it a preview of things to come in 2014 or 2015? Will two tornadoes or hurricanes hit the South in 2014-2015 and hit the same places or opposites like Florida East and West coasts or two tornadoes hit the south or two hurricanes hit the South U.S. at the same time? Will one hit in the South on the dates given for 2014 and then on 2015 on the same dates and full moon and Sunday another hits there in the same place or two different places. The dates of these events might be the ninth of Av (=August 4-5, 2014 and on that same lunar date of 2015), Rosh Hashanah, feast of Tabernacles on a solar or lunar eclipses in October 8-9, 2014; August 4-5, 2014, March 20-21, 2015 or April 3-4-5, 2015 or the ninth of Av in 2015. See Proverbs chapter 6.

Going back to my dream of my grandparents back woods and the monkey eating a wooded pigeon and then a flood could have a deeper meaning than once thought. The Chinese Monkey sign rules our Leo sign or star time and cusp. The pigeon could be a bird connected to Gemini who's cosign is Virgo the Virgin woman. Put these things together and you have Leo cusp star time and Virgo star Time which equals September 27, 2014-2015. Star time is when the sign is actually behind the sun as they are today because of the precession of the equinoxes.

The "sooner and later changes" that Nostradamus predicted in dates could mean these events don't happen in 2015 on those dates in question, but on September 27, 2014 or December 21-25, 28-29, 2014. The one prediction for 2015 maybe an earthquake on New Madrid, Missouri on September 27-28, or December 21-25, 28-29, 2015.

The seven year periods of time from 9-11-2001 plus seven equals September 2008 near the exact date of 9-11 when the stock market crashed. Add another seven years to that date and you have September 2014 when the stock market may crash literally by the tidal wave exact seven years from the past date or the dates of December 21-25, 28-29, 2014-2015.

The Cherubs I saw on January 4, 1983 showed the what to two Iraq (=Babylon) wars both of which were the first month (=January 16-17, 1991) and March 19-21, 2003 (=Julian first month) could mean the anniversary of a army as terrible as with banners (=flags or anniversary) when the second Iraq war started on March 20-21, 2003. Add the Chinese cycle years to that date and it equals March 20-21, April 4, 2015 or September 24-26, 2014-215 which is the first month and 24th days and the dates of Rosh Hashanah on the Jewish Civil calendar. Add four days as four returns of Song of Solomon 6:13 to the polar opposite of March 20-21, 2015 and it equals September 20-21+ 4=September 24-25, 2014 when these events happen or on December 21-25, 26, 28-29, 2014 and 2015.

Daniel 10:4, 12:1-13 may predict the death of Billy Graham who led many to Christ as the stars of heaven show millions that a just and righteous man did on earth some 2625 years from Daniel's time of 606-605 B.C. to September 24, 2020-2021 or its polar opposite September 24-28, 2014 or 2015. The "time, times and a half" equals three and a half days from September 20-21 or 24 to September 24-27, 2014 or 2015. The 2625 days equals Daniel's chapter 12 dates of 1290+1335=2625 days or years as Ezekiel 4:6 tells us a day for a year. Colossians 2:16-17 predicts these same date as a Jewish or Christian Sabbath days (=September 26-27, 2014 and 2015 or on Rosh Hashanah in 2015 or the feasts of tabernacles in that year on this Holiday). Just like in 2003 A.D. these same dates are times of great trouble and great blessing as Ecclisastes 7:14 predicts. The word "lot" in Daniel 12:13 is where we get the word "lottery" from. It is also where we get the word inheritance and portion of one's family's birthdays of five as in Fantasy 5 lottery in Florida wins on one of those dates in September-October or December 21-25, 26, 28-29, 2014-2015. That is double shame and double blessing as 2002-2004 plus 12 years equals 2014-2015. See Zechariah 9:10-14 and Isaiah 61:7. My family's birthdays are: 15, 19, 20, 22 and 27. Will those lots win on September 21-28, 2014 or December 21-25, 26, 28-29, 2014 when we mourn greatly and celebrate greatly?

Irvin Baxter told on his TV show how the four horsemen of Revelation chapter 6 are the four powers left on earth in the end times. In my book I list three, but I believe he is right because I left our democracy as the fourth from Communism, Islam and Catholic. The democratic nations are UK, parts of Europe and New Zealand and Australia, which two I feel is safe there for awhile. But I don't see the U.S. and Israel on that list even though the may come back a third or fourth time in 2014-3005 A.D. to become a nation four times as Song of Solomon 6:13 predicts.

Proverbs 30:30-31 predicts a U.S. President born in the Leo the lion sign which President Obama was born in on August 4-5, 1961 was the Leo sign and the sign of the Sheep or Goat in Chinese astrology as is our year 2015. My Dad was born in the Chinese Year of the Sheep or Goat and died in the Chinese Sheep or Goat polar opposite in 2015 when some or all these events happen. My mother was born in the Chinese sign of the Dog and died in the Chinese sign of the Dog. He would face trouble in the Leo cusp star time and Virgo star time both on September 27, or December 21-25, 28-29, 2014 or 2015. The great living translation or the NIV Bible list those verse as greyhound as a Rooster which in Chinese astrology is ruled by Virgo which star time is September 27, 2014 or 2015. The greyhound or dog rules our Libra which is September 27, 2014 or 2015. To the Jewish Civil calendar September 27, 2014 is the start of our year 2015. See Proverbs 30:30-31. The ancient Egyptian carving from the temple Hathor is held by hands (=27=September 27, 2014 or 2015) of women and kneeling bird headed men. Does this mean Gemini signs ending June 20 to 27 cusp is changed to the Virgo star time on September 27, 2014-2015? Or does it mean Mercury that rules Gemini and Virgo its cosign and are the days of Wednesday-Thursday in Latin for the end in September 27, 3005. A.D. The kneeling of the bird headed men might be that its changing dates or submitting its self to September 27, 2014 or 2015 in the Virgo star time and is the Libra sign of the Dog.

Nostradamus predicted that from the roof the ancient work is done and the great man ruin. Could that quatrain mean two things? One, Oswald shooting at JFK from near the roof or sixth story of a seven story building. It also could mean the ancient carving (=work) on the roof of the temple Hathor that predicted the JFK assassination. See C6:Q37. Nostradamus also predicted one falls at noon (=JFK) and another at night (RFK- midnight). See C1:Q26. The "misty woods" referred to in the former quatrain may be the ranch the mob boss in the swamps (misty woods) who gave the orders for two nuts to carry out the assassination which were Oswald and Rogers. See the book "Man ion the grassy knoll". That mob boss was leader or king of the south as Daniel chapter 11 predicts killed JFK from seven hills (7 mountains or stories of Revelation chapter 17 as was the Texas school book depository. Yes Oswald killed JFK, but was put in place with the other man as two nuts to carry it out. Ezekiel chapter 30 predicts a Pharaoh arms of President or king his brother is the other arm polar opposite JFK and RFK. JFK and RFK were born polar opposite of May-November and died polar opposites of Sagittarius and Gemini and noon and midnight. With JFK being Catholic goes along with being killed by Oswald on a seven story building or seven hills that Rome, Italy is also built on where the Pope rules from. JFK return is doubtful but if a UFO lands on earth and JFK walks out then beware of him and his knowledge. Also beware of a UFO landing and a husband and wife steps out with two books or more with wisdom that is evil. They are the antichrist and false prophet and the son and daughter of satan.

Revelation chapter 22 in Chapter/Year codes is 2002 A.D. and is the 27th book of the new Testament. Add 12 yearly cycles of Chinese astrology to that and it equals

September 27, 2014 or 2015 or some other year like 3005 A.D. when many great events happen on. The book of Song of Solomon Chapter 8 in Chapter/Year codes in 2008 A.D. Add the polar opposite to that and it equals 2014 A.D. when a vineyard of books and wisdom are revealed by angels coming to share his voice to those in the garden just as Psalms 68:17 and Revelation 3:22 predicted the angel of the Lord would speak to people and tell them where to buy my books. The angel is bluish-white and makes you smile ear to ear.

Ezekiel chapter 30 predicts a Pharaoh arms of {President or king with his brother on the other side polar opposite JFK and RFK) were polar opposite on birth days and days of death not only in time of their killing one at noon hours and the other at midnight hour.

Matthew chapter 24:7-8 predicts earthquakes in diver (=different) places, famines and pestilence's as when a woman has sorrows or "birth pangs". The tidal wave that hits the Eastern U.S. Coastline would sure do that. An estimate of 10 million dead along with power outages, food shortages and disease from the dirty water and sewers will be terrible and chaotic.

Another event on that same date plus or minus 30 days is that a great red dragon or President Putin of Russia the red (communist state=red) that draws down three nuclear tip missiles on Israel for its attack on Iran Russia's ally. See Revelation chapter 12. The tail of the Dragon (=Draco the dragon constellation) in the north stars area see drawings 1-6 in chapter 6 of this book draws down a third of the stars upon Israel and one of the White house when Polaris is the North Star and a 1000 years later on September 26-27, 3005

A.D. has the ox leg on the carvings pointing at ox horns and at Virgo- Libra or Wednesday-Thursday. It starts at Cepheus the king on the throne or the Great White Throne judgement about a 1000 years from now. See drawing three in chapter 6 of this book. This time is when the Milky way comes from Taurus and goes to Sagittarius, Scorpio, Aquila, Sagitta and Libra as the many stars shown in the Milky Way are shot at each other. Aquila the eagle who shoots many missiles or stars at Iran is Israeli jet fighters that attack Iran. The constellation Sagitta "the arrow" is one missile shoot at the White House in Washington, D.S. The third is two or three nuclear missiles shot at Israel by Russia because of it many planes attack on Iran on September 27, or December 21-25, 28-29, 2014 or 2015 plus or minus thirty days. See drawings 1-6 in chapter 6 of this book.

Acts and Joel chapters 2 in the Bible predicteds blood moons or solar eclipses on Jewish feast days during the time of great evangelistic movement as the TV show It's Supernatural showed on one of its shows in late June early July 2014. They claimed this very prophecy of Joel and acts chapters 2 as young, old and in between receiving power of the Holy Ghost as healing, Prophesying and gospel preach during this time of May- September of 2014. Then "afterwards" the end comes for some in the form of these predicted events exactly as predicted. The word "afterwards" could mean the first Holy Ghost movement in 30 A.D. near when Christ died on the cross to now in 2014 when there are blood moons and darkened sun in Lunar and Solar eclipses. Two lunar eclipses on feast days on April 15, 2014 and October 8-9, 2014. Then in 2015 a solar eclipse on March 20-21, 2015 and a lunar eclipses on April 3-4-5, 2015 and

September 27-28, 2015. That would be afterwards of the 30 A.D. Holy Ghost coming to when it comes again exactly as Sid Roth guest mentioned on his show in late June or early July 2014.

All Bible verses in Isaiah chapter 29, Amos chapters 1-2, Obadiah 1-6, Deuteronomy 32 (song of Moses) and Luke's 21:9-11 predict 32 years from when the woman flees into the South East (Florida) on September 27, 1981. Adding 32 years to 1981 on September 27 and it equals September 2012-2013, in which Luke 21:9-11 predicts "by and by" or two years counting each year or not to September 27, 2014-2015. My mother, dad and I arrived in Florida's Ocala city at McDonald's on September 27, 1981 at 12-1 p.m. Ariel mentioned five times in Isaiah chapter 29 could mean 4x8 or 32 years from 1981 September 27 plus or minus 30 days. The book of Amos in the Bible predicted for three or four transgressions equals 4x8=32 years added to 1981 equals 2012-2013 plus or minus 30 days. The three and four great transgressions is repeated eight times or 8x4=32 years+1 or 2= 2014-2015.

A man born on October 15, 1954 name counselor from Germany or Kurt Nostradamus predicted as a man many think is good, some think is evil and yet some don't know. He was born in Camden, N.J. during hurricane Hazel in which his eyes colors is hazel. He was born at 8:11 p.m. in 1954 the Chinese year of the Horse the same as September 27, or December 21-25, 28-29, 2014 plus or minus 30 days is the Chinese year of the horse. Nostradamus also predicted in C1:Q55 a polar opposite of Babylon will have many confused when heaven seems unjust and great famines and pestilence's come upon the kingdoms (U.S. and Russia).

The NBC nightly new in late June 2014 reported a great confusion over Iraq (=Babylon) because our enemies and fighting are enemies. There will not only be confusion over Iraq (=Babylon) but also in the kingdoms of the U.S. and Russia who destroy each other leaders and a great tidal hit the U.S. along with two storms and two earthquakes one in the U.S. and the other in another part of the world. Fighting Isis is very confusing to the U.S. leaders, but also the antichrist and false prophet coming in the UFO landing in sight of men and bringing books of wisdom will be very confusing. People will think good is evil and evil is good as Ecclisasetes and other parts of the Bible predicts. In Ecclisastes it predict in the last days you won't know what evil will come upon the earth, law, lawlessness or neutral. That same book in the Bible also states it is good to know not to be over righteous or overly lawless, but neutral as a born again Christian in which fear cometh forth of them all. Fear in law, fear in lawlessness and fear in the lukewarm- neutral is fear cometh from them all. But it claims it is important to go the balanced way or neutral not meaning Christianity is evil, but like a born again Christian loves all as the only great commandment of the Bible that is important. Not to be just full law or full lawlessness. Don't be full lawless and full law. Solomon wrote that this is a good thing to hold on to. See Revelation 13:13 for the UFOs landing in sight of men and bringing books described in my book "The Experiment at Philadelphia" as the first 14 chapters. If I am the antichrist, false prophet and satan I wouldn't reveal satan's plans in advance and destroy them for coming true or take the sting out of them. He may try to destroy my publisher thus people will be on their on to defend against the antichrist, false prophet and satan. I betrayed Satan, antichrist and false prophet to let you saints know the truth behind their plans for your future. Believe me satan, the antichrist and false prophet are not please with me for doing this, but are very angry at me.

One minister on the Jim Bakker show in late June 2014 said that Solomon was a type of antichrist. This is true but only partly. Song of Solomon 1:5 tells of Solomon as part black and part white (=comely) meaning he is good and evil being not only a type of antichrist, but a type of Christ. Jim Bakker on his show in late June 2014 said he was positive something will happen this fall of 2014 and next fall in 2015. That's what I believe are dates of September 26-27-28, 2014 with an earthquake and then next year another earthquake on those same dates on or near a full moon. But I give the winter dates they most likely will happen on in December 21-25, 28-29, 2014, 2015, and 2024. The Jim Bakker show from Branson, Missouri is the opposite side of that sated from New Madrid, Missouri that is hit by and great earthquake in September 27, or December 21- 25, 28-29, 2015 plus or minus 30 days. The former and latter dates on September 27, 2014 and December 25, 2014 or 2015 is when the volcano erupts and send a tidal wave to the East Coast of the U.S. along with an great earthquake in San Francisco or Seattle a year ago and the New Madrid earthquake on December 25, 2015. They are the "double" blessing and double shame for the U.S. and Israel. See the books Isaiah 61:1-7 and Zechariah 9:10-14.

The three shepherds dies in one (=first month=September or in one month's time) might be President Putin, President of Iran and President Obama all killed in this war.

Isaiah chapter 18 predicts a great gift (=The Holy Ghost) is given to Israel and the world near or on a new moon when river flooding happens or will happen and hit the U.S. in May- June or September-October of 2014. Now, in late June 2014 we have river flooding in the Mid-West in the U.S. Remember June is the first month to God's creation calendar. This could be what the Isaiah chapter 18 predicts means along with the other predictions told of in this book happen on or near a new moon on September 24-28, 2014 or 2015. The fire on the mountains and trumpets blowing meant Rosh Hashanah to the ancient Israeli who did those things on the Jewish Civil New Year's Day and give gifts to one another celebrating by the Jewish people all over the world where they were scattered from Israel in 70 A.D. and 2014-2015 September 27 or December 21-25, 28-29, plus or minus 30 days when they are again destroyed and scattered. That date is the end and beginning of good and evil and are when Billy Graham dies and people (Jewish) give gifts one to another. See Revelation chapter 11 and Luke 21:34-37. The Jewish people will on Rosh Hashanah in 2014 or 2015 being partying, over eating, drinking, the cares of this life and give gifts one to another just as predicted. Are these prophecies that of not only 2014-2015, but also 2024 when Yellowstone Park super volcano erupts Christmas Eve or Day December 24-25, 2024 when also people are over eating, over drinking and enjoying the cares of this life. Are these dates of Christmas Eve and Day in 2024 and 2060 the Dragon Years that the Mayas were predicting not for December 21, 2012, but for those dates. Mayas lived in Central America where we get our name from meaning the land of the "plume'd serpent" or "land of the "plume'd

Lucifer" after the snakes or serpent seen in their pyramids or writing that they worshiped. These dates could also be in winter, on the Sabbath Days of Saturday-Sunday as Matthew 24:19-20 predicts when women with child or John the Baptist birthday of December 24-25, 2024 or 2060 to beware. Isaiah chapter 18 1993 river flooding on the U.S. and present or gift sent back to Zion or Israel was a peace agreement that Israeli President Rabin return to Israel on or near the new moon in September on Rosh Hashanah. Will this time in 2014 see a gift of the Holy Ghost come to the U.S. and the other dates when John the Baptist was born has God shake the heavens and earth with great volcanoes, earthquakes, wars and storms? If the Rapture time is a time of stopping time and wars, and other events happen in 2014-2015 or 2024-2025 it would fulfill ancient prophecies of Zechariah 11:10, 17, Habakukk 3:4, 9-19, Luke 21:25-28, Isaiah 6:12-13 look at the sky for signs in the sun, moon and stars standing still will give people long life's. And if the tree of life is restored it will give eternal life psychically along with paradise on earth. But the sight of the sun, moon and stars standing still for three days may throw nations and men's heart into failure, fearful sights and distress for the things that are coming upon the earth. Looking up will bring those fears and the coming of the son of man with great glory and power seen hiding behind hurricane storm clouds, volcano ash and smoke and nuclear bombs being dropped at the sight and sound and destruction of them will scare people to death. The one volcano off Africa West Coast may erupt causing a tidal wave to hit Eastern U.S. coastline and drifting smoke and ash over Florida and making the hiding of God's power and great glory in the heavens when you look up. This event of time stopping in Habakkuk 3:10 means exactly this that time has been stopped for the sun moon and stars to stand still. If it stops in day time you will have day time for three days. If it starts at night time or twilight or dawn you will have those things for three days. But remember and don't panic they will start moving in three days. The reason they stop is because Venus rotates clockwise which is a curse on the earth with diseases and short life spans, but when they start up again the life span should be 500-1000 years of longer life with the tree of life restored. And all diseases will be healed. These events are also prophesied in Wisdom of Solomon 7:16-21 Apocrypha pages 190-191 by Edgar J Goodspeed. Zechariah chapter 11, Daniel chapter 2 and Genesis chapters 6-7 predict a covenant made with Noah and the world that he will never stop the earth's rotation again along with the sun, moon and stars. The stars that stand still and start at the light of those arrows means September 24, or December 21, 2014 or 2015 will see Venus rotation stop thus stopping all planets and moons for three days making them stand still. Then at the light of Ballistic missiles shot at Iran, Israel, Russia and the U.S. the sun and moon start rotating again. That may occur three days after Israel attacks Iran or on September 26-27-28, 2014 or 2015 plus or minus 30 days or December 21-25, 28-29, 2014 or 2015.

One preacher mentioned that a generation was 51.4 years long. Add 51 years to November 22, 1963 and come exactly to November 22, 2014 on a new moon. The circle seen with a man in it and a jackal on top or dog both on top of Libra could mean a new moon or full moon in Libra by as Libra man (President Putin) shoots an arrow Sagittarius (first sign of Chinese astrology and it rules Jupiter that is given the number 3) or the numbers 1-3 (=archer of arrows half horse=2014) at Scorpio (=Washington, D.C.) in the Libra sign runs from September 23-October 22, 2014. The Dog or jackal on top of the circle could mean the Libra sign of 2-7 after the moon numbers equals September 27, 2014 when President Putin assassinates President Obama. The many missiles from the sky at this time could be many missiles nuclear or not that Israeli, Iran, Lebanon, Gaza, Russia and thee U.S. fires at one another shown as the Milky Way and these exact same signs a perfect prophecy coming true. See drawings 1-6 in Chapter 6 of this book for details.

Those drawings shows Sagittarius, Sagitta, Libra and Pisces all meaning 1-3 or 1 missiles from a Libra man (President Putin) fired by the same man as two fishes under water or subs) that shoots three nuclear missiles at Israel and one other under water fish (=two fishes or subs by a cord of one man=Libra) fires one sub nuclear missile at the White House (=Scorpio=Washington D.C.) that assassinates President Obama and the U.S. and/or Israel retaliate and fires a nuclear missile at Moscow killing President Putin. Those three signs and constellations all ruled by Russia's longitude zones. The Milky Way are many stars (=missiles) going toward Taurus or Persia-Iran with jets shooting many missiles or stars at Iran by Israel and Iran fires back many stars or missiles back at Israel (=Libra) from Lebanon, Syria, Gaza, Russia and other enemies. And Sagittarius and Scorpio rules both Iran and Washington, D.C. that fight one another with its ally Russia and Syria along the Milky Way going toward Taurus not seen on the drawing, but the rest are. Also Israel is in the Libra zone and its leader

Benjamin Netanyahu was born in the Libra sign on a new moon (=his end near a new moon September 24-28, 2014 or November 22 or December 21-25, 28-29, 2014-2015) and the U.S. is the symbol of Libra of two parties of government. The Pisces zones where the White House is are ruled by Jupiter (=three missiles at Israel) that rules Libra (=Lupiter=3 missiles shot at Israel).

The Canary Islands where this volcano is that causes the East Coastline of the U.S. with a tidal wave is in the Gemini Zone which rules the Chinese Horse Year and Gemini rule San Francisco and Seattle. Will the two earthquakes of 2014-2015 be the earthquake of this volcano of the Canary Islands and/or San Francisco or Seattle and tidal waves in both or one?

The word "Know" or "knew" in the Bible sometimes means sex between a husband and wife. We get the word "knowledge" from those words which meant all wisdom (=knowledge) is that of sex when a husband and wife join as one.

The drawing with Sagittarius the half horse half archer of arrows shot at Scorpio next to a duck or Goose is ruled by Iran and Russia and the arrows it shoots (Sagittarius) at Scorpio rules Washington, D.C. in a assassination of President Obama 51 years after the assassination of JFK and in the Horse year of 2014 on September 26-27, 2014 or December 21-25, 28-29, 2014 plus or minus 30 days and the jackal or dog on top equals Libra from 7-9 p.m. in the Libra sign of September 23-October 23, 2014 or 2015 fired by a Libra man whose tail draws down a third (=three) of the stars on Israel. President Putin we seen was born on the seventh day of Libra or October 7 in the Chinese Year of the Dragon whose tail goes down to the Libra man on top of Libra in a circle with a jackal or dog on top. President Putin was born in the Chinese Year of the Dragon and shoots one missile at the White House on the day of a new or full moon (=circle) in the Libra sign in 2014 or 2015. The drawing with a lion's two front paws on a box (=coffin) with three wavy lines in it below Libra and near the other box with three wavy lines in it with the jackal's tail goes down to a circle or new or full moon on that same dates or in March-April 2015 when these prophecies come true. Than as Isaiah 6:12-13 predicts men to be removed far off for the forsaking of the land and Matthew 11:12 predicts a "tenth" and John the Baptist birthday of December 24-25, 2024 the Chinese Year of the Dragon and December is Latin for Tenth just as predicted. Was this the year and month the Mayas were claiming as the end when God shakes the heavens and earth when Yellowstone park super volcanoes erupts? It warns men to flee the U.S. before then and live in New Zealand or Australia. Isaiah chapter 6 in Chapter/Year codes is 1906 when the great San Francisco earthquake hit along with fires on April 18-19, 1906 the same Horse year as 2014. Don't go or live in these places in 2014 and in 2015 near New Madrid, Missouri. See drawings 1-6 in chapter 6 in this book. The three wavy lines on both boxes on this ancient carving can mean a nuclear attack that shakes the ground and heavens like a wavy line, an earthquake that Richter scale is a wavy line and a storm which is wavy seas or wavy lines. Remember these prophecies and if they come true the last one in 2024 will too and if you haven't been moved to New Zealand or Australia then it will be to late for aircraft can't fly in volcano ash, smoke and gases. And everyone fleeing to Canada or Mexico won't make it and life of hell will be upon the Americans in riots, looting, stealing peoples food, just one big great hell the U.S. will face because they turned their back on God.

If there are one or two tidal waves to hit the East and West Coasts of the U.S. it would literally destroy both Stock Markets and they may drop from 3000-12000 points or more. This is exactly as Revelation chapter 6 predicts great inflation as when a loaf of bread could cost you as whole day's earnings. If people are making 80-500 dollars a day then a loaf of bread for a day would 80-2500 dollars, which would account for great inflation, famines and along with famines comes pestilence's exactly as Revelation chapter 6 predicts with Libra or the scales of money in the Libra sign which runs from September 23- October 22 or December 21-25. 28-29. 2014 or 2015. The date of September 27, 2014 comes into that time span in which a archer of arrows is predicted which could be Sagittarius half horse and half archer of arrows. The year 2014 is a Chinese Year of the Horse, which makes even more sense of what Revelation was trying to predict. Things would really get bad with bridges, companies and stores are washed away and the road trucks won't be making delivery and thus quick inflation and famines and pestilence's. The following book of mine has this book excerpt from "The Experiment at Philadelphia," "Predictions for 2015 Revised Edition" mad "End Time Signs II" by Kurt B. Balky all available now at this web site WWW.Authorhouse.Com. The electric would go off the sewer and water go off or be poison making hell on earth while between the two coasts are river flooding, wild fires, tornadoes, droughts and earthquakes like in New Madrid,

Missouri between September 27, 2014 and September 27, 2015 or December 25, 2014 and December 25, 2015. Revelation 6:12-13 predicts between solar and lunar eclipses there would be many stars fall from heaven and great earthquakes. The many stars could be many missiles Israel, Iran, Syria and other terrorist states and people shoot at each other. And if you add the .4 of the 51.4 generation to JFK assassination it would come to March-April 2015 or its polar opposite September- October when there is a blood moon or lunar eclipse on Feast of Tabernacles when some or all these events happen. Be ready! Watch! Just as Jesus predicted! If the Lord tarries from 2024 to 2060 or even to 3005 or beyond be patient with Him because his clock and time is different than ours. For example, December 21-22, 2060 is the Chinese Year of the Dragon, the same as the Mayas were suppose to predict on December 21, 2012. Maybe they meant December 24-25, 2024 or December 21-22, 2060. We could have miscounted them. The 2060 dates are Chinese Dragon, winter, and Sabbath Day to the Jewish people and the Christmas Holidays when someone important was born (=with child=John the Baptist=December 24-25 Dragon Year) or near then exactly as Colossians 2:16-17 predicted. Remember Matthew 24:19-20. Or did they correctly predict these events not on 2012, but two years past 2012 or 2014-2015?

In one of my books I mention that July 16-17 is very active for plane crashes and heavenly crashes. For example, TWA flight 800 crashed on July 16-17, a comet crashed into Jupiter on July 16-17 and JFK Jr., plane crash happened on July 16-17, 1999. Then on July 17, 2014 Malaysia flight 17 crashed. There's definitely a pattern. Could Malaysia Flight

17 equal July 17, 2014? The flight number was 17 the same date of the past three July 16-17 air crashes and it crashed on July 17, 2014 exactly as predicted.

The BTK serial killer was named in code and living in the plains of the U.S. See my book entitled: "Predictions for 2011- 2019" buy Kurt B. Balky, which the same quatrain predicted his name also predicted great heat and drought in the plains and/or West Coast. That book is now available at this web site: WWW.Authorhouse.Com.

It may be smart to cash in all your stocks before September 26, or December 21-25, 28-29, 2014 and put them in CD's or savings account in a bank far from the East and West coasts or buy gold with it and put in a large safety deposit box in a bank far from the East or West coast and move it to New Zealand or Australia before December 21-25. 28-29, 2024. Also don't be in these areas on these date and watch out for New Madrid, Missouri.

The time, times and a half we read could be 35 years added to the beginning of Revelation chapter 1 in year/codes or 1981+35=Septemeber-October 2015-2016-2017 by the Jewish Civil calendar. When you hear that Billy Graham has died and see some on top of roof on September 24-27, 2014 or in December of 2024 then run away from these places inland, but not near New Madrid, Missouri. The same signs will also hold true in December of 2024 right before Yellowstone Park super volcano erupts and destroys the U.S. You may want to make that trip to New Zealand or Australia sooner to make sure your not killed and remain safe and move all your belongings and money there before it becomes nothing in the U.S. There is earthquakes, volcanoes, and storms and religious persecution in these two nations, but its nothing like others or will it ever be that bad, I pray. These signs to flee from the U.S. and/or the East Coast and earthquake places mention are the same signs the Jewish should watch for happening to the U.S. along with someone of the rooftop, dreams, visions and angel visitation along with the events happening in the U.S. The Jews should flee to the mountains of Petra, Jordan. If the events happens suddenly in December with the death of Billy Graham then flee that day or by 3 and a half days later with your possessions. If they happen in 2015 then flee to the same place of Petra, Jordan. Don't say to the angel it is an error as Ecclesiastes predicts or else you will lose your life and possessions. Daniel 12:7, 11-13 predicts time. times and a half of three and half years added to 1290 and 1335 days changed to years equals a little over 10 years. If you add 10 years to December 21-25, 2014 it equals December 21-25, 2024. Also when you subtract those numbers of days added together equals 2020-2021+3.5 years equals 2024 when the end comes for a great nation the U.S.

In the book Astrology: "The Space age Science" by Joseph F. Goodavage pages 186-187 it tell of a remarkable event with the assassinations of Lincoln and JFK. Lincoln was elected in 1860. JFK was elected 1960. Lincoln was shot at Ford's theater in the head and the assassin ran from the theater into a warehouse. JFK was shot in the head by Oswald from a warehouse and ran into a theater. Lincoln was shot a Ford's theater and JFK was shot in a Ford Lincoln. Lincoln had a sectary named Kennedy and JFK had a sectary named Lincoln. They both told the two presidents not to go. Both Lincoln and JFK married pretty 24 year old brunettes who spoke French. Lincoln had family who became a U.S. senator another cousin who was mayor of Boston. Lincoln had Levi Lincoln graduate from Harvard who became U.S. attorney general. Another family was a minister to London for four years.

JFK had some of the same family similarities. Teddy Kennedy became a U.S. Senator Robert Kennedy a Harvard graduate became U.S. Attorney general and Senator of New York. John Kennedy's grandfather Mayor of Boston and his father was ambassador to London. Both Lincoln and JFK were elected to congress in 1947. See my books entitled "The Antichrist" "End Time Signs II" "The Seven Thunders" "The Divine Code II" and this book for other amazing predictions.

It may be true that the U.S. as a Christian nation, but it was discovered by Jews in 1492 when the Jews were kicked out of Spain and joined Columbus a Jew to sail to another place where they would be safe. Thus the U.S. is a Zionist nation founded by Jewish people. Then later came the Christians to this new world the Jewish people discovered also a safe place from kings that told them when and how to be religious. The exact opposite of what the laws are now. They were perfectly right the way are constitution was written not how lawyers twisted the words away making for the very freedom the Christians wanted to preach and live the way they want without a king (=U.S. government) telling otherwise as they do now (=now).

On the star chart in chapter 6 in this book it shows the stars positions on how they predicted these events in the stars for December 21-25, 2014, 2015 and 2024 at noon as Isaiah chapters 16-17 predicts or at midnight or 1 a.m. as I Thessalonians chapter 5 and Revelation chapter 16 which is midnight to 2 a.m. Eastern Time in the U.S. When it is supper time here on the East Coast of the U.S. it is 12-2 a.m. in Israel, thus, the sup or supper of God and a thief in the night. Every time you read night in the Bible it can be translated "midnight". Amos 5:7-8 predicts these same dates in the morning and other verses at night (=midnight) as Isaiah chapter 17 predicts. See Matthew 25:1-13. The star chart in Chapter 6 of this book in drawings 1-6 can equal midnight even though Gemini, Orion, Taurus and Auriga are not seen, but equals those stars as a story or prediction for things to come in December 21-25, 2014, 2015 and 2024. It also can mean noon time June 20-25, 2015, 2024 and 3005 at all the same times of 12:18- 1:18 a.m. Eastern U.S. time. See Revelation 16:15, Isaiah 16:3, 17:14 and 17:6. The two or three berries and the four and five berries of this prophecy of Isaiah 17:6 might just means the years ending in 2-3 nothing happens, but in the years 4-5 or 2014-2015 many predicted events happen in the grape harvest of September or two-three months from then the predicted events happen from September of 2014 and 2015 in November-December of those years.

Nostradamus in his quatrain C6:Q35 predicts two names of two serial killers and the unabomber where he was living. It also gives the exact amount of dead love ones each would kill. Such as the Zodiac killer was five. The BTK killer was 13 even though he was only charged for 10, and the Uanbomber who killed three. How this quatrain does this is by codes seen in my other books entitled "The Experiment At Philadelphia" "Predictions for 2011-2019" and "End Time Signs II". The quatrain give five zodiac signs that spells out the Zodiac's name and the five he killed scream out of their grave for justice on him. The BTK killer has in that quatrain Jupiter, Mars and the Sun in the plains with fire in Forrest and cities because of a great drought and heat which start when he is caught or is going on during his rampage or years after he was caught. The BTK killer was caught on February 6, 2005. Jupiter is given the number 3, Mars the number 9 and the sun the number 1. All together equals 13 murders he did kill. I am only sorry that I couldn't deliver this information sooner even though they would of laugh at it and call me a cook. The Unabomber killed three which is the number of Jupiter. And the white wool and bear in Nostradamus' quatrain in Greek the word white or wool is near the word for "wolf". And in Daniel chapter 7 it predicts a monster killer as a bear with its mouth with three ribs in it. Put the two together and you have Bearmouth, Montana the only place in the U.S. that is called Bearmouth. And in Montana there's a place called "Wolf Creek". Put your finger between the two and you are pointing to Lincoln, Montana where the Unabomber was living before he was caught and killed three people with his pipe bombs that are like a candle shape with a wick or fuse in the end that some were sent by mail as a letter exactly as the quatrain predicted.

The Pig, woman kneeling near seven stars, 12 stars and a ram's head or goat's head with a sun or moon disk between the horns on a raft may have several meanings. See drawing 6 in chapter 6. One, is Erich Von Daniken death and birth or revealing as we have or will read. He was born of the Chinese year of the Pig the same as President Reagan was. The rams' head or goat's head on a raft could be the day President Reagan was born on February 6, 1911. That date us the Aquarius sign which is the "water-bearer" seen on the carving as the raft. That date is also the Capricorn star time which is the sea goat or the goat's head on top of a raft (=sea). It also could mean the sea-goat as Capricorn in the Chinese year of the Goat or Sheep in 2015 and in March 1981 the sign of the Ram or Aries sign when President Reagan was shot in 1981. The table with four snakes on it near the raft with a goat's head and sun and moon disk between its horns could mean Surgeon's operating of President Reagan at the time of Aries the ram's head on the carving. The snakes represents the Medical emblem of a staff with snakes around it. See drawings 6 in Chapter 6 of this book. The Chinese Pig Year is not only 1947 when Hillary was born on October 26 could mean her as U.S. President that flies in a airliner and for some reason falls into the sea and her body is never found. I looked at moon placement and the moon is in Scorpio on December 25, 2024. Does President Hillary Clinton take a trip then or tries to flee this disaster or in March-April of 2019 or 2024? which is the Aries sign and lightning or mechanical trouble or the smoke, ash and gases down the plane when Yellowstone Park's super volcano erupts. October 26, 2024 has is the Scorpio sign when Hillary Clinton was born. It could also mean this accident happens in March-April of 2019 or 2024 the Pig and Dragon Years in Chinese astrology. Her husband took this same trip in April and came back alive having the prophecies fail or they were meant for Hillary Clinton another one from Little (=small) Rock (=Edom) Arkansas. See Obadiah 1-6, Daniel 11:19-24 and Amos 2:14. July (17?) of 2019 or 2024 could also be this trouble for the Clinton's Bill or Hillary.

These signs could also mean Erich Von Daniken birth in the Chinese year of the Pig in the Aries sign of the ram or goat. He was born Aries 14, 1935, which equals the Chinese year of the Pig and in Aries sign of the ram or goat. He was born then and may die then or revealed then and may die then in 2014- 2015 on those dates or others dates given.

According to the book entitled "The only astrology book you'll ever need" by Joanna Martine Woolfolk in December 25, 2014 the moon was in Pisces the water sign or raft seen on the carving near the Pig and woman kneeling. On December 25, 2015 the Moon is in Cancer the water sign again with the raft. Von Daniken may have been born in the Virgo zone which is an earth signs as the second beast to come up out of earth as the False Prophet and the other again him. Von Daniken, coming up from the seas when he dies on these dates or revealed on these dates or both are just as Revelation chapter 13 predicted. More on him as little later.

In the years 2014 and 2015 there are ancient prophecies of double trouble and double blessings. See Isaiah 61:1-7 and Zechariah 9:10-14. The two trouble may mean earthquakes, storms, wars or attacks, tidal waves and volcano eruptions in two years both in December 21-25, 2014-2015. The two blessings may mean Venus turns counterclockwise making paradise of earth and long lives of 500-1000 years old. The second blessing would be the tree of life be stopped from hindering eternal life and cures all disease. The tree of life is made up of Lithium and hydrogen or 1-3=Trinity. The double trouble and double blessing could also be two tornadoes side by side as we saw in 2014 in the U.S. and two storms hitting or near Hawaii islands. Will two storms hit Florida at the same time this year or 2014-2016? Or will there be four storms in those years like what happen in 2004 all hitting Florida or the South. In the Chinese cycle years 12 years equals the same sign and 12 years added to 2004 equals 2015-2016 according to the Jewish Civil calendar. The double blessing is winning the lottery (=Daniel 12:13) and succeed with great success of these books by making copies sold like the book of Ecclesiastes predicts a multitude of business (=sales) is a blessing and success.

In his book "Chariots of the Gods" by Erich Von Daniken he is constantly putting down God Almighty. Is this the man or antichrist that speaks like a dragon and have heads with great blasphemies and the antichrist who speaks great blasphemies on God Almighty. See Revelation chapter 13 and 17. Erich Von Daniken and his colleagues constantly teach God Almighty was mistaken by our ancient forefathers as human ancient astronauts in UFOs. Erich Von Daniken blames God Almighty the Jewish God for evil because of his wrath and destruction of Sodom and Gomorrah. He also questions is that a good God that does that? Erich Von Daniken claims ancient astronauts came long ago from other solar systems and had sex with humans on earth and taught them all the wisdom of fairy tales, legends, fables and stories handed down in written or carving forms or put into buildings or images or just stories for itching ears that lust like an orgasm for all these things the mother devil and all her women children did. See Paul's writing in the Bible for detail of these things as he calls them correctly as doctrines of devils. My book, "The Experiment at Philadelphia" in the six or seven footnotes gives a book that claims angels did come down to earth and teach and do all these things to the heathen or Gentiles they created, but only as a temptation for the last days under the phrase "MYSTERY BABYLON".

These things are exactly what I wrote about in my early life. I thought Von Daniken was right! But God showed me he was wrong and would within an hour (=42 years) from when that book was published first by Erich Von Daniken in 1965-1967 would equals 2007-2009 when he brings the final temptation of MYSTERY BABYLON to the people on earth in his latest book "History was wrong". I knew back in 1976-1977 that he would do such a thing in a new book which is "History is wrong" or another to come later. I don't have to even read it to tell you what is will basically say which I learned over the years. But I will read it and give a report of it in this chapter. Stay tuned! Is that book the covenant or one week covenant and the covenant with death Israel and the world falls into at the end? Who ever said the covenant was a peace treaty? See Daniel 9:27 and Isaiah chapters 28 and 29. It may be a book for a length of time of seven years (=one week=years) or 10 years from when the end comes from 2009, which equals 2016 (=2015 Jewish Civil Calendar in the fall) or 2019-2020 as I wrote about in my other book "End time Signs II. Erich Von Daniken reduces Almighty God to a poor weak human alien that does stupid things or ancient astronauts or Extraterrestrials. I first was fooled by this ancient astronaut theory and God corrected me by I reading "The sons of God return" by Kelly Seagraves see my bibliography at the end of my book "End Time Signs II." Then after being fooled by it I quickly went into the covenant of what the antichrist would do, say and write in which I also thought was right, but found it as "THE STRONG DELUSION" that II Thessalonians chapter 2 predicts and a very great lie like never before. Combine the two and you have a divine deception or delusion as

MYSTERY BABYLON and THE STRONG DELUSION. And remember Daniel 9:27 and Matthew chapter 24 predicts the love of many wax cold because of iniquity and as Daniel 9:27 predicts the antichrist breaks the covenant because of the overspreading of abominations (=sins). This may mean that satan will come as "the prosecuting attorney" in the end when he is thrown out of heaven. This means satan is true and full law and doesn't like any sinning. This is why he satan is in heaven accusing the sins of all including mostly the Saints to be judged because of their sins or iniquity or abominations.

The book of Haggai in the Bible predicts three troubles or times to be strong on the 24th day of the ninth month which to the U.S. would be December 24-25, 2014, 2015 and 2024. The 3005 time of trouble would be different in the month of September on September 26-27, 3005 A.D. All the documentation in this book for those dates for September 26-27, 2014 or 2015 or 2024 may not mean those years, but those dates in September 26-27, 3005 A.D.

I had a dream last night of August 12-13, 2014 that I saw someone hold a sign up with the word or name "Mabus" that Nostradamus used in his quatrain for the third antichrist in which no one could understand. In the dream I suddenly knew what the name was and called to them not to throw it away for I knew what it meant. But when I awoke all I knew was what I just told you I couldn't remember the name or word. It could be a digested dream or a false dream that satan will use about me or I use against him. I really have come full circle going from lawlessness to full law to full lawlessness and back to full law. Dead twice as Jude in the Bible predicted of me born near a storm or raging sea.

The beast (=false prophet) that comes out of the earth and has two horns like a lamb, but speaks great things (=against God and the Church) like a Dragon we have and will see means Erich Von Daniken who was born in the Aries signs of the Ram or Lamb with two horns meaning he has two people inside him that of the false prophet who leads the female devils in UFOs to start the Gentile races after the flood starting at Babel or Babylon. The Jewish people were the pure blooded good race created directly from God and all Gentiles were the pure blooded evil race created directly from devils. This is why God is Jewish and the Jewish people are God's chosen people. The second person in Erich Von Daniken is the antichrist and the great Dragon rules them all and puts all his wisdom and power in them in that one man who comes up out of a earth and sea as we have or will read. The false prophet was originally conceived in Los Angeles on May 19-20 long ago which makes her a Taurus the earth sign (=coming up out of the earth). She was born nine months later in the middle of China in the double Aquarius zone which is the "water-bearer" or water or sea sign she comes up out of also. Thus, another way she and he can be coming up out of the earth and sea. The great antichrist was conceived in Giza, Egypt where the great pyramids and sphinx are and was born in Bimini in the Bahamas off the East Coast of Florida which is the double Pisces zones which are a water or sea sign. With those two as one as Gemini are twins or one and rules the Chinese Horse Years of 2014 and 2015 rules the Sheep or Goat Year in Chinese astrology makes them two in one in perfect wisdom of the dragon with power over much coming up out of the sea and earth being revealed by a erupting volcano in the earth and into the sea as a tidal wave.

Another point that book brings out is the number nine is almost everything. Remember me explaining in my book entitled "The Experiment at Philadelphia" how three sets or three equals all things in the Universe. That equals 999 and not 666 or 777 which we think as good and bad numbers. See that same book and read pages 104-108. The number 9 is the great God Almighty.

The Bible predicts in several places that in the end times many will be saying "Peace, Peace" and "Peace and safety" then comes sudden destruction. Could this mean the Israeli war with the Palestinians in Gaza, the Russian war, the Iraq war and others one or all of them agree to peace in this summer or earlier fall of 2014, then Israel attacks Iran suddenly and soon after the peace agreement, then sudden and very great destruction?

Revelation chapter 12 might give a date to that sudden destruction like Isaiah chapter 48 predicts after a woman is dead and hears not and knows not. Revelation chapter 12 could be that woman born in the moon and dog year and dies in the sun (=Leo sign=July 30, 2006=Dog year). The moon is given the numbers 2-7 or September 27, 2014 when these sudden destruction comes. My dream of Shania Twain and a person next to her as one+2=3 days or 30 days plus or minus Shania's birthday of August 28. Those dates are September 27, 2014-2015 and July 30, 2006 the woman's death and date when many things are fulfilled on her birthday, but being dead she knows not or hears not. Revelation chapter 12 Dragon and 12 stars equals the days of my mom's birth year and death year polar opposite the Dragon is the Chinese Year of the Dog on September 27, 1922 and July 30, 2006 in the Leo sign which is also connected to the Dragon or satan and Sunday when see died is the Sun ruled by Leo. The 12 stars of Revelation chapter 12 and that chapter number 12 could mean the two Pisces (=12th sign) in the Eastern Coast of the U.S. where the flood tries to kill her son twice there when he was born and after she dies. Or does this dream mean three years, 30 days and three months from Shania Twain's birthday of August 28 and 2013 when my grandfather was born and was 2013+3=2015-2016 by the Jewish Civil calendar will come adversity and prosperity on December 24-25, 2014 or 2015. The movie "Psycho" had the Bates Hotel may have her traveling to or near the way to San Francisco where in 2014 or 2015 on or near Christmas day suffers a terrible earthquake.

The third of the stars satan draws down on Israel from heaven by its tail as predicted on Revelation chapter 12 and directly shown on the stars of heaven. Draco the Dragon is a crocodile who spends much of its time in the water like fishes do that Pisces is a sign of two fishes ordered by a Libra man to launch nuclear missiles on Israel and the U.S. The crocodile goes under water looking for his prey just as a Russian sub would be catching it off guard and by surprised. The sub being under water would launch 2-3 nuclear ballistics missiles under the ocean that come up and go into the sky and arch over to where their target is. This is what being pulled down from heaven as stars look like when falling from heaven. If the nuclear missiles are cruise missiles they would not go up into the sky but stay low below radar. The third of the stars Revelation chapter 12 predicts the dragon tail (gives orders to launch) would be 2-3 nuclear missiles. Libra has six stars in it and a third of those equals two, with third as three or 2-3 missiles. Those two stars are the conception dates of the antichrist and Jesus Christ born nine months later in June 24-25. Their conception dates are September 19-27, when they were conceived September 19-27, the Virgo sign and Libra sign or cusp. Thus, these events happen in the Libra sign or cusp on a Libra nation (=Israel and Moscow) by a Libra man (=Putin) in the Libra sign and zone Israel and Moscow are in. See my book "The Nativity" drawing 10 for the picture of this and the whole book that explains these things predicted exactly in the Bible, stars, Nostradamus and ancient Egyptian art. Also see the six drawings in chapter 6 of this book.

The one week of Daniel 9:27 maybe just that seven days from when a cease fire or agreement is made by Israel and Gaza and the Palestinians. It also could be one week or 21 days of Daniel 10:13 predicts when Billy Graham dies and then one week or 21 days later all these predicted events happen. If Billy Graham dies September 6-7-8, 2014 add 21 days to it equals September 26-28, 2014 when these events of this book come true. If it is literally seven days before September 24-28, 2014 when Billy Graham dies or three and a half days or seven days equals September 19, 23-24, 2014 and September 20-21 or 24, 2014 is when these events happen. If a peace agreement is reached in September of 2014 or 2015 or in 2024 and people start saying "Peace, Peace" and "Peace and safety" then watch out for sudden destruction just as predicted in the Bible. If Billy Graham dies September 6-8, 2014 then 21 days later these events happen on September 26-27-28 or at least some of them happen then. The chapter 9 and 27th verse of Daniel seems to me to be a date of our ninth month of September and the 27th day when this covenant of peace or of wisdom starts or comes out in 2014 or 2015. Will Israel make peace then with the Palestinians? Or is the ninth month 27th day that of December 21-25, 28-29, 2014 or 2015?

After these things another great event may happen like Yellowstone Park super volcano erupting destroying the U.S. and part of the world with one quarter of the earth's population dies because of it, famines and pestilence's and earthquakes and storms and wars just as Revelation chapter 6 predicts. One quarter of the earth's population equals 1-2 billion people.

During some of these dates and years the sun, moon and stars will stop for exactly three days and will stand still and not rotate. Then exactly three days later they start up again at the light of thy arrows (missiles) as the Bible predicted and Venus will rotate counterclockwise making paradise of earth and long life spans of 600-1000 years people will live for. And if the tree of life is turn right then people and all diseases will be gone and you will live forever if born again Christian or to the Great White Throne judgement a 1000 years from now (=2014).

In Daniel chapter 7 it predicts the antichrist and false prophet thrown into the lake of fire at this time and the son of man and saints will have their land taken away, but their lives prolong by living 600-1000 years old. Their dominion Daniel chapter 7 predicts taken away is the U.S. and Israel, but if the saints heed these warnings and flee to New Zealand and Australia and live a 1000 years or more their land is taken away, but lives prolong. But with that prophecy predicting beasts have their dominion taken away but lives prolong living only in the U.S. as weird beast and animals and birds and just demons who are not aloud to leave that place to hurt or do any mischief. Daniel chapter 7 mention several time "ancient of days" and the son of man and the Saints. If I live to 3005 A.D. I will be 1051 years old (ancient). The antichrist and false prophet (=Erich Von Daniken=beasts) dies and the end of the U.S. happens then the antichrist and false prophet are thrown into the lake of fire at one of these dates (December 21-27, 28-29, 2014, 2015 or 2024. The U.S. left desolate only demons and strange beast live there fulfilling these prophecies of Daniel chapter 7. With the antichrist and false prophet thrown into the fire and the U.S. destroyed and the devils left are put in desolate U.S. and are not allowed out of that place for a about 1000 years prolonging their lives but their dominion taken away (the world) and they are confined to the U.S. (=Babylon) as Isaiah chapter 13 predicts as well as Daniel chapter 7. Satan is bound in hell for 1000 years in chains and a seal put upon him so he can no longer deceive the world. See Revelation chapter 20.

The great hail predicted in Revelation may have several meanings. One is that it would be great hail from a storm. Another great rocks from Yellow Stone Park super volcano eruption, and the other is parts of the sun in a nova hitting the earth. Revelation chapter 6 predicts men to hide in the caves from the terrible hail. This wouldn't be the end but could be from Yellow Stone Park super volcano eruption. The smoke, ash and gases from that eruption may last three days/months/years and no light of the sun comes upon the U.S. and possibly other parts of the world for that same time span causing great famines and pestilence's and possibly a small ice age or nuclear winter.

Irvin Baxter on his TV show told how in the book of Revelation chapters 8-9 predict events that happened in the first Iraq war in 1991, which I predicted before hand in my books or writings. The "darkness at noon," the third of the sea turned to blood or the oil released from Kuwait by the Iraqi army, a third of the stars are not seen because of the smoke from the oil well fires and so on and so on. See my book "The Experiment at Philadelphia" Appendix D and remember most of those predictions were written before the events happened.

My books revealed the names of killers or murderers from four named storms and by numerology or codes hidden in the Bible and by the killers themselves. They were Andy (=Zodiac), Charley (=Charley Manson), Francis (=Frances), and Opal or O.J. Simpson. The Boston Strangler killer was not Albert DeSalvo, but George Nasser who's first name George may be a future storm to hit Florida by 2014-2015-2024 with that name or the first letter of that name or "G" storm.

Erich Von Daniken wrote the book "Chariots of the Gods" which was reprinted by Bantam Books in 1971-1972-1973 and took off in sales. He is the false prophet and antichrist satan tried to get me to be instead I betrayed satan and turned to God and revealed this mystery in truth about ancient astronauts and UFOs and the science and physics that may come to deceive the world with a strong delusion. His theory makes you lustful like a sexual lust for a sexy woman just as Revelation chapter 17 predicted. I knew early in my Christian life that he was the false prophet and what he would do at the end as the "one hour of temptation" that revelation predicted. If a day is a 1000 years to God then one hour is 41 years added to 1971-1972-1973 equals 2013-2014. His publisher Bantam Books that bought the paperback rights in those years had the address of 666. Is that the 666 number of the false prophet who lives in seven (many) hills or mountains and makes a mark (=letters) of 666 in books to deceive all the world? Could those marks being books printed out of Bantam books that equals 666? I believed they moved from that address but were there when Erich Von Daniken's books (marks) were published by them in the U.S. In WWII Hitler was the Antichrist and his ally of Italy was the false prophet. This is a secondary fulfillment of these prophecies. Remember John said there are many antichrists even though the main ones are the three or four antichrist's and false prophet's those of the many authors who wrote more about ancient astronauts that turn peoples lust for their doctrine to MYSTERY BABYLON and UFO's (=flying saucers or sorceries). See Revelation for these prophecies.

I betrayed satan twice once with Erich Von Daniken books of ancient prophecies he wanted me to publish, but I resisted and refused and turned to God of Christianity. As I torn up my notes and manuscript of that theory I actually heard angels rejoicing. Then I fell for the strong delusion of science and physics that he deceived the world with and again I resisted and refused satan offers and turned again to God Almighty and Christianity being dead in sins twice and born again two times one on September 6-8, 1976 and the other early May 2007. In Erich Von Daniken's new book out this year of 2014 or in 2013 it sound like the final phase of the antichrist and false prophet. Is it to published by Bantam

Books? And does it led people away from the Church and Christianity? Will he teach religion is evil and the UFO's beings are truth? That's saying good is evil and evil good as the Bible warned about in the last days. He uses old wives tales, legend's, fables and stone images and writings which are all called and done by heathen gods the serpent's or dragon's, which is Satan. They are doctrines of devils just as the Bible predicted people in the last days would teach and preach on and about as false teachers and false prophets and false Christ's (=false gods). See my book entitled "The Experiment at Philadelphia" for these teachings and where a book in it is mentioned that these ancient things were done, but not by God, Jesus or the Holy Ghost, good angels, but by devils not to enlighten humans but to cause a strong delusion in the last days leading to apostasy and falling away from Christianity and into lawlessness which is what is exactly happening from the dates of 1965-1967 when the book "Chariots of the Gods was published till one hour of temptation that Revelation predicted or 42 years from then to 2008-2009 when his book "History is wrong" teaches along with religions being all wrong. Making Erich Von Daniken both the false prophet and the antichrist. In a moment I will give a brief book report on that book. But I guarantee it will be like my book just mention first 14 chapters tells of. I know this cause way back then God was teaching me these things and I knew what the False prophet would teach and what the antichrist will teach and they both could be one as Erich Von Daniken coming up out of the waters or seas and out of the earth exactly Revelation chapter 13 predicted. Here is my report on the book entitled: "History is wrong."

Even though his book entitled "History is wrong" by Erich Von Daniken is anti-religious it doesn't fit the first 14 chapters the antichrist and false prophet will do like in my book entitled "The Experiment at Philadelphia." If you count Erich Von Daniken book "History is wrong" that came out in 2009 and call it the covenant with the antichrist or death as Isaiah chapters 28-29 and Daniel 9:27 predicts it would equal seven years added to 2009 which equals 2015-2016 when he (Erich Von Daniken, Billy Graham or me) dies withholding the power of the antichrist or man of sin or iniquity or lawlessness or son of prediction (=doom!). That same year could be when Erich Von Daniken writes the new book that match my 14 chapters written by the antichrist. Or it could be when UFO's land in sight of men and give the world the 14 chapters on one or two books. Betty Hill was taken aboard a UFO and claims to have seen a book on board and wanted to take it with her. The one demon said the others don't want you to do that. See book entitled "Interrupted Journey" and the movie made of it. Was that book the first 14 chapters of my book entitled "The Experiment at Philadelphia"? If I die at these dates and my books go out of print or are taken off the market or the super volcano at Yellowstone Park destroys the U.S. then there really will be a great withholding power removed and all evil will break out especially with my books gone. But if they stay in print it will stop or withhold the power of the evil one. Erich Von Daniken in his book "History is wrong" claims Gods and all religion were started by humans coming from other solar systems and heavenly places to satisfy their sexual lust and created people on earth in which our ancestors mistaken for Gods or thee God, but were just human ancient astronauts. One chapter in Erich Von Daniken first book was entitled "Was God an astronaut?" The antichrist may still come just as a famous writer or an unknown writer and write the first 14 chapters of my book I mentioned with great writing style and advance science and psychics and really deceive the world. What all of Von Daniken books do is to make God Almighty a weak UFO being rather than a great good God of heaven for the whole Universe. Please watch these things closely and keep my books in mind and don't say they are in error even to an angel that may come and tell you about them. It may work out that a few do this and take it seriously and survive to the end as the Saints of God at 20,000 or 144,000 and billions of people come to faith with Jesus Christ. It may cause satan to stop his plans to do these things because more people will come to Christ the more if he lands in a UFO in front of people and has the book or anyone writes the book with more science and psychics in it to make it look like the truth.

Erich Von Daniken lives or use to live in a very great mountainous area of Europe. He was born in the Aries sign in on April 14, 1935 the Chinese Year of the Pig and in Aries sign of the Ram or lamb with two horns on it as Revelation chapter 13 predicts as two people in one as the two horns as the false prophet and the antichrist. The "lamb" could mean religious leader of new with new ideas and ways to believe. His religion is that the heathen gods are gods of the UFOs and are to be followed, but Matthew chapter 24, Mark chapter 13, Luke chapter 21, John's letters and II Peter 2:1-3 predicts those gods as devils of UFOs who use old wise tales, fables and legends that the many ancient astronauts books do just as predicted using doctrines of devils to fool the world. His newest book does just that claiming his book the Holy Bible is all wrong and religions are all wrong. The main antichrist might come up out of the sea as one from flight 370 that went missing or JFK' Jr., who's plane went down in water or JFK that had a fatal head wound as predicted. The Malaysia flight 370 his body was never found. See Daniel 11:19-24. The Aries sign is the sign of a Ram with two horns exactly as Revelation chapter 13 predicts the false prophet as a man with two horns like a lamb who speaks like a dragon and a dragon gives him power and wisdom. Erich Von Daniken might not only be the false prophet of revelation but also the antichrist of Revelation and the Bible. His new book cover is saying you been taught all wrong by religion. That's exactly how I knew and wrote the antichrist would say and write. Even if he doesn't use science and physics to do it then he still is telling the world that religion is wrong or opposite the truth and is using UFOs (sorceries-flying saucers). When you add 41.6 years to 1971- 1973 it equals 2013-2014 counting each year or not and adding the sixth month as another year. Revelation chapter 13 predicts two beasts one coming up out of the sea and one out of the earth. Flight 370 crashed in to the ocean or sea where the antichrist would come back to life if that prophecy comes true. JFK and his son was shot by a fatal head wound as Revelation chapter 13 predicts and his son crashed into the sea. If UFO's brings back any of these two watch out for the strong delusion.

Erich Von Daniken the last I heard was living in a place of many hills (=seven hills) in Switzerland, which is ruled by Virgo the planet Wormwood that satan was before he came to earth. When he fell the planet wormwood between Mars and Jupiter it blew up and the asteroid belt is its remains. Satan then went too Venus by forced or violence and came to the earth with the seed of his son to pregnant a woman at time of conception at Gaza, Egypt which is where the great pyramids and sphinx are and are the dates of September 19-27 in cusps and signs of Virgo-Libra. That place is in the Virgo-Libra zone making the 666 name, number and mark (=symbols of those planet and signs). On the carving from the temple Hathor it shows a pig with a kneeling woman with seven stars and 12 stars near the, with a raft with a ram's head with a sun or moon disk between them. The Year 1935 that Erich Von Daniken was born in was the Chinese year of the Pig the same as 2007 when adding the 12 cycles years as the 12 stars to it. The polar opposite it equals 2013 the Chinese Year of the Snake that Revelation calls the antichrist, false prophet and satan. And the raft with a ram's head with a moon or sun disk in its horns could be April 14, 1935 when Erich Von Daniken was born. His last book came out in 2009 the Year of the Tiger the polar opposite of the Monkey (=2015-2016) starting in September-October 2015 is about how everything is wrong and good equals evil and evil equals good is just how satan was predicted to come in the last days. If Erich Von Daniken dies and a UFO lands with him coming out with two books than watch out. But he may just remains on the earth for a 1000 years as Ellen White predicted a long reign of the antichrist then look out for his future books.

The raft (=flood=tidal wave, hurricane) with a ram's head and horns with ox horns near a kneeling woman and seven and 12 star by her and a Pig next to her and a table with four snakes on it. Is that a medical table and snakes known for healing and surgery to Erich Von Daniken who is now very sick of July 30, 2014. Erich Von Daniken was born April 14, 1935 the Chinese year of the Pig or its polar opposite the Snake as satan the deceiver. Add six times twelve year Chinese cycles to April 14, 1935 equals April 14-15, 2007. Add the six or seven stars as seven years to that date and it equals April 14- 15, 2013 and April 14-15, 2014 when a blood moon fell on Passover that year. Polar opposite that in a new moon on September 24-27, 2014 or in October he will die and be revealed. These things represents the stars, snakes, raft and ram's head and horns and ox horns and Pig. The Ox Year is 2009 when Erich Von Daniken published "History is wrong". I have not read that book yet, but if he says in it how religion is all wrong and backwards then it fits my prophecies of the antichrist and false prophet and satan. If he died before he can write a book that mine books claims he would then as II Thessalonians chapter 2 will come true perfectly. The mystery of iniquity already works only the withholding will know it to he be taken out of it and the Holy Ghost reveals the real antichrist. Mystery Babylon will be reveal, the 666 number be revealed. The seven heads and hills will be revealed, UFOs will be revealed and all mysteries will be revealed in all my books. Daniel predicted the antichrist to come to this area known as the Revived Roman Empire (=Switzerland) and deceives the world with UFOs and science and psychics which he would certainly do if he lived except the Holy Ghost with held him and revealed his plans in advance to take the sting out of them or stop them altogether. This would prevent or help stop the Strong Delusion that deceives the world. Irvin Baxter as mentioned earlier claimed that Revelation chapters 8-9 were of the first Iraq war where modern day helicopters are described in Chapter 9 and the third of the trees, green grass and stars would be darkened or burned up. Those helicopters are secondary fulfillment of those prophecies along with the stars, trees and green grass darkened or burned up. The first interpretation of those things is that of monsters let loose from hell and the bottomless pit that have seven heads that breathe out fire and look like what the prophecies predicted of them. These monster will be let loose near the end of the 1000 year period. As for the stars not shining could be two different events. One is that of a volcano eruption and the other is the stopping of the rotation of the earth leaving a third below the horizon and can't be seen. Another is the oil well fires in Kuwait that went burning for months causing "darkness at noon" and the darken the third of the stars. The green grass and trees burned up could also be from those oil well fires or are the green grass and tress in the U.S. burned up because of the rotation stopped and neutralized the electricity. Another interpretation is that of super volcano eruption in Yellow Stone Park and showers down hot rocks like Revelation 6:12-17 predicts causing people to flee to caves and the fires burns for three days until the electricity comes back on. The other interpretation of that could be wild fires in the mid-west to the west because of the drought causes wild fire to burn a third of the U.S. or mid-west and west of the U.S. Revelation chapter 9 predicts those monsters from hell and/or the helicopters against Iraq's leaders is a king over them named Abaddon or Apollyon, which some Bible translate "the destroyed." Irvin Baxter said on his TV show that a king or leader of Iraq in the first Iraq war was named Saddam Hussein, which in Arabic his first name "Saddam" is named "the Destroyer." This maybe why a king is mentioned as Saddam and not a queen or women who created those monsters let loose at the end of the 1000 year period. The third of the sea turned to blood equals a oil spill that Iraqis did into the Persian Gulf from Kuwait and killed wild life in it for about a third of Kuwait. In many books I bought on the first Iraq war I saw pictures of Kuwait that shown darkness and said dark at noon exactly as the Bible predicted. Another was the horrible sites of Kuwait and a soldier saying, "Almost Armageddon." Daniel chapter 10 predicts Daniel in the midst of this place of Baghdad and Iraq and being killed twice in 12 years and seeing something so scary and frightening that he fell down dead twice. The 21 days Daniel prediction in Daniel 10:13 predicts in reverse 12 years instead of 21 days and for three times 12 as there were three weeks. The first Iraq war happened in 1991+12=2003, the first and second Iraq wars when Daniel saw shock and awe in both wars that scared him to death as like being in the center of hell like one reporter said. Add the third 12 to 2003 and you have 2014-2015-2016 to the Jewish Civil calendar. This maybe when Daniel was praying for his people the Jewish people that an Iran-Israeli war happens and Iran and Israel are destroyed. If people don't repent and become born again Christians these bad events for the U.S. and Israel will remain and happen to them. If they do Jesus Christ will come back for 1000 years of peace and joy.

If the UFOs return and help mankind but only as a great temptation to live lawless lives so all can go to hell where they are fed into the mouth of satan a beast there just like the Twilight Zone shows "To Serve Man." It may so happen that if something goes wrong and my books are no longer available then the UFOs are free to do what they want. What they want is three fold just as God is a Trinity. The three are the full lawlessness life, the neutral life and the full law life. Just as Ecclesiastics 11:2-3 predicts you will not know what evil shall come upon the earth in the last days. The demons or UFO beings may bring one of the three or all three to the people of earth. They may bad mouth my books for being lukewarm teaching people to be either full lawlessness or full law, but not lukewarm.

If the UFOs returns after the Rapture they may declare that the Rapture was evil, so you should beware of it an preach and teach full law. They might even do this by the Catholic church claims any one who doesn't follow them is evil and should be persecuted tortured and killed. The Catholic Church for the 1000 year period may do those things to any one who is not catholic as they have done in the past two milleniums. If the UFO beings and the Pope agree to be lawless or full law then they will spread that over the entire earth to all who don't do those ways of life to be persecuted, tortured and killed. If the withholder lives the 1000 years then he may prevent these things from happening. If not they will come full blast at you heaping many burdens and troubles on you for a 1000 years by revealing satan plans in advance to take the sting out of them or stop them completely. The UFO being claims that the first Rapture took all evil to heaven then see what they say is true good equals evil and evil equals good as my book entitled "The Experiment at Philadelphia" and the first 14 chapters tells in advance satan's plans for you and the future. If satan is bound up in hell and put a seal on him to not deceive the world any more then we will have a peaceful good 1000 year period. The deception will be stopped at that time as Revelation chapter 20 predicts from the time many were behead and claim for 1000 years to avenge their blood. God may do this at the end by throwing anyone not written in the Lambs book of life into the lake of fire to burn for eternity. If the 1000 year kingdom is peaceful due to this Rapture then at the end many will become born again Christians in the billions like Daniel chapter 12 and Revelation chapter 7 predicts.

The big foot sightings and other monster sightings may just remain a mystery because they come from UFOs and can disappear at once or go up into the belly of a UFO. I once read that a town in Europe were terrorized by a big hairy monster for a certain time long ago and finally one night they saw the big monster go up into the under belly of a UFO and he was gone. One other reports told of hunters tracking big foot in the snow only to have the tracks stop in the middle of the field with no big foot around. Other reports of big foot claimed he smelled like sulfur which is fire and brimstone form hell where demons and these monsters live. People who died and went to hell and came back to life said it smelled as sulfur down there along with other horrible smells. People being taken aboard UFOs say they sometimes would seem strange creatures aboard them. These are the monsters or demons that are being sighted around the world. Moth Man, Sunk Man, the Abominable Snow man or what ever they are they are all demons and probably will never be caught unless they want to. Another interpretation of the dream I had about showing many people the back woods of my Grandparents property could be this: Shania Twain with one person near her mean

August 28, her birthday, plus 30 days plus three months and three years from the year my Grandfather died in 1976. This equals starting from 2012 the Chinese Dragon the same as 1976 the date of December 24-25, 2015. In Revelation chapter 12 it predicts of a woman would flee into the south for three and a half decades and minus three days equals December 24-25, 2015-2016. Remember the Jewish Civil calendar start the new year of 2016 in September-October 2015 making it exactly 35 years from 1981 when we moved down here from up north to when another flood tries to kills me like in birth exactly as Revelation chapter 12 predicts.

To repeat again be ready, prepared and watching for these signs to travel somewhere else or else you and the family and all belongings might be destroyed. Those signs are both for the U.S. and Israel. The signs are Billy Graham is dead, or Erich Von Daniken is dead or I am dead for shortly after the wrath of God will come in Volcano eruptions, tidal waves, great earthquakes, storms and wars. Then when you see someone of the rooftop, had dreams of floods or tidal waves, visions of them and angel visitation telling you to flee if the earthquake of San Francisco and/or Seattle happens on December 21-25, 28-29, 2014. If smart you would move now (=August 2014) from these areas of San Francisco, Seattle and the Eastern Coast line of the U.S. If your not affected by that event take it as a harbinger for the events of December 21-25, 2015 by leaving the East Coast and from New Madrid, Missouri. And if those events happen in 2015 then really be ready to move to New Zealand or Australia before December 21-25, 2024. Don't be in the U.S. at that time and plan to settle into those two places for good. As for Israel if you see these same things hitting the U.S. when

Billy Graham dies flee to Petra, Jordan or New Zealand or Australia before the first harbinger hits the U.S. in the form of a great earthquake in San Francisco or Seattle. The war between Israel and Iran may spread to Russia and the U.S. and thus if Iran doesn't have nuclear weapons yet Russia sure does and will use them on Israel if Israel attacks Iran. Russia has a covenant, which maybe the seven year covenant that Daniel 9:27 predicts with Iran signed sometime in the past three or four years that if Iran is attack Russia will act as though Moscow was attack. Israelis should also look for dreams of war, visions of war, angel visitation of war and telling you to flee before December 21, 2014 and you see someone of the rooftop. Be smart now (=August 2014-2015) move now to New Zealand or Australia. Don't anyone say to the angel it is in error about my books or some thing else or you will loose your life and the works of your hands. The angel makes you smile ear to ear. See Ecclesiastes and Revelation 3:22. God so help us all!

On the ancient carving from the temple Hathor there is a ox leg pointing down towards Virgo-Libra where near that point is three ox horns seen. The constellation Cepheus is the king on the throne. Was this predicting that the end will come on 3005 A.D. when the North Star is 1000 years past the 2001 A.D.? That date which was 3005 A.D. when the great white throne judgement happens a 1000 years past 2001 A.D. when Polaris was the North Star in 2001 A.D. till 3005 A.D. when the North Star is approaching the feet of Cepheus. The Cepheus constellation is a man on a throne or the great white throne judgement on the latter dates just as the stars and Bible predicted. September 26-27, 3005 A.D. is not only the Chinese Ox year, but also a

Wednesday-Thursday as Virgo-Libra equals in symbolism. See drawings 1-6 at the end of this book for details in the North Stars and these ancient prophecies. Amen!

I may have painted a dark picture of the 1000 year period in this book and my other book "The Seven Thunders." The other alternative 1000 year period may be long healthy life with no crime, wars, terrorist attacks but fun and joy for everyone for the 1000 years. No return Christ or Rapture of good people but as II Peter 3:1-18 the Lord tarries His return for a 1000 years so many (=billions) may come to Christ as Revelation chapter 7 predicts. It maybe that we are now in the seven year period when Christians and Saints and Jewish people are under attack exactly what we see in Iraq right now (August 2014).

Nostradamus in his quatrain C1:Q55 predicts a unjust heaven and confusion. Could this mean that the Rapture is soon to come, but not for Christians, Saints and the Jewish people but for all evil people like Isis and all the other terrorist groups and possibly all Palestinians, Arabs and anyone who is doing evil in the world to be suddenly taken up to heaven and the birds eat their dead bodies just as Jesus predicted in Luke chapter 17 and He also predicted in the end times that the first would be last and the last first. This would mean evil men and women and children would go up to heaven first before the Christians, Saints and Jewish people do. All evil Kings, Queens and Presidents that are evil will also be removed as Daniel chapter 2 predicts along with Song of Solomon predicting certain queens are set up over nations that had these evils kings, queens and presidents. The new ones will start each nation again but with the exact constitution of the U.S. and its economy and law systems making for a great new world for the 1000 years. These things seem like a unjust heaven and confusion about the Bible just as that quatrain Nostradamus wrote C1:Q55 comes true especially in Iraq known as Babylon where Isis is doing unspeakable things. These prophecies will be great confusion for many and seem unjust and maybe rejected by the Christians, Saints and Jewish people, but you can't deny they happen that way no matter how unjust it seems like Isis in Iraq (=Babylon). There are differently two different Raptures one for evil people and one for good people. The first may have two parts to it right now (=October 2, 2014) with the killing of Isis and their dead bodies left unburied and eagles and/or vultures eat them just as Revelation chapter 19 and Luke chapter 17 predicts. And John 16:1-2 and chapter 20 predicts persecution of the Saints by beheading them which Isis did and two happened in the U.S. and they think they are doing God's service and will go to heaven with certain virgins. That was fulfilled exactly and may also have a secondary fulfillment when a great Rapture of all evil people happen. That is the last first and first last. The U.S. was founded or discovered by Columbus who was a Jewish person with his passengers and/or crew were Jewish who were kick out of Spain in 1492 A.D. And later on Gentile Christians started the U.S. which is Judaism the Gentiles were called after the Jews were called that but then rejected Christ and the name and fruits went to the U.S. The U.S. and Israel will be destroyed and abandon for ever as Isaiah chapter 13 predicts for Babylon (Iraq and/or the U.S.) where demon spirits live for the 1000 years. Why God did this is because the U.S. turned its back on God and Israel. For Israel destruction is the same reason they turned their back on God and God destroyed them. They may rebuild again or two times or may not. But the 1000 years will be of great joy, prosperity and happiness for all people. Three days of darkness and neutralized electricity for that time may or may not happen, but a counterclockwise rotation of Venus at the end of the three days along with God taking away the Cherubs that hinder or stop the tree of life we will all live for ever and in the end of the 1000 year period the true Rapture of good people happen without them dying. That's why Bible prophecies predict two ways of two Raptures. One their souls are taken and bodies left and the other their bodies and souls are taken up to heaven and they never die. The curse on humans, the earth, animals and all things will be gone. And at the end of the 1000 years will be the great white throne judgement for those in heaven that behead God's people and the innocent. This is why Revelation chapter 6 the Saints under the alter in heaven ask God how long will you be till you revenge our blood which Revelation chapter 20 tells as beheaded. This means it a long time (=1000 years) until God judges those Isis people and terrorist groups for their evil just as the Bible predicted and makes those beheadings now in 2014 until 3005 A.D. when God judges them. May God Bless us all!!! Remember anyone not written in the Lamb's book of life in heaven will be throne out of heaven into the lake of fire for ever. The only way to get your name written in the Lambs book of life us by becoming a born again Christian as Chapter 7 of this book tells you how.

The two authors named Cris Putnam and Thomas Horn who wrote the two books: "EXO-Vaticana" and "The final Pope is here, Petrus Romanus" claimed on one TV show that the Maya's didn't predict the end of the world or age on December 21, 2012, but that the Pope would change and two new people would come upon the scene within two years. Everyone declared the Mayan prophecies of the end as December 21, 2012 A.D. But nothing happened! Will two more years come and two people or one as the twins of Gemini (=Horse) on the Chinese Year of 2014 (=Horse) which rules Gemini appear upon the world scene? That person maybe be a Horse sign born and third son of a family of five and which prophecies come true on December 21-25, 28-29, 2014 (=+2 years to 2012-2013 equals 2014-2015-2016) when Billy Graham dies and within three and a half days he will win the lottery of Fantasy Five with his birthright of those five birthdays of his family. Then on December 25, 2014 there will be a great earthquake in San Francisco and/or Seattle which are in the Gemini zone, which the Chinese Horse and Year equals 2014 A.D. See Revelation chapter 11, which predicts two twins to come to earth and predicted the end times (knowledge increased of end times when people travel to and fro and give gifts to one another) as that chapter predicts along with Daniel 12:4. Those dates are the Christmas Holidays and people travel to and fro, give gifts one to another and party by over eating and drinking as Luke 21:9, 34-37, Daniel 12:4, Amos 1:1 and Revelation chapter 11 predicts by and by or two years from the Mayan date of December 21-25, 2012-2013+2=December 21-25, 28-29, 2014-2015-2016. Then on the one year anniversary of that quake will come two more one in the Gemini zone and one in the Pisces or Aries zones. The Canary island's volcano eruption and causes and earthquake and tidal wave to hit the U.S. East Coast on December 24-25, 2015 as

Daniel 9:26 predicts along with a New Madrid, Missouri earthquake and a Iran-Israeli war may come to pass then or the year before. December 25, 2015 is a full moon as the coded earthquake theory of mine come true again for the third time. See my book entitled "Predictions for 2013-2014," by Kurt B. Bakley available at this web site: WWW. Authorhouse.Com. Daniel 9:26-27 predicts the end because of many sins people have committed as abominations that cause desolation on Hanukkah or its symbol day to our calendar as December 24-25, 2014-2015-2016, 2024. I showed in the introduction how the seventieth week and three and a half years and 2300 days were fulfilled in by the Greek antichrist in 171-165 B.C. ending on Hanukkah in 165 B.C. that started that Holiday. Will God hate that Holiday in December 24-25, 28-29, 2014-2015-2016, 2024 and destroy many for their sins? Or will many repent and change and they go on for a long time. Be warned now and turn to Christ now or else all will be destroyed. Remember that if you die in those sins on these dates it is the end of the world to you. Reread Chapter Seven in this book again.

For sometime now I showed how Genesis 3:15 predicted Jesus' death on the cross as the spike through the feet which all movies and stories show. But Genesis 3:15 predicts the heel to be bruise not the feet as I put it meaning the same, but it wasn't the same. Two preachers showed focalized heels of a crucified man with the spike going sideways through the heels an exact fulfillment of Genesis 3:15. These prophecies relate to the Roman Catholic Church in which hammered the spike through Jesus' heel by the Romans and JFK who was Catholic (=Roman Catholic Church) who had his head wound exactly as Genesis 3:15 predicted.

Jesus predicted that as the days of Noah and Lot so shall be in the end. In Noah's days God saved the good people of Noah and his family and killed all the rest of the people in the world with a flood. If this first Rapture takes out all evil people and leave the good it will be as the days of Noah exactly as Jesus predicted. And the Holy Ghost reigns over the world with much gold, silver and oil for 1000 years and making all nations left prospering again for those 1000 years. And the days of Lot judges were approving gay sex just as our Supreme Court of judges did in October of 2014 by leaving it go until the states that many do allow gay rights. Exactly as the days of Lot and don't look back when you run from the capitals of Washington, D.C. and Jerusalem because fire and brimstone will come and blind you or kill you as it did to Lot's wife. The dates to run or flee are December 21-25, 28-29, 2014 or 2015 or other dates and years given in this book and my other books. If you see Jerusalem overrun by armies and/or these other signs I give then flee and run to the mountains or in the U.S. from the East Coast and San Francisco and/or Seattle and New Madrid, Missouri when earthquakes happen on December 21-25, 28-29, 2014 and 2015. Also look for people on roofs, angels in dreams or visions or in person warning you and the earthquake in San Francisco and/or Seattle happening first in 2014 then watch out and flee before hand on December 21-25, 28-29, 2015 when a tidal wave hits the Eastern U.S. Coast line then or the other dates give in this books or my other books.

The "pillars of smoke" and thee "afterwards" and "before" the coming of the terrible and notable day of the Lord happens certain events will happen as described ion this book as earthquakes, tidal waves, wars, storms, volcano eruptions annd other events as predicted in Joel chapter 2 and Acts Chapter 2. The "pillars of smoke" can mean mush-room clouds cause by nuclear explosions in which Zechariah chapter 14 predicts what happens top as human when a nuclear bomb explodes. Remember that over 2000 years ago well before we ever knew what a nuclear was or could do. A volcano eruption could also be a prediction of pillars of smoke going up in the sky making the sun dark as sack clothe of hair. See Revelation 6:12. Thee Greek word for "hair" is 5155 in the Greek dictionary of The Strong's Concordance. In that word it mentions "mohair", which is an Sngara Goat or the Chinese Year of the Goat or Sheep in 2015 when fig tree are not ripe and the stars of heaven fail like the shaking of as fig tree which is unripe in late fall or early winter in 2015 which is the Chinese Year of the Goat or Sheep. In those two chapters of Joel and Acts both predict these events before the great and terrible and notable day of the Lord comes. And Joel predicts "afterwards" that God will pour out His Spirit of the Holy Ghost on all people making then to repent and becomes a born again Christian and the animals, lands and all things will be peaceful and good just as Joel chapter 2 predicts. Those events are afterwards of the many bad things but the bad things and the pouring out of the holy ghost are good things but before the return of the Lord a 1000 years later in which billions of born again Christians enter into Heaven at the Rapture of good people at the end of the 1000 years of peace, prosperity, good health and great joy. They not only be born again Christians, but Baptist in water and the Holy Ghost. See Revelation chapter 7. Revelation 6:12 predicts as darkened sun near a blood moon that are special. They are the four blood moons of April 14-15, 2014, October 8, 2014, April 4, 2015 and September 27-28, 2015. The two blood moons of April 4 and September 27-28, 2015 has afterwards these troubled events happen on December 21-25, 28-29, 2015. See Joel 2:28 Then the curse of the earth and people will be gone for a 1000 years before the return of the Lord in the air, (He never touched ground) and people are all Rapture psychical bodies and all making no death for them that Thessalonians and Corinthians predicted. Luke chapter 17 predicted the death of evil people where eagle and vultures eat their dead bodies like that of Isis now (October 10, 2014) and possible on a greater scale when this Rapture happens. My angel visitation in August of 1995 that had three birds around his neck riding a bicycle crossing over to Bates Street or Avenue in Eustis had the middle bird with two red tip wings. Was this a prophecy of between two or four blood moons or afterwards there would come these events of pillars of smoke caused by nuclear bomb or a volcano eruption or wars and storms and then a pouring out afterwards of God's Holy Spirit? Isaiah 6:12-13 predicts a "tenth" added to chapter/year codes of 1906 when the San Francisco earthquake happen in the Chinese years of the Horse the same as 2014 on December 21-25, 28-29, 2014 is the Chinese Year of the Horse 10 years afterwards of 2004 when on Christmas Day if its our local time on December 25, 2004 a great earthquake and tidal wave hit the island s and nations around the Indian Ocean. Will 10 years latter we see a great earthquake and tidal wave hit the U.S. on December 25-26, 2014. I don't know if they count their earthquake on December 26 or 27. IF it was declared on the

26 then a day earlier would be the day of this earthquake and tidal wave to hit Sand Francisco and/or Seattle? But they are close together and same Chinese Years.

In the Fatima prophecy in which three little girls seen the Virgin Mary in the 1900's it was noted that she gave them three prophecies for the future. Two have already been fulfilled but the third hasn't. Some say because it revealed that the Roman Catholic Church was evil and they didn't want the bad publicity. But during the 1990's there were several TV documentaries on ancient prophecies leading to the end. On one of those TV documentaries it told of a horrible vision the three little girls seen from the Fatima prophecy. It like to scare them to death. The Catholic church being evil wouldn't do that. But it also mentioned in that third prophecy that there would come a time when no engines works. I far as I know every engine needs electricity. IF Venus is stopped in its rotation and the earth stops too, it could make all electricity neutral just as the movie "The day the earth stood still." That certainly would scare people to death as Luke 21:25-26 predicts. But remember this it is only stopped for three days and when it starts again it will rotate counterclockwise making long lives and paradise of earth with the ground and animals and people. So you need not be afraid. In the book of Habakkuk in the Bible it predicts when arrows fly at Israel and the U.S. as missiles then the sun, moon and stars will again rotate. That same book predicts a hiding of His (God) power. Could this mean clouds cover due to the arrows or missiles and mush room clouds or a volcano eruption or a storm at that time blocking (=hiding) the vision and power of God to see the sun, moon and stars stand still. In Luke 21:25-26 it predicts men's hearts failing them for fear of what coming upon the earth because of signs in the sun, moon and stars standing still for three days. You now know this mystery and need not be afraid, but rejoice of the coming good times for a 1000 years. See my book entitled "End Time Signs II" chapters 77-78 for more details on this event and remember Zechariah chapter 11 where it predicts God breaking a covenant He made with all people after Noah's flood which also had the stopping of the rotation of the sun, moon and stars for three days but couldn't be seen (=hiding of His power) because of the rain clouds starting the flood. Genesis chapter 6-7 predicts this covenant God made with Noah and all people that he would never stop time again. But Zechariah chapter 11 predicts He will break that covenant.

In Matthew 24:32-35 it predicts the end of the world as a fig tree and a generation from when the fig tree or Israel is reborn. Hal Lindsey in his book "The late great planet earth" said the fig tree represents Israel and a generation is 40 years. So he added a generation of 40 years to 1948 and came up to 1988 when the Rapture of Second Coming happens. Nothing happened in 1988. But could he have meant a fourth rebirth of Israel in 2965 A.D. plus 40 years equals 3005 A.D. Remember Song of Solomon n 6:13 four returns of Israel to become a nation again. In 1948 and 1988 Israel has only been return twice as Song of Solomon 6:13 predicted as two armies destroy the temple. Two more returns of Israel in the 1000 years period with the fourth on 2965 A.D. as the fourth plus 40 year generation equals 3005 A.D. as the end of the world. The fig tree was the tree of knowledge of good and evil in the garden of Eden in the Virgo sign or cusp time. That timing is from August 21-23 to September 21-27 and star time from September 21-23 to October 21-23. In Chinese astrology the Virgo sign equals the Rooster sign which is not only 2005 A.D. plus 1000 years to 3005 A.D., but is also 2965 A.D. When we add a 40 year generation end time generation to 2965 A.D. it equals 3005 A.D. ruled by the Chinese Ox. The Chinese Ox year is equal to Capricorn sign and month of January which both names and sign means "door" or "gateway." I mention in my books how I heard knocking at my door in morning time and got up to answer only to find no one. Was that a sign that meant the door or gateway to heaven as the final Rapture and end of the world would be on the Ox year of 3005 A.D. in the Virgo sign or star time from August 21-23-September 21-23-October 21-23, 3005 A.D.? If the exact time is early morning in Israel at 6-8 a.m. it would equal 12:18-1:18 a.m. EDT or EST on the East Coast of the U.S. The Chinese Rooster sign or Virgo sign or star time of August 21-October 22 is when at 1:18 a.m. EDT the end comes just as Colossians 2:16-17 predicted. See my book The Divine Code 3 Revised Edition. Matthew 24:33 predicts these signs as being at the "doors" plural. Could it have meant January and Capricorn names as "doors" at the end in the Ox Year and Virgo sign or star time in August 21-23-October 23, 3005 A.D.?

Nostradamus predicted in his quatrain C9:Q83 that 20 degrees when the sun is into Taurus there will be a great earthquake, darkness and Rapture (=evil rapture of infidels dies and go to heaven asking mercy for their sins to God and the Saints in heaven) when the theater is full. Los Angeles and San Francisco which near where the woman was going or show in the sign in of the Bates Hotel register could be where one or two great earthquakes hit in 2014-2015. The 20 degrees into the Taurus sign by the sun could mean May 10 or June 9-10, 2014-2015 when these events happen. It also could mean 20 degrees by a star chart on the polar opposite of June or December 21-26, 2014-2015 when over head at midnight or 10-11 p.m. 20 degrees is into Taurus in the night sky. Those times are when the movie theaters would be filled in Los Angeles or San Francisco on Christmas Day of December 25-26, 2014-2015 Los Angeles or San Francisco time making our Eastern U.S. time as December 26, 2014 or 2015. Los Angeles is ruled by Leo the lion sign that is ruled by the sun that stops Venus and the earth from rotation causing great darkness for three days as that quatrain predicts. My dream of my grandparents and me showing the backwoods of their property and Shania Twain equals 30 days, 3 months and three years form her birthday of August 28 starting form 2012. That gives the exact date of December 26, 2014 or 2015 when these events happen. The year 2016 equals the Chinese Monkey Year that rules the Leo sign which December 25-26, 2015 equals 2016 by the Jewish Civil Calendar. Will these events happen May 10, June 9-10, 12, 20, 24-25, 27, 29, 9th of Av, 2014, 2015, 2024, 2060, 2061 and 3005 A.D.

My book entitled "Predictions for 2013-2014" predicted pestilence's or diseases happening in the fall of 2013 or 2014. On the Jim Bakker show in late October 2014 showed a clip from a man named Mark Biltz that he showed a chart of the first ebola patient in Texas on September 25, 2014 which was the first day of Rosh Hashanah spread by fruit bats, apes, monkeys and pigs (=swine flu as my book predicted?) The man died on October 8, 2014, which was the second blood moon this year on a Jewish feast day or Holiday. Just as they predicted signs from God came on September 25, 2014 and October 8, 2014 with pestilence's. Will earthquake soon come as the prophecies predict? By the way September 24, 2014 is near the first day of fall as book just mentioned predicted for 2014. See the book "Blood Moons" by Mark Biltz and my book mentioned above. It is unclear at this time that the earthquakes, volcano eruptions, tidal waves, stopping the rotation of the earth and a Iran-Israeli war with the U.S. and Russia get involved is for December 21-25, 26-29, 2014 or 2015 or the dates given in this book for when these events happen.

Luke 21:25-26 predicts signs in the sun, moon and stars and seas roaring sending distress among nations in great trouble making so fearful men suffer heart attacks. The "roaring seas" can not only men a storm buts also a tidal waves. Those verses could also mean the rotation of earth stops which would really scare men to have heart attacks and the third thing is storms and/or wars or attacks in Iran, Israel, Russia and the U.S. The U.S. could suffer a double trouble with a nuclear bomb shot at the White House and then a tidal wave hit later that time. See Isaiah 40:1-2.

Do you remember me telling you in my book "The Experiment at Philadelphia" about 999 equals all things of the trinity of 3 being Omnipresence, Omnipotent and Omniscient. The book entitled "Astrology: A Space Age Science" pages 105-106-107-108 and 197 by Joseph F. Goodavage The author of that books claims the same thing about the number 9. The 999 is a upside down 666 and both equals 9 when adding up their numbers as nine or add the two numbers to equal 9. The same is true of seconds, minutes, degrees, breathing, heart beats a minute or hour, the Sidereal Great Year seen in drawing three in Chapter 6, the number 333=9, gestation, a degree of the sidereal Year along with 30 degrees of it and the whole of it as 360 degrees or nine. The author of that book wrote about chance, chaos and order in page 197 and other parts of that book. He seems to think everything is controlled and not by chance, instinct, fate or free will. Just as the 9 controls all things and can't be chance or coincidence.

The books of Jeremiah and Limitations written in the Bible by Jeremiah the prophet predicts warnings to the Jewish people of Israel to turn to God and repent and humble themselves and live for Christ as a born again Christian or else God will judge and destroy them and the land. If they do that then God won't judge them and do those things. The false religious prophets of Jeremiah's time when he wrote these prophecies and warning were claiming God will protect and deliver the Jewish people and their land from their enemies. They had dreams, visions and the Bible prophecy showing this but its was false and the opposite of all of what Jeremiah predicted. These same things hold true for Israel and the U.S. in 2014-2015 and 2024. Those prophets and teachers that taught that may be the Christian preachers and writers and teachers today saying the same thing that God will protect Israel even 82-92 per cent of all Jewish people there today are secular (=non-religious). Matthew chapter 24 predicts many false prophets and false Christ to come in the last days. Jim Jones, David Koresh, Reverend Moon, John Doe and a few others are not many false prophets and false Christ's. The name Christ is where we get the name of Christians from. And many false Christs could mean the many TV preachers and local Church teachers totaling 1-2 billion people or more people that follow them and they themselves are in the 1000s if not more. That's many false prophets and Christ's in the last days. Like Ellen White wrote in her book that in the last days many will be saying a great revival in the Church and that God is moving greatly, but it is the work of another spirit which is satan. Was this what Jesus predicted in Matthew chapter 7 as in the end judgement people will say to Him we have cast out demons in your name, we have prophesied in thy name, we have healed in thy name and we have preached the gospel in thy name, and Jesus says depart from me you who work iniquity. Pat Robertson, Jimmy Swaggart, Fredrick Price, Benny Hinn and some others could be these people in which Jesus refereed to. They have done all those things but are not Christian or truth of Christianity. These doesn't mean all Christian preachers but many are false just as predicted. I read Jimmy Swaggart and Pat Robertson's books on their life's mad there seems to be no spiritual born again experience to both of them. They have head knowledge of Christianity, but no born again knowledge. Yes they did preach the gospel, cast out demons, heal, prophesied in the name of Jesus, but worked iniquity in money and other sins. They spoke in tongues and gave words of knowledge, prophesies, healed and cast out demons but were not of the Lord, just as Jesus prophesied in Matthew chapters 7 and 24 as false teachers and preachers or prophets. I said this before and will say it again that two co-host of Pat Robertson 700 Club did these very things in the name of Christ yet years later said they were true Christians. How can they do these things in the name of

Christ and not be born again is that they aren't true born again preachers and are false Christ's and false prophets. It is the work of another spirit-satan.

Song of Solomon 6:13 predicts four returns of Christ and Israel after it was destroyed in 585-587 B.C., 70 A.D., 2014- 2015 A.D. and 2050-2059 A.D. (=Psalms 150=2050-2055 A.D.=return not destroyed or 2060-2061 A.D. as Isaac Netwon predicted) two or three of which is 40 year generation from when certain prophecies happen till the end of those prophecies being 30 A.D.+40=70 A.D., and 2015+40=2055 A.D. and 2965 A.D.+40=3005 A.D.

II Peter chapters 2 and 3 predicts false teachers which is what Matthew chapter 24 meant at the end times many false prophets and teachers and Christ will appear as prophets and authors on ancient astronaut books that lead many to false gods claiming to be known as God or Christ who may come out of UFO's landing in sight of man as Revelation 13:13 predicted.

Satan will put Christ as satan and satan as Christ and good=evil and evil=good as I explained in the first 14 chapters of my book "The Experiment at Philadelphia." It will be quite convincing and parts may even be true, but the lies will destroy Christianity and hurt and deceive Christians and the Jewish people. Many of the ancient civilization worshipped a goddess and not God. A "goddess" is a female god and could even be a female and male together as one in the end as a great wedding and feast in heaven occurs. Jesus' planet Venus is known as the goddess of love and is a female sign of Taurus.

The four horsemen of Revelation 6:1-17 and the seven seals could be this book of seven chapters (=seven=seals) that are started to be open in 2014-2015 A.D. The four horses men of that chapter are a white, red, black and pale colors. The scales are predicted in that chapter along with a scroll of clouds in the heavens appear which could be a mushroom cloud from, and nuclear bomb on the White House shot by a man born in Libra the Scales and is a "red" horsemen of communist nation known as "red" in the Chinese sign of the Horse which rules from now (October 27, 2014) to January 19-20, February 18, 2015, which is when the Chinese New Year begins. Is the "black" horse that of Africa? And is the "White" horse with one arrow or archer that of one nuclear bomb shot at the "White" house in the year of the Horse or the next year of 2015? The great sword given to the Red horsemen could be a nuclear bomb he shots at the White House from Russia's President Putin born in Libra and is red as a communist. The Black horse could also mean President Obama who is black at the time of trouble from black Africa in which animals and fruit bats effected Ebola from there to the U.S. The sixth seal of Revelation chapter 6 predicts a solar and lunar eclipses in 2014-2015 on Jewish feats days and it can also mean these events on a new or full moon. Next year (=2015) there is a solar eclipse on March 20-21, 2015 and a Lunar eclipses on April 4, and September 27-28, 2015. There also was a partial solar eclipse in October of 2014. The seventh seal of Revelation 8:1 predicts a silence in heaven for about a half hour. If a day or 24 hours equals a 1000 years to God then the hour would be 41.666 years added to 2964-2965+41=3005-3006 A.D. as the end. Add about 40 years to that date of 2964-2965 A.D. and it equals 3005-3006 A.D. The half hour would be the polar opposite of an hour or a half hour or year or the polar opposite of

April 4, 3005 as 95 days into the year and 270 days left in the year. The polar opposite that is September 26-27, 3005 A.D. when the end comes. A half an hour could also mean half of 41.666 or 20.833 from the time of the end to the end in September 26-27, 3005 A.D. That would make 2984 A.D. The start of signs of the end and a half hour or 20.833 years or about that time to the end in September 26-27, 3005 A.D. The half hour of Revelation 8:1 could also mean half a year from predicted events that don't happen on those dates till the dates when they do happen. If nothing happens between now (October 27, 2014) and the end of 2014 A.D. then a half hour could be half a year till they do happen in April-June 2015 on the dates this book and my other books predict.

The unripe figs that fall from heaven like falling stars in Revelation 6:12-13 could be many missiles or bombs dropped on Iran by Israel then many missiles fired at Israel by the Palestinians and/or Russia with two or three are nuclear bombs. The "unripe figs" would mean these events would happen in winter time or late winter early spring in 2014-2015 when figs are not ripe, but leaves form on them and other trees on March 20-21 and April 4, 2015. See Matthew chapter 24, Mark chapter 13, Luke chapters 17 and 21. Are those years the times of the end as Luke 21:9-11 predict as "by and by" or two years of end times events, but the end is not yet. The stars of the Milky Way seen in chapter 6 could mean Pisces where they are shot at or from which the double Pisces zones is in Washington, D.C. who is attacked by one nuclear bomb and shoots many nuclear bombs at Iran or Israel does that in the Chinese Horse Year of 2014 with Sagittarius as a half man half horse with an archer of arrows (missiles and bombs). The Sagittarius sign is from November 22 to December 22 and star time is from December 22 to January 19, 2014-2015.

The word "hour" in Greek is 5610 which also means day, instant, season, short, tide and high time. If one day is a 1000 years or 30 degrees or half it (=half hour at 15 degrees) then the half hour of silence in heaven could mean peace and quite on earth for about a 1000 years before the end. In creation the summer solstice was pushed back one hour or a 1000 years, which is half of 15 degrees or about a half hour. See my book "The Experiment at Philadelphia" for the one hour difference on the summer solstice. If a sign moves through the signs of 15 degrees each for three signs or one age it equals 15 degrees three times or 45 degrees as one hour each making creation time off by about 1000 years, which 2014-2015-3005 A.D. equals when peace on earth happens which is when the small book with seven chapters and the seventh seal is open in heaven at the end of the 1000 years of peace on earth. Satan is let lose for a short season or little while at the end and gathers many against Jerusalem when God rains down fire and brimstone on them all.

It could be that all the events predicted in this book for this year of 2014 in November-December might fail to come true and happen in March-April-May-June of 2015 when the Holy Ghost is poured out on all people like in 30 A.D. after Jesus Christ ascended to heaven. Nostradamus C9:Q83 predicts a great earthquake when the theater is full and a great darkness when the sun is in 20 degrees of Taurus which is May 10, June 9-12, 2015. See Joel and Acts chapters 2 in those books of the Bible for these dates and predictions. Zechariah 11:10 predicts God will break His covenant with all people at this time. If that covenant is the one He made with Noah never to again stop time that may be what the darkness is in Nostradamus C9:Q83 when He does stop time again. Signs of these things coming are when you hear Billy Graham dies, which could be in September 27-28, 2015 when there is a blood moon and a tidal wave hits the East and/or West Coasts of the U.S. God made that covenant with Noah on May 19-20, which could be the dates of these events come to past. They don't all have to happen on one or two dates, but could be spread out over the years even 1000 years on those certain dates.

Will Iran, Israel and the U.S. and face trouble on certain dates in the years of 2014-2015? In Jeremiah 51:11, 46 it predicted this:

"And lest your heart faint, and ye fear for the rumour that shall be heard in the land; a rumour shall both come one year, and after that in another year shall come a rumour, and violence in the land, ruler against ruler.

Make bright the arrows gather the shields the Lord hath raised up in spirit of the kings of the Medes; for his device is against Babylon, to destroy it; because it is the vengeance of his temple." Jeremiah 51:46, 11 (Old King James Version).

In this prediction it could mean when the Secretary of defense of the U.S. said a rumor of war that he thought Israel would attack Iran in the spring of 2012. Nothing happened. But the prediction in Jeremiah 51:46 predicts nothing will start then, but "another year," or translated "next year" (2014), a rumor of war will come at or near the start of the year, or spring and/or autumn-winter and summer in 2014-2015, then violence in the land and ruler against ruler. Is this book the second rumor in 2014-2015 or will someone make a statement in 2014-2015 about a Israeli attack on Iran and then violence in the land and ruler against ruler? The "Medes" predicted in Jeremiah 51:11 were the ancient Iranians and "Babylon" in that same verse is a spiritual name for the U.S. and Israel just like the book of Revelation 11:8 claims Jerusalem is spiritually known as Egypt and Sodom.

Obadiah 1:1 predicts "Edom" is to give a rumor and gather up war against it and then send a ambassador (=messenger=angel and/or leader is sent to the U.S. or Israel) to it to set up a time of attack and the angel to proclaim new knowledge of end time events when the constellation Auriga The Charioteer is seen in early morning in April-June in 2015.

"The vision of Obadiah. Thus saith the Lord God concerning Edom; We have heard a rumour from the Lord, and an ambassador is sent among the heathen, Arise ye, and let us rise up against her in battle." Obadiah 1:1 (Old King James Version).

"Seek him that maketh the seven stars and Orion, and turneth the shadow of death into the morning, and maketh the day dark with night: that calleth for the waters of the sea, and poureth them out upon the face of the earth; The Lord is his name;" Amos 5:8 (Old King James Version).

"The chariots of God are twenty thousand, even thousands of angels; the Lord is among them, as in Sinai, in the holy place." Psalms 68:17 (Old King James Version)

"But thou, O Daniel, shut up the words, and seal the book, even to the time of the end: many shall run to and fro, and knowledge shall be increased." Daniel 12:4 (Old King James Version).

"Edom" mentioned above can mean Israeli enemies along with its friend the U.S. which is an Israeli ally. Edom was started by Esau which is the twin brother of Jacob and Esau was a great enemy of Israel. And in spiritual sense Esau (=U.S.) is a great friend to Jacob (=Israel). The "rumor" in Obadiah 1:1 could be the second rumor from 2014 to 2015 as in told of in Jeremiah 51:46. The "ambassador" predicted in Obadiah 1:1 can be translated "messenger" or "angel" the same as Song of Solomon 8:13 and Revelation 2:29 predicts as a spirit that comes from God and tells people of these books on the date or near it when Israel attacks Iran.

The "many" that travel to and fro and knowledge is greatly increased in Daniel 12:4 can mean 20,000 angels (=many) that travel from heaven to earth to 20,000 people when many people (=millions) on earth travel by car, plane, trains and boats for their spring or summer vacations and much knowledge of the end times is increased in these books as Daniel 12:4 predicted.

Then in I Samuel 2:6-10 and II Samuel 11:1-2 they predict these things at these times of rumors, knowledge and angels:

The Lord killeth, and maketh alive; he bringeth down to the grave, and bringeth up.

The Lord maketh poor, and maketh rich: he bringeth low, and lifteth up.

He raiseth up the poor out of the dust, and lifteth up the beggar from the dunghill, to set them among princes, and to make them inherit the throne of glory; for the pillars of the earth are the Lord's, and he hath set the world upon them.

He will keep the feet of his saints, and the wicked shall be silent in darkness; for by strength shall no man prevail.

The adversaries of the Lord shall be broken to pieces; out of heaven shall he thunder upon them: the Lord shall judge the ends of the earth; and he shall give strength unto his king, and exalt the horn of his anointed." I Samuel 2:6-10 (Old King James Version).

"And it came to pass, after the year was expired, at the time when kings go forth to battle, that David sent Joab, and his servants with him, and all Israel; and they destroyed the children of Ammon, and besieged Rabbah. But David tarried till at Jerusalem.

And it came to pass in an eveningtide, that David arose from off his bed, and walked upon the roof of the king's house: and from the roof he saw a woman washing herself; and the woman was very beautiful to look upon." II Samuel 11:1-2 (Old King James Version).

These prophesies can be translated that when New Year's Day comes, or "after" or "afterwards", kings go to war by the new Gregorian calendar, the old Julian calendar, the Bible calendar or Jewish civil calendar and in spring time or when spring time starts, or in the fall (September-December) when the Jewish Civil calendar starts. Some translations of the Holy Bible translated it this way, "The following spring, the time of year when kings go to war." That is to say in the spring time the following year after the first rumor in 2014 or 2015 "after" or "afterwards" when the year expires in the spring or when spring time comes again is when kings go to war. The Spring time predicted starts in March 20-21, 2015. "Afterwards" or "after" would be March-April-May-June 2015. By the old Julian calendar its also starts on March 20-21 or on March 1 or March 24-25, 2015. Passover starts April 4, 2015. The Bible calendar would start March 20-21, 2015 when it's a new moon. The new Gregorian calendar starts the New Year on January 1, 2015. The Jewish Civil calendar starts on September 14 or September 27-28, 2015. The dream we will read in a later chapter would put the dates of these events at January 3-4, 10- 11, 14-17, 24-25, 28-29 or February 1-4, 10-11, 14, 28, March 1-7, May 9-11, and June 9-12, July 18-19, August 4, 11, 28-29, and on September 7-8, 11, 19, 26-27, October 15, 31, November 1-2, 11, December 7-14, 20-31, 2014-2015 plus or minus three days. If these events don't happen in 2014 then in 2015 on the dates or holidays, fast days or feast days given they may happen. The holidays, feast days and fast days may be the same ones mentioned in this book and my other books, but on a different date.

The dying and maketh alive in those verses of I Samuel chapter 2 can mean Jesus Christ death and resurrection on April 6-9, which could be April 6-9, 2015 when these events happen. The "horn" mentioned in I Samuel chapter 2 can mean Auriga, Taurus, Gemini and Orion as when these events happen, which is when those constellations are seen in the early morning in April-June 2014-2015. The word "them" and "saints" can mean God's two witnesses come alive at this time or way in the future who were born December 24-25 and June 20 who died and went to hell by now (2012) and in the future come up out of hell (=dunghill) and be God's two witnesses from then till the end. Amos 5:8 and Revelation chapters 1-5 predicts seven stars which is in, or is Taurus, the sign that runs from April 20-May 20 and May 21-June 20 star time is a bull with horns, in which I

Samuel chapter 2 predicts as a time when these events make one rich in May 2015. One star that is apart of Taurus is also apart of the Auriga constellation. And Gemini and Orion are right near both Taurus and Auriga. See Psalms 68:17, Amos 5:8 and Nostradamus C9:Q83 (=May 10 or June 10).

Daniel 10:4 predicts the first month and 24th day plus 21 days before or after or on it as a time of trouble between Israel and Iran (=Perians). The start of the Year to the Bible is March 20-21, 2015 when the year expires and New Year's Day begins. The first month and 24th day Daniel 10:4 predicts as trouble with Iran (=Persia) equals April 14, 2015, which is twenty four days later. Fourteen-fifteen days before April 3- 4, 2015 equals March 20-21, 2015. Twenty one days after the New Year's Day of March 20-21, 2015 equals March 31 and April 1-2, 2015. See Nostradamus C1:Q42. Tony Perkins was born on April 4, 1932 and died in 1992 both on a leap years like 2012 and both in the Chinese Monkey Year which 2016 is. He being born then would put his birthday exactly of those days when these events and disasters could happen the coming year in spring. Is this the second or third bird omen that the movie describe told of? The *Psycho* movie began November 11, 1959 which polar opposite comes to our year 2013. It was finished in 1960 and released in June which equals our June of 2013 or 2014 or 2015 when these events could happen on. See a upcoming chapter for more details of Tony Perkins who played Norman Bates in the movie *Psycho*. The predictions of these events in Joel and Acts chapters 2 would be Pentecost which in 2015 is May 24-25. And the words "after" in Samuel and "afterwards" in Joel can mean after April when Jesus died and was resurrected till May when these events happen. As just mentioned the days of Pentecost in 2015 are May 24-25, which were originally May 27-29 in 30 A.D. Each set of dates could be when some of these events happen, which was originally when the Holy Ghost came on Pentecost. Noah's flood was the second month and 17th day, or May 6, 2015, or the original date of Noah's flood on May 19-20 or November 10-11 when these events happen. The ninth day of Av that Zechariah 7:3, 5, Song of Solomon 6:10, 13, and Proverbs 6:11 predicts when two armies or "armed man" come and people "travelleth" (=to and fro=Daniel 12:4) on their spring or summer vacations is when these events happen. The ninth of Av is the same date as when the two ancient Jewish temples were destroyed in 585-586 B.C. and 70 A.D. those dates being of an "armed man" and when people "travelleth" as Proverbs predicts. On July 27-28, 2015 is the ninth of Av. It changes each year by the Jewish Bible or civil calendars because they have and go by a lunar calendar. Nostradamus' quatrain C9:Q83 predicts that 20 degrees into the Taurus sign these events will happened which could mean May 10, 2015 or June 9-10-12, 2015 (=star time). Or the polar opposite of June 2015 equals December 21- 25, 26, 28-29, 2015.

There was a report in October or early November 2014 that Iran was going to sign an agreement not to make a nuclear bomb. Whether this is true or not and they do then many will say "Peace and safety" and "Peace, Peace", the sudden trouble comes when Isis and/or Syria or Iran attacks Israel. See Isaiah chapter 17 and Jeremiah chapter 6. It could also mean that no war happens and the sudden destruction is that of a great earthquake, Volcano eruption, tidal wave and storms hit Israel and/or the U.S. suddenly in

2015. There could be a terrorist attack on the White House or some other place in the U.S. on these dates in 2014-2015.

Predictions can be for the past, present and future. The dates predicted can fail may come true in the future over a 1000 years. And those prophecies of the future that fail may have come true before in years of the past. See Ecclesiastes 1:9 predicts to know the future look at the past. This is why I give so many dates in my books because I am predicting many events past, present and future the way prophecies were always written like Matthew chapter 24 predicts the prophecies to happen in winter (=also autumn), summer and spring as one date and event. Not only is there more than one date but more than one event, Thus, I write prophecies the way I do just as the Bible claims.

Each date I give is not guessing, but following these rules and each date is on an anniversary of a past of some important events. I am not guessing just passing on the truth of them all. This theory of past failed dates and events may equals Isaiah chapter 21 predicts of the two nights and inquire twice, return, come in the Leo the lion star time of September 27, 2015 when great earthquakes, tidal waves, storms, volcano eruption, terrorist attacks and wars happen. I failed at these prophecies on September 27, 2003, but 12 years later by Chinese astrology equals September 27, 2015 when they come true. That date is 2016 to the Jewish Civil calendar to our calendars and year and 35 years (=time, times, and a half=35 years) when my mother (=woman of Revelation chapter 12) flees into the wilderness or south from the north on September 27, 1981 her birthday. We arrived in Ocala, Florida on September 27, 1981. Add 35 years to that date and it equals September 27, 2015. All of this chapter and book and all my other books predict events on my mother's birthday of September 27, 2015. That date is a Sunday, a full moon, a Sabbath Day, a holyday (= feast of Tabernacles), a lunar eclipse or blood moon on the anniversary of my warning to my brother and rumor of these events in 2014 to that same date in 2015 just as Revelation chapter 12, Colossian 2:16-17 and Song of Solomon 6:10 predicted.

The two rumors of Ezekiel, Obadiah and Jeremiah 51:46 may just be September 27, 2014 when I warned my brother of a tidal wave then and he laugh it off. Then I warned him again in 2015 as a rumor of these events for September 27, 2015 and it all comes to past.

My dream I mentioned in my other books of me showing my back woods of my grandparents to many people and seeing a monkey eating a wood pigeon, Shania Twain and a person beside her then a flooded area may have a deeper meaning than what I told of before. That is my Grandfather's birthday is in 1893 and my Grandmother's birthday is 1896. My grandfather's birth year is the Chinese year of the Snake or 2013, the same as Shania Twain born August 28, 1965. My Grandmother's birth year is 1896 the Chinese Year of the Monkey as is 2016. Shania Twain last name is two plus one person next to her in the dream equals 3 years or 30 days added to her birthday and year of the Snake which is 2013+3=2015-2016 plus 30 days added to August 28 equals September 27, 2015-2016 on the Jewish Civil calendar. The monkey eating the wooden pigeon refers to the Monkey Year of 2016, which begins in September 2015 to the Jewish Civil calendar when it is Virgo star time on September 27, which is ruled by a Rooster in Chinese astrology that is in the family of birds or the wooden pigeon seen in the dream. Will a tidal hit that wooded area behind my grandparents home which is 40-50 miles inland from the Ocean. Or is it the storm or two that date that floods the area or both storm and tidal wave.

Revelation chapter 1 in chapter/year codes equals 1981. There are 22 chapters in the book of Revelation. Add 22 years to 1981 equals 2003 as the end of Revelation. In Revelation chapter 22 it predicts many events to happen suddenly leaving no time to change you mind by an angel of Jesus as the bright and morning star that is Venus ruled by Libra and is 2x6=12 years added to 2003 or September 27, 2015.

Isaiah 61:7 and Zechariah 9:10-14 predict double trouble. Could that be prophesying two great earthquakes, two volcano eruptions, two tidal waves (=East and West Coast of the U.S.), two storms and two terrorist attacks and/ or wars on September 27, 2015?

When ever Billy Graham dies play Fantasy 5 in Florida for four consecutive days from when you hear he died. Play the numbers 15, 19, 20, 22, 27 each of those four days.

If Yellowstone's Park super volcano is one of the two volcano's eruptions it may destroy all of the U.S. (Babylon) except Florida on September 27, 2015 as Isaiah chapter 13 predicts. Then as Daniel chapter 7 predicts the antichrist and false prophet are thrown into the flame or lake of fire and their children the demons have their dominion taken away, but their life prolonged. See Revelation chapter 20. What this means is that demon possession is stopped in all the world except for the desolate U.S. except for Florida. Satan is bound in hell with chains and a seal is put upon him so he and the demons can't deceive anyone for 1000 years. But God may spare the U.S. and/or Israel and it's MT. ST. Helens volcano that erupts the volcano in the Canary Islands that is the other volcano that erupts and causes a great tidal wave to hit the Eastern Coast line of the U.S. But if He doesn't and they go down in war, tidal waves, storms and volcano eruptions would come true and three days/ weeks/months/years of darkness will come upon the U.S. and parts of the world causing great famines and desolation's destroying a quarter of the earth's population as Revelation chapter 6 predicts. Mt. ST. Helens Volcano is near a small town called "Ariel" which in the Bible means "lion of God" in Isaiah chapter 29. That town is near Seattle which may see a great earthquake and/or that volcano erupts on September 27, 2015 if San Francisco and Los Angeles is spared at that time. The "lion" would be Leo the lion star time and cusp of September 27, 2015. The book of Revelation in the Bible was written to the seven churches in western Turkey. They are in or near the end of Virgo zone and beginning of the Libra zone where below them are the great sphinx and pyramids that are right on or near the Virgo-Libra zones which are on the cusp of them on September 27, 2015. The Sphinx and great pyramids are the symbol of Revelation of God at that date.

Daniel 12:13 predicts in the end days on September 27, 2015 that a "lot" will be cast to a great blessing with the two great wraths of God happens as Ecclesiastics predicts a day of prosperity is the same day of adversity. The word "lot" in Daniel 12:13 is the word we get for 'lottery" and is connected to the words "inheritance" and "portion". Those two words are connect to birth rites of one family of five which Virgo is given the number five in numerology or five birthday numbers equals the lottery number for the day Billy Graham dies who led millions to Christ and righteousness as Daniel chapter 12 predicts is when those lottery number come to past on Florida's Fantasy 5 lottery ticket. Adding three and a half days to his death as Revelation chapter 11 predicts could also be the days of those lucky lottery numbers, Play those numbers five days from where you hear Billy Graham dies in advance for five consecutive days of Florida's Lottery Fantasy 5. My dad told me if I was a prophet then walk on water or something to prove it. I heard more than once people say if someone is a prophet than predict the next lottery jackpot. Well here it is.

If prophecy were written as one date and one event it would be easy to fail or succeed. But the test of a true prophet and prophecies is a multitude of dates and events over a 1000 years or thousands of years into the past and till the future. That's the way they are predicting and how we should interpret them.

On November 10, 2014 at 2-4:30 p.m. a Monday I saw two or three messengers. One was on a tricycle going through a green light from third street on down the road and crosses over to the over side where is near my chest doctor office for sleep disorders is. The other two were a black man on a bicycle going down the road with a red bird or something red near his left shoulder and neck. Then a another man is on the island of the road where he is lifting his shirt up to show his bare chest and pointing at his chest or heart. The meaning of these angel visitations is the third street and tricycle both mean three as three days added on to the Leo the heart star time on September 24+3=September

27, 2015. The island which divides the road on where two of the angels were seen equals the next years from 2014 when I saw these three angels equals 2015 on September 27, 2015. The Leo sign or star time rules the heart and chest. The black man on a bicycles with a red bird on something on his left shoulder or neck might be a volcano eruption or two on that date on September 27, 2015 (=2016 to the Jewish civil calendar) and two (=bicycle=two years away from 2014+2=2016) with red lava and caused by a black spirit of satan. The red bird or whatever by the neck and shoulders of the black man may mean a volcano eruption with black (=black man) and red lava coming from the neck of the volcano on a blood moon (lunar eclipse on the feast of tabernacles) on September 27, 2015. The neck rules our sign Taurus which is where the Yellowstone's park super volcano is and near Mt. St. Helens volcano in the Taurus zone.

Leo the lion rules the heart and chest and is given the numbers 1-4 and 5 when the end of it star time happens on September 22-23. The 1 and 5 could be the year 2015 and the four and five could be four or five days added to September 22- 23+4-5=September 27, 2015 when these events prophesied all happen. The ancient carving from the temple Hathor shows these same dates as a lion or Leo below Libra the scales looking back at its tail from the beginning of Libra. The beginning of Libra is September 22-23, 2015+4-5 days=September 27, 2015 (=1- 5 or 15 or 2015) that Leo is given numbers for. Remember this is Leo star time not the Leo sign. The ancient Egyptians knew of the precession of the equinoxes way back then and prophesied future prophecies of when the events would happen by star time meaning when the sun is actually in that constellation.

See drawing five in my book "Predictions for 2015 Revised Edition" or see it in the book "The Orion Mystery" by Robert Bauval & Adrian Gilbert page 207.

The bicycle with the black man on it with something red near the neck as the blood moon or two on September 27-28, 2015. The moon is the number 2 and Leo the lion or chest and heart (man pointing at his chest or heart) are the numbers 1-4, and 5 and zero as the symbol of the sun is with a dot in the middle. Mars that is known as the red planet is red and the number 9 as the ninth month of our calendar which is September. Putting it all together and it equals September 24+3=27, 2015. The 3 days added is the first angel on a tricycle or three coming from third street. I saw these angels between 2-4:30 p.m. Do they represent three plus two or five days past Leo star time. The heart the one man on the island dividing the roads was pointing at his chest and heart which is leo the lion sign rules and is the fifth sign (=five days). Also the three wheel tricycle is three and the bicycle is two, added together equals five as well. They both equal five, which equals five days added to the end of the Leo sign star time on September 22, 2015, which equals September 27, 2015 five days later on the next year after I saw these three angels as the island dividing the road to cross over as one did means one year has past from November 10, 2014 to September 27, 2015 when a black and red lava blows up and comes out of the neck of the volcano on a blood (=red) moon on September 27-28, 2015 as the black man had some things red on his neck. The black man may not only be black and red lava coming from the neck of the volcano, but also three days and/or three years of darkness coming from the volcano's smoke and ash and three days of darkness from when the earth stopping its rotation which Luke 21:9-11, 25-26 predicts as signs in the sky that scare people into heart attacks when the stars give the signs of as a special blood moon and the stars stand still and the sea is roaring would be tidal waves when two hit the U.S. along with two storms with the seas roaring against the shores. At this time it is best to get out of the country before they shut down all air ports because planes can't fly in smoke and ash from volcanoes. Try to get to New Zealand or Australia at that time. If the rotation stops on September 27, 2015 then don't go till three days later because it may neutralize the electric making all electric stop for three days when no engines run like the Fatima prophecy revealed and the movie "The day the earth stood still". The hail predicted in the book of Revelation could be the many rocks or lava thrown into the air and falling like stars to the earth near or on a solar eclipse (=darkened sun) and lunar eclipse (=blood moon=red on back of the black man's neck) when people give gifts to one another on Rosh Hashanah on September 13-14, 2015 when a solar eclipse (=darkened sun) happens. See Revelation 6:12-13 and Joel and Acts chapters two near a solar eclipse (=September 13-14, 2015 as a darkened sun and a lunar eclipse or blood moon=red) on September 27-28, 2015 predicts not only this great hail but a great earthquake at this time. Will Yellowstone Park's super volcano erupt at that time on September 26-27-28, 2015 on or the polar opposite 2-4:30 p.m. or 2-4:30 a.m. The Chinese Year of the Monkey start then to the Jewish Civil calendar and its rules the Tiger and Monkey its polar opposite. Those two signs are the hours of 3-5 a.m. or p.m. Leo the lion is ruled by the Chinese Monkey which Year begins on September

13-14, 2015 as the Year 2016 and hours that equals 3-5 p.m. when the one or two volcanoes erupt on 3-5 p.m. or a.m. September 26-27-28. 2015. Two and 2:30 may also be the time or from 2-6 p.m. or a.m. or about 3-4:13 p.m. or a.m. Nostradamus wrote in his quatrains C3:Q4-5 predicting when the down fall (destruction) of the lunar ones are not to far from each other, cold drought, danger around the frontier where the oracle has it source. The opposite of the lunar eclipse (blood moon=dead and destroyed) on April 4, 2015 is the same date in polar opposite as September 27, 2015 making it close to each other of the lunar ones. Also the solar eclipse and lunar eclipse not far from each other by 14 days happens in September 13 and September 27, 2015 which Joel, Acts chapters 2 and Revelation 6:12-13 predicts as a darkened sun (=lunar eclipse) and a blood moon (=lunar eclipse). There is also a solar eclipse and lunar eclipse on March 20 and April 4, 2015. The cold, drought and danger (=at the White House with a nuclear attack) in the frontiers (south=wilderness= Florida or Pacific North West could be two earthquakes and volcano eruptions like Mt ST Helens and/or Yellowstone Park super volcano eruption. It also could mean because of the darkness from the volcanoes eruption causing tidal waves that hit Florida hard, the earth stopping its rotation darkness, cold will come and possible ice-age and danger to the White House where the oracle has it source. In the next quatrain of Nostradamus C3:Q5 it predicts between March and April eclipses are seen and oh what a loss, but two great influences comes on both sides of the sea and land. The two earthquakes, two tidal waves, two volcano eruptions, two storms and two attacks or wars will cause a great wrath of God for not heeding the harbinger of 9-11-01. There will be a great loss of life then if everyone doesn't repent and humble themselves and accept Jesus as their Lord and savior and live for Him forever. And afterwards but before the Lord's return there is a great pouring out of God's spirit comes from the Holy Ghost just as predicted on Joel and Acts chapters 2.

The book of Zechariah chapter 14 in the Bible predicts great earthquakes and attacks by nuclear bombs starting on the day the feast of Tabernacles. What date is September 27-28, 2015, the start of the feast of tabernacles.

Chapter Six

The Carving

The following four of the next six drawings are part of the ancient Egyptian carving from the ceiling of the temple Hathor in Denderah, Egypt dated 100-300 B.C., or 1800 B.C. or a copy of one in 5000 B.C. The two other drawings are star positions that predicted exactly what the Holy Bible, Nostradamus and ancient Egyptian art shown in the signs and constellations as ancient prophecies fulfilled today and up to 3015 A.D. and beyond. Please reread chapter 4 for the explaining of this carving with letters A-H, along with star positions for ancient prophecies read the whole book.

See chapter 4 for details and how I interpret this drawing of the book entitled "Secrets of the great pyramid" By Peter Tompkins page 173 with arrows and letters A-H used by permission by HarperCollins Publishers.

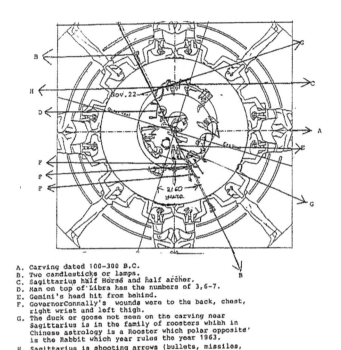

A. Carving dated 100-300 B.C.
B. Two candlesticks or lamps.
C. Sagittarius half Horse and half archer.
D. Man on top of Libra has the numbers of 3,6-7.
E. Gemini's head hit from behind.
F. GovernorConnally's wounds were to the back, chest, right wrist and left thigh.
G. The duck or goose not seen on the carving near Sagittarius is in the family of roosters whibh in Chinese astrology is a Rooster which polar opposite' is the Rabbit which year rules the year 1963.
H. Sagittarius is shooting arrows (bullets, missiles, planes) at the exact spot where Libra ends and Scorpio begins, which is November 22. If you add 51.4 year generation to November 22, 1963 it comes to November 22, 2014 the Chinese year of the Horse and on the anniversary of the JFK assassination. Will there be another assassination then or some other events happen as described in my book The Seven Thunders at .Authorhouse.Com. Add the .4 equals from November 22, 2014 to April 4, 2015.Or December 21-25, 28-29, 2014 and/or 2015. Or the polar opposite of it on September 27, 2015.
Drawing One

Drawing One

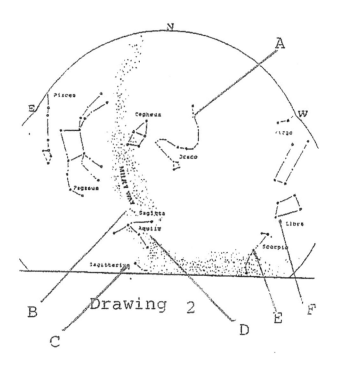

Drawing Two

The above drawing of the stars seen at night or twilight or morning or at 12 noon behind the sun and not seen has the following fulfillment's of ancient prophecies: One, is Aquila the eagle or jet fighters of Israel shooting many missiles or arrows (=Sagitta) and the Milky Way at Taurus not seen but the many stars (=missiles) are seen going through Taurus which rules Persia (Iran) and Israel Born May 14, 1948 in the Taurus sign. See B and D. The year 1948 in Chinese astrology rules the year of the Rat and its polar opposite is the Chinese Year of the Horse which is

2014 when these events happen. Taurus (=Iran and Israel) shoots many missiles at Sagittarius, Scorpio (=Iran) and Libra (Israel, Russia and the U.S.). See The Libra sign is President Putin's birthday on October 7, 1952 the Chinese Year of the Great Red Dragon as Revelation chapter 12 predicts to draw down a third of the stars (three missiles) on Israel a Libra zone land. See A, B, C, D, E, F. Sagittarius is half Horse half man as a archer or arrows shot at Scorpio. The Scorpio sign rules our Washington D.C. and Sagitta The arrow is one missile shot by the other Russia sub off the coast of the White House.

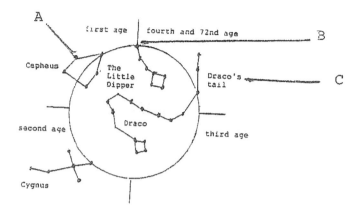

Drawing Three

The above drawing shows the present, past and future prophecies of the stars mentioned in the Bible. For example, the Great Red Dragon tail (See B.) draws down a third of the stars or missiles on Israel which was the North star long ago when the great pyramids and sphinx were built and the time of Adam and Eve from 2500-4000 B.C. and today of September 27, 2015 A.D. has Polaris as the North Star. See C and B. The present day Polaris our North Star of the Bear constellation represent Russia the bear who bring down three missiles or stars with his tail of Draco the Dragon the same Great Red Dragon Revelation chapter 12 predicts by President Putin who rules a Great Red communist nation and is born in the Chinese Year of the Dragon, The future prophecies is the constellation Cepheus 1000 years from now (2015) that judges all people from his great white throne as Revelation chapter 20 predicts. See A. Simply amazing!

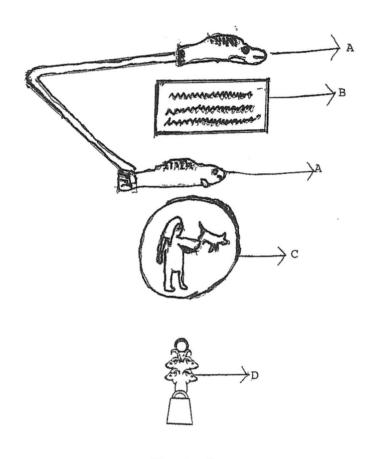

Drawing Four

The above drawing shows from the ancient carving from the ceiling of the temple Hathor in Egypt two fishes tied by a rope with a box (=coffin=death) near it with three wavy lines in it. See A, B. Pisces rules the eastern part of the U.S. Could this be a prophecy of two Russia subs off the coast of Israel and the U.S. that launches 3 nuclear tipped missiles on Israel and one of the U.S. on the White House? And Pisces double polar opposite are the Aquarius zones also part of far Eastern Russia. Pisces is given the number 1 and 3 and as two fishes tied together by their tails equals both the same nation fires those missiles from under the sea like fish swim in. The circle the woman is in holding a jackal or dog could mean a Dog President or George W. Bush would launch missiles on Saddam Hussein a Taurus or woman and on or near a full moon (=circle) near the end of Pisces which he did on March 19-21, 2003. Adding 12 years (=Pisces=12th sign) from then equals March 20- 21, and April 4, 2015 when predicted events are suppose to happen on a solar eclipse (=sun darkened by sackcloth) on March 20-21 and the moon turned blood red in a lunar eclipse on April 4, 2015 and September 28, 2015. The three wavy lines in the box equals stormy seas or tidal waves as one wavy line. Then an earthquake as the Richter scale as another wavy line and wars or attacks that causes the heavens and earth to shake as the third wave line. But as Nostradamus predicted in C1:Q56 that changes would be made sooner and later. These eclipses in 2015 along with the events would be changed or happen in September 27, 2014 or plus or minus 30 days. The woman in the circle holding the jackal or Dog could mean Taurus the woman as Iran and Israel goes to war with each other in the Libra sign of September 22 to October 23, or December 21-25, 28-29, 2014 or 2015. See C.

Drawing Five

The lion seen below Libra on the carving above shows
three wavy lines in the box that the lion has two front paws
on (see D) and is looking back at its tail near Libra. The
Dragon's tail goes down to the man in the circle on top of
Libra with a jackal or dog on top of it. See A and B. Could
this mean the time of the end of Leo the lion star time from
September 27 looking back to the end of Leo star time
on the cusp of September 22-27 when Leo star time ends
and Libra begins as well as Virgo star time begins. See C.
Libra rules Russia and President Putin who was born on the

seventh day of October the Libra sign seen above the lion in the drawing above. The circle on top of Libra can mean a full moon on September 27, 2015. Will President Putin shoots three nuclear missiles at Israel (=Libra zone) and one nuclear missiles at the White House then or shortly after as 3 or 21 days later? Libra is given the numbers 1, 3, 6, 7, which could mean Putin the seventh shoots 3 missiles at Israel and one at the U.S. in the cusp of the sixth month and seventh month of September 22-28, 2014. The small ox and bird and Ox head with a sickle seen near Leo the lion, Libra, Virgo all may mean the end in the Ox year of 3005 A.D. on September 27. See E.

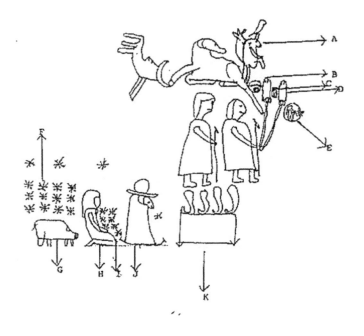

Drawing Six

The above drawing shows Pisces' two fishes tied by a rope and its two tails (See B) of the dragon or jackal has its tails going down to the man in a circle on top of Libra with a jackal or dog on top of it. The Jackal (=7-9 p.m.?), Baboon (=Monkey Year of 2016 begins in September 2015) and bird (=Rooster=Virgo sign or star time of September 27, 2015) are back to back with the bird on one of its heads. See A. This mean Leo born leader gets into a fight with a Dragon leader in Leo, Virgo and Libra signs, star signs and cusps, which equals September 27, 2015, 2024 or 3005 plus or minus 30 days and three years from August 28, 2013+3 years and 30 days=September 27, 2015. That date is the end of Leo cusp star time and President Obama born in the Leo sign with

Virgo Star time in the Libra sign that starts September 22-23, to October 23, 2015. And again we see the woman in the circle holding a jackal or dog near Pisces. See E. Pisces is the 12th sign ore 12 years from when a Dog President launch a great attack on Iraq in March 20-21, 2003. Add 12 years to that and on a new moon or full moon (=circle) Taurus the woman in the circle may go to war on March 20-21, 2015 a solar eclipse (=circle) or on April 4, 2015 a Lunar or blood moon eclipse on September 27, 2015 or a full moon on Christmas Day 2015. The box with three wavy lines in it may mean at this time three trouble come. See C. It could happen earlier near another lunar eclipse or blood moon in October 8- 9, 2014 plus or minus 30 days. The pig, woman kneeling, 12 stars, 7 stars, a raft with goats and ram's horns on it and a table with snakes on it could have special meanings. Those meanings are Hillary Clinton born on a Chinese Pig Year the same a former President Reagan was who a young man tried to kill near Easter 444 days after the hostages were held and release when President Reagan took office. The snakes on the table could be surgeons working on Reagan who was shot by a young man near Easter in 1981. See Nostradamus quatrain C9:36 and letters F, G, H, I, J.K. on the carving shown in Chapter 6 of this book above. Is the lightning in that carving and quatrain predicting a plane crash do to it in March-April of the Pig year of 2019 or 2024? Six years from the Chinese Pig year is 2025, which starts in Israel in September or October in 2024 and the date December 21-25, 28-29, 2024=2025.

There is one other possible future and that is a UFO lands and out comes a man named "Muhammad" the leader of Islam or its beloved prophet or the man comes out of the

UFO and calls himself Allah the god of Islam. With Israel destroyed and Jerusalem and the temple mount and Dome of the Rock destroyed in the nuclear war on September 27, 2015 then he may rebuild the Jewish temple and sit in it as God or Allah with an image of himself standing in the Holy of Holies. The Muslim religion declares such a future history as the one or tenth leader comes and destroys all of Israel then they enter the 1000 years of peace as Muslims when their leader returns. He may take the name Venus Virgo Libra or its mark or number and have access to much gold, silver and oil to help the remaining nations come out of economic mess if they just convert to Islam and its law and worship that man then they can buy or sell with ease. If they don't do that then they will be persecuted, tortured and killed especially if they are Christians and Jewish people. The image that he sets up maybe TV or internet that both sees and hears from inside the temple that everyone worships the speaking image (=vision=TV). But again with this book and my others this possible future may also be ruin for no one would fall for it Christian, Jewish or others. The Muslims though would be excited and follow him blindly for he came out of nuclear war or volcano eruption and lives and carries on the Muslim belief. These would make for a short term future or a long reign future of this man according to prophecies.

Chapter Seven

Come to Christ

Forget about what the antichrist and false prophet say and write, which I showed in the first 14 chapters of my book *The Experiment in Philadelphia*, if they come. What they say will poison the mind. But fear God and keep His commandments just as Solomon wrote in Ecclesiastics 12:13-14. Jesus said if you love Him you will keep His commandments. See John 14:15. He also said He is the truth and the life and the only way to the Father and heaven. He is purely the Son of God and perfect in every way and righteous. All of us have failed in our life, some many times, and in many ways. Maintaining a balance of the two, as the antichrist may teach, is also wrong as Jesus taught in Revelation 3:16. He said, regarding those who are lukewarm (balance), that Jesus will vomit out of his mouth anyone and any church that is that way. Yet Jesus gives us a second chance at life. What a great and beautiful thing that is!

The second chance comes when you are ready to repent of your sins, ask Jesus into your heart and life and live His ways for the rest of your life. Say this simple prayer and mean it with all your heart:

Dear Jesus: I repent of all my sins. Please forgive me for all of the sins I have committed in my life. Come into my life and heart and be my Savior and Lord and I will live for you forever. Amen.

Imagine this: after you said that prayer all the mistakes you ever made in life are forgiven completely. There will be no more fear, shame or guilt or remembrance of them ever again. This is because the blood of Jesus dying on the cross has saved you and given you that new freedom from those things bothering you ever again. You have a new life in Jesus and can live and die knowing that and have no fear of past sins or death and hell. You are born again!

Change your lifestyle after you said that prayer and live for Jesus. Go to a Bible-based church every Sunday. Pray every day. Read the Bible everyday. Do not sin and keep all the laws of the land. When you get this second chance do not waste it or throw it away because it is precious. Love Jesus and worship Him every day and live for Him. Most of all, keep the two greatest commandments, which is to love God with all your mind, soul and heart and most of all love your neighbor as yourself. You will find a loving good friend in Jesus when these things are done. Pray for the baptism in the Holy Ghost and tell others of Jesus. Give copies of this book and my other books to others as witnessing tools. See the web site: WWW.Authorhouse.COM for all my books and future ones to come and it will tell you how to order them. Separate yourself from the world for the world is not friendly with the ways of God. And remember, no one or things can take your salvation away. God bless all of you now and forever. Amen.

A few things should be stated about Christianity today. Do not point the finger at other people's sins, point the finger at you. Judge yourselves and not others or people even those in authority. Judge not lest ye be judged. Examine yourselves and not others. See Luke 6:37, Jude 8-11 and

Matthew 7:1-5. Sinners will see the positive light in you and follow Jesus. I know the Bible says to tell people of their sins, but it also says these things just mentioned. When Jesus was here He never judged the sinners, but judged very hard the religious leaders for their judgement of others over every little thing. The Holy Bible says not to bring up other people's sins. Jude says that even the archangel Michael didn't accused the Devil of anything when over a dispute over the body of Moses. If he doesn't judge the Devil himself how much more should we not judge people.

Do not give to get. That is the wrong way to teach people to give. I know the Bible verses that teach those things, but I also know the Bible says to give and not to expect back. See Luke 6:29-30 and Matthew 10:5-42. Freely you were given your gifts and freely you should give them to others not for money. See Matthew 10:5-42.

Do not come to Christ for prosperity, success, fame and power as many teach today. Come to Christ humbly and without these motivations or expectations. Christianity can be very difficult if followed correctly. See Matthew 10:5-42. Family and friends can turn against you. Living without the world as your god and all the sins it brings can be extremely difficult to give up. This is why James said be not friendly with the world because it is at enmity with God. See James 4:4.

Beware of Eastern religions and all other religions and spirituality movements no matter how good they sound for they are not from God, but are ancient Gentile gods who are devils as explained in my book *The Antichrist* as MYSTERY BABYLON. There were only Ten Commandments in the Bible and you know what the first one is? It's not do not murder, or do not steal, or do not commit adultery, as important as those commandments are and are of the ten. The first commandment was "to have no other gods before me (The Jewish God the one and only true God). God wouldn't of said that if there weren't other gods and wouldn't of put it at the beginning of the Ten Commandments if it were not very important. Look at all the trouble today in the world. The trouble is not true Christianity! Its other gods and other religions, which God explained in the Bible as devils (=gods). See my book *The Antichrist* for more details of those other gods.

People in this generation don't want to hear "the devil made me do it" or "the devil told me to do it" as it is so far and hard to believe these horrible killers telling us that is what really happened. Yet this generation loves to blame God for everything. The BTK serial killer claimed demons drove him to do it. And everyone mocked that answer. Another family member found several of his victims and he said when he found them brutally murdered he right then and there "lost his religion." Like God did it instead of demons. One famous hit song in the past was called "losing my religion." One person once said when trouble occurs it either drives people away from God or nearer to Him. And believing is everything. It's the mighty power in good and it is the mighty power in evil, just believing. Believing can change your life and keep you out of hell or it can bring you down to hell forever. That's why Jesus taught so much about faith and believing in the Bible. It is also why the Bible calls Christians believers and non Christians unbelievers.

In the past four decades we seen God, prayer, the Bible, Nativity scenes and Ten Commandments removed from our schools, public buildings and court houses. What have we seen ever since? A great murderous killings in schools, public buildings and courthouses. God is not mocked. He is not just sitting back while you take Him out of everything. If you don't want God in these places and things He will let the Devil and great lawlessness come in and that is exactly what happened. You got your wish of not having God in these places and now you have the Devil. But you say don't blame the Devil for those great murders, but you blame God. But you don't believe in God? What is your excuse then? This generation is like Romans 1:22 claims as "professing to be wise became fools."

Questions have raised as to whether the U.S. is a Christian nation and if Christianity should be allowed in any part of it especially public and federal buildings. The lawyers have gotten so many confused about this. A little girl was thrown out of school for saying grace. When Bibles or Jesus are not allowed to be read or spoken of to anyone or by anyone in public and federal places, is that freedom? That's a simple question. Is that freedom? Is it? NO!!! And we all will agree this nation was founded on just that--freedom. When you offend atheists by Nativity scenes, Bibles and Christianity and take them away what about the Christian's rights who you then offend?

Just Look at whom you elected President of the U.S.? You elected President Obama, who he and his wife are ashamed of the U.S. He goes over to Europe and makes friends with all of our enemies and blasts the U.S. for being proud. He, or one of his spokesmen, said the U.S. is not a Christian nation or founded on Christianity. Even a democratic news anchorperson said what would our enemies think of us with him saying such things? The latest poll in Israel says only eight percent of Israelis like President Obama. That makes 92 percent of Israelis who dislike him. He promise to be good friend with Israel before he was elected and the first day in office he gave an interview to an Arab TV network that shows captured Americans being beheaded by terrorist. President Obama refused nation prayer day to have any Christian preacher come into the White House to pray on a certain day which many U.S. Presidents have done on that day for decades. He never invited Billy Graham to the White House who's been in the audience of every U.S. President since the 1950's or 1960's. Yet on the Muslin Holy Day President Obama had a big party and celebration at the White House.

One neighbor I witness to about Jesus Christ said that if Jesus were born today He would be a bastard. I tried to tell them He was virgin born, but they mocked that. Such blasphemy! After I got done witnessing to them I said even if I am wrong do you want to take a chance on going to hell? Before I even finished the sentence he answered in a quick strong angry voice, Yes! Yes he will take the chance.

One man I was talking to about being born again said he liked a bumper sticker he saw that said: "I was born right the first time." I immediately thought of Paul's writing in the Bible that the preaching of the cross and salvation is utter foolishness to the unbeliever. You just can't understand why the whole world is foolish in Christianity and you are right can you?

One man I met once said he couldn't believe in a God that let his wife slip in and out of consciousness during Child labor. The man said that it is right there in the Bible that God would make women suffer during childbirth. And it is, but is that any reason to hate your creator or not to believe in Him?

Another man I met I said to him "have a Merry Christmas." Before I could even get the finished sentence out of my mouth he said back: "I'll have a merry Santa Claus Christmas!" He didn't even want the mention of Christmas just like many don't want Nativity scenes at Christmas time. What in God's name is the world coming to? These things are such hatred of God from this perverse and twisted generation. People quote Lennon the evil Russian leader, or Karl Marx, the founder of atheistic communism, long ago over his saying of how sickening religion is. And people today love *The Da Vinci Code* book that mocks and blasphemies God.

People who say the Bible is contradicting, vague and has inconsistencies are just ignorant. If they had any knowledge of it they wouldn't say those things. In one of my books remember me saying that I wondered at people who say things about the Bible and wonder how much research and study they did on it. The answers are always none. They say these things simply because they feel that way, not because of study and research. Let's throw our feelings out the window and look for solid truth to these things. Let's not base important things and decisions on feelings.

It is easy to knock something, but hard to prove it. I am sick of seeing Skeptic Magazine editor or owner on TV knocking prophecy. Anyone can do that. That is very easy. Why don't you try to prove it instead of saying it is vague and self- fulfilling prophecies when prophecy does come true? They all say the Bible is so vague or could be made to say anything and they put no stock into prophecy. Then when a detail prophecy comes true they say a coincidence or self fulfilling, meaning if you say you will get the flu on February 18 you will get the flu on that date because it's self fulfilling. Give me a break! You have no knowledge of prophecy so don't speak cause you ignorance shows. If you say enough times an earthquake is about to happen is that self-fulfilling? Then they say quickly "well there always been earthquakes." If a storm is prophesied and it happens is it a wild coincidence or self fulfilling because there always been storms? This type of thinking is not wise, but stupid. The study of Bible prophecy for the first Coming of Christ alone is amazing. All those details can't be vague or coincidence or self-fulfilling. See study Bibles in the rear for a list of those prophecies and Hal Lindsey's book The Late Great Planet Earth. Judas could of betrayed Jesus for any number of pieces of silver, but it was predicted 30. Jesus could have been born any other place, but Bethlehem, but was as predicted. His parents didn't even live in Bethlehem. You can go on and on about the many predicted events of Christ's first Coming. Read the list of them and their fulfillment's in those sources I just gave. You will be just amazed. See the Ryrie Study Bible pages 1879-1882.

Let me say something about TV preachers and your local preachers. And that is a few may be phonies and many may have sin in their life like we all do, but they are the only ones preaching Jesus Christ. They lead people to repent of their sins and accept Jesus Christ as Lord and Savior and to read the Bible, pray and go to Church. Do you do that? Does your family or friends do that? Do the people you watch or listen to on TV or radio or CD, movies, books or whatever do that? NO!!! If you took a survey of the people in all churches I think you will find a great many are there in church directly or indirectly by the TV preachers teaching them so. Jesus' Disciples came to Him one time and said they caught someone doing something in Jesus name and they forbid him not to do that. Jesus told them forbid them not for those who are with me are not against me.

Another note: The mystery Babylon as described in my other books as the birth of the Gentiles from women devils mating with Jewish men was true and not the antichrist writing. It is now made known as Romans 16:25-27 and Malachi 4:6 claimed for the obedience of faith for all. It was made known so the fathers (Jewish) love their sons (Gentiles) and the sons (Gentiles) love their fathers (Jewish) just as Malachi 4:6 predicted. So go in faith, obedience and love among all races both now and forever. See my other book *The Antichrist*.

A final note: At the end of this world and when the Second Coming of Christ happens there could be great storms, wars, volcanoes, earthquakes and other troubles happening in the world, but then it may not be. That year or two or three years before or a month or two before may see peace treaties, not many storms or earthquakes, a SDI system deployed, prosperity and many saying Peace, Peace and Peace and safety. Then one day many will be looking up to see a strange light by the Sun and soon after our Sun novas and the end. See Jeremiah chapter 6; I Thessalonians 5:3; Luke 21:25-36; Matthew 24:37-42. Is the saying of "Peace, Peace or Peace and safety" a prediction of two years of peace from 2012 or 2016, then a very great and sudden destruction? If President Obama reaches a Peace Treaty with Israel and the Palestinians between now and 2012-2013 or 2014-2016 then watch out for sudden destruction. The great antichrist was predicted to come and make peace then he starts an awful war. Was that prediction that of a Peace Treaty with the state of Israel and the Palestinians then war or sudden destruction? Or does it mean now with President Obama winning the Nobel Peace prize and then in 2010 attacks or helps Israel attack Iran then a tremendous war breaks out? That's exactly what the Bible predicted the antichrist to do all along. I don't think it is wrong for President Obama to help Israel to attack Iran, I think it is right. But what will happen after that attack is the big question. In these end times reverse is true of some things. You can do right and still be wrong and you can do wrong and be right. But as I said earlier the end time antichrist doesn't have to come cause all was fulfilled in WWII in Hitler.

Today many lay and wait for some TV preacher or local preacher or some Christian to fall to some sin and they then accuse them as being hypocrites and why they don't follow Christ and Christianity. That's just the point! Follow Christ and not Christians, men, women and children. If you put your trust in them they are sure to fall. But if you put your trust in Christ He will never fall. Read the four gospels of the New Testament and see for yourself how perfect Christ was His whole life. People will always let you down, but Christ will never let you down. Put your trust in His righteousness and not in peoples' righteousness.

But remember Jesus Christ is the true meaning of life and not vanity or emptiness. He loves you deeply and wants you to accept Him as Lord and savior. Come to Christ...

Amen!

Appendix A: Recent prophecies fulfilled

The following are excerpts of my books "Predictions for 2013- 2014" and "The Seven Thunders" that you will find interesting even though some have already failed others reveal great things. They were written by August 29, 2011 ("Predictions for 2013-2014") and December 24, 2013 ("The Seven Thunders").

Coded earthquakes

Over the years I have noticed a pattern in earthquake (and tidal waves?) predictions. There is a code that can sometimes predict earthquakes. It doesn't happen all the time, but every once an awhile it does. The code is based on Song of Solomon 6:10 "banners" and the Greek word for commotion or earthquakes and the words near them, which are: "second", "Augustus", and "moon" or "brilliancy" (=full moon).

This code worked two times is the past 20 years. How it works is that a major earthquake happens somewhere in the world in one year than on the same date, plus or minus one day, the next ("second") year another major earthquake happens on the same date and on a full moon.

Like I just said this code has happen twice in the past 20 years. It happened once in the great Northridge, California earthquake of January 17, 1994. Then on January 16-17, 1995, a year later, in Kobe, Japan another earthquake happen almost to or on the exact date as the first and it was on or near a full moon.

The second time this code has come true was in December 26, 2003 when a major earthquake hit Iran the day after Christmas. Then on December 26, 2004 ("second") another major earthquake hit Asia along with great tidal waves the day after Christmas and that date was a full moon. I actual thought a week before Christmas if we would see another earthquake the day after Christmas in December of 2004.

If this code is correct and the Bible quote and Greek words mean anything then on August 10, 2014, plus or minus three days a major earthquake (and tidal waves?) will hit some where in the world. Another will strike somewhere in the world on August 10, 2013, plus or minus three days, a year earlier.

Song of Solomon 6:10 predicts this second earthquake as happening in the morning, fair moon or full moon, as the sun and as terrible as an army with banners.

"Who is she that looketh forth as the morning, fair as the moon, clear as the sun, and terrible as an army with banners?"
Song of Solomon 6:10 (Old King James Version)

When you look up the word "banners" in the Greek dictionary of the *Strong's Concordance of the Bible* it is near the word for memorial (anniversary). That word means on the anniversary of a past event another events happens on that date connected to when armies come with their flags (=banners) in victory.

Will a major earthquake strike somewhere in the world on August 10, 2013, plus or minus three days, then on August 10, 2014, plus or minus three days another great earthquake strikes somewhere in the world on a full moon ("fair moon")? And that second one is on a Sunday (clear as the sun) and in the morning (=EDT or EST or morning time of the place where the quake hits) on the second anniversary ("banners") of the first one. This is just as Song of Solomon 6:10 and Greek words 4579, 4580, 4582, 4572 and Hebrew 226, 234, and 1713 in the *Strong's concordance of the Bible* in the Greek and Hebrew dictionaries predicted. The flag or banners used in these verses and dictionaries can mean a signal or sign of coming danger when armies are approaching. Is that signal of the two armies of the past when Jerusalem was destroyed in July-August of 585 B.C. and 70 A.D.? Will earthquakes, wars, attacks, storms and commotion's such as school shootings or public shootings happen on these dates of July-August in 2013, 2014 and 2018? Are the exact dates from Zechariah 7:3, 5 and 8:19 in the fourth and/or fifth month of Av in the Bible's calendar, in which two armies we will see attacked Jerusalem on the same date years apart? The fifth month of Av on the 9th day is when the fast and the two armies attacked Jerusalem. Will on those dates on the 17th of the fourth, or 9th of the fifth, or 19, 21, 26-27, 15 of the seventh month in 2013, 2014 and 2018 we seen again attacks, wars, earthquakes, tidal waves, storms, commotion's and public shootings? Those dates are June 25, July 16-18, 22-24, 2013, August 14-17, 2013, September-October 2013, July 5-7, 13-16, 2014, August 2-6, 2014, September-October 2014, July 20-22, 28- 31, 2018 and August 19-22, September 19, 21, 26-27 and October of 15 or September-October 2018 or on new moons in those years and months as shown in a latter chapter. The other dates are July 16-17, 2013, 2014, 2018, August 2, 19 and 28-29, 2013, 2014 and 2018 and September 7-8, 19, 26-27, 2013, 2014 and 2018. July 16-17 has several past disasters happen from the sky on those dates. Like TWA flight 800. The comet that hit Jupiter. And JFK, Jr plane crash all happened on those days. August 2, 1990 was the Iraq invasion of Kuwait. August 19 is when Adam was created. And August 28-29 was when satan fell from heaven. And Zechariah 7:1 and 8:19, and Haggai 2:18 tell of the fourth day and 24th day of Chisleu, which is our months of November-December and when Hanukkah is in 518 B.C. and 520 B.C. The *New Living translation* of the Bible tells us that December 7, 518 B.C. was when the fourth day of Chisleu was. That along with Haggai's date when it was written in 520 B.C. equals the Chinese Year of the Snake on December 7, which in 2013 A.D. and is the fourth day from a new moon (December 3). Could December 6-7, 2013 be a time of double trouble and blessings as those books of Haggai and Zechariah predicts? The year 2013 is the Chinese Year of the Snake the same as 520 B.C. See my other book entitled *The Experiment at Philadelphia* for more details of these events. See the book *Armageddon* by Grant Jeffrey for documentation of this fifth month and ninth day when two great armies came and completely destroyed Jerusalem. For the date December 7 see the book *Today's*

Parallel Bible with NIV;NASB;KJV;NLT page 2173 and look at the NLT version on that page and notes below.

The "these so many years" of the fifth month and seventh month that Zechariah 7:3, 5 predicted the Jewish people fasted and prayed on was from the years 585 B.C. to 515 B.C. In 585 B.C. the Jewish Temple was destroyed on the ninth of Av (fifth month) and was the Chinese Year of the Rat. The polar opposite of the Rat is the Horse that rules 2014 A.D. and 70 A.D. was the Chinese Year of the Horse the same as 2014 A.D. In 515 B.C. the Jewish people had finished rebuilding the Jewish temple and dedicated it. That year is the Chinese Year of the Dog, which 2018 and part of 2019 A.D. is. These same 70 years from 585 B.C. to 515 B.C. are the "many years" predicted of Zechariah 7:3, Daniel and Jeremiah and may also be connected to the same time period to the time of the end as shown in the chapter five. The moon phases in 518 B.C. when Zechariah chapter 7 was written is very close to the same moon phase as 2013 making the fourth day of the ninth month be December 6-7, 2013 just as I mentioned above. Moon phases are different each year making lunar calendars different each year along with their feasts and fasts days. The moon phase in 515 B.C. is very close to the same moon phase of 2019 when in January 21, 2019 there is a full moon and lunar eclipse. See the book: *Canon of Lunar Eclipses 1500 B.C.-A.D. 3000* by Bao-Lin Liu and Alan D. Fiala. And Zechariah 8:19 predicts the tenth month, which to our calendar is in December-January (=January 21, 2019?), is when something happens.

According to the book *As Above, So below*, by Alan Oken page 157 Emperor Augustus was born September 23, 63 B.C. The year 63 B.C. was the Chinese Year of the

Horse the same as 2014 A.D. We get the name August from the name of the Roman Emperor Augustus. We also get the name Sunday from the sun and the full moon from the phase fair moon as Song of Solomon 6:10 predicts. See chapter 7 for names of the days of the week and month's names. On August 10, 2014 is a Sunday, full moon, August and the Chinese Year of the Horse exactly as predicted.

And as Song of Solomon 6:13 predicts the end will come four years (=four returns) after that on August 10 or August 28-29, 2018, or January 21, 2019, which is still the year 2018 to the Chinese calendar?

"Return, return, O Shulamite, return, return, that we may look upon thee. What will ye see in the Shulamite? As it were the company of two armies." Song of Solomon 6:13 (Old King James Version)

The "four returns" of that verse can mean four years added to 2014, which equal 2018 into 2019. The word "return" can mean return to a new year four times or four years later. And the "shulamite" mentioned may be connected to Solomon's name that means "peaceful" and "complete, whole and full under Hebrew words 7999-8004 in the Hebrew Dictionary in the book *Strong's Concordance of the Bible*. The two armies Song of Solomon 6:13 predicts are the two armies that came in July or August in 585- 586 B.C. and 70 A.D. to destroy the Jewish Temple and scatter the Jews. It is called the ninth day of Av, or the month before on the Bible's calendar, and both times those events happened on the same date even though to our calendar it may have been different dates because the Jewish calendar is lunar and ours is solar.

These two earthquakes in August of 2013-2014 might be the only major events of those months of July or August. The wars, terrorist attacks, storms, shootings, volcano eruptions that darkens the skies, famines, pestilence's and other commotion's might come later on as the Bible predicts "by and by" and the beginning of sorrows starts then in 2013-2014. See Luke 21:9 and Matthew 24:8.

Other predictions for 2013-2014

The flu epidemic of 1918-1919 that killed millions in the Spring of 1918 and peaked in the Fall of 1918 may again happen in those months or December of 2014 into 2015. The years 1918 and 1919 are the Chinese years of the Horse (=2014) and the Year of the Sheep or Goat (=2015). Will we see a new and very deadly form of a flu on those years in which Jesus predicted as a pestilence or epidemic of diseases or flu, which He said would come around when great earthquakes are happening around the world in different (divers) places during a war (=WWI)? See Matthew 24:7:

"For nation shall rise against nation, and kingdom against kingdom, and there shall be famines, and pestilence's, and earthquakes in divers places." Matthew 24:7 (Old King James Version)

The epidemic or pestilence maybe caused by horses, sheep or goats or birds (=Gemini=Horse=2014) and flying (=Gemini to) things as the Chinese Years of the Horse and

Sheep or Goat may predict. Revelation 6:8 predicts a great out break of disease to happen caused by animals. And with the Horse of Chinese astrology being our Gemini sign it could mean birds that the ancient Egyptians believed was connected to the Gemini sign causes this epidemic to start. The world wide epidemic could be for 2018-2019. Read my books of predictions on those years in *Predictions for 2015, 2018 and 2019* coming between now (2011) and December of the year 2012. Will this sicknesses or pestilence's cause sores and fever as Revelation chapter 16 predicts? Or are those predictions of Revelation chapters 6 and 16 that of the "Black death" that hit Europe centuries ago and killed a third of all Europe? Revelation chapters 6 and 16 predicts a quarter of the population killed in which a third is very close to that. Revelation chapter 9 predicts a third of mankind killed by animals carrying disease coming from the bottomless pit where most UFO researchers claim UFOs come from. My book *The antichrist* shows how UFOs are demons coming up out of hell at the center of the earth where there is fire and brimstone. Brimstone can be translated sulfur in which some people claim UFO beings smell like and hell smells like and strange beasts seen on earth smells like (big foot?).

Revelation chapters 6 and 16 predicts people dying with high fever (heat) and black sores on them exactly as Revelation 6 and 16 predicted. It even predicted the disease coming from animal, which the black death was caused by fleas on rats. One cable channel claimed people saw lights in the sky releasing gases into the air and black shadowy figures at the edge of town in the fields (crops-sickle) shortly before the black death appeared. Was the lights UFOs or demons releasing the disease in gas in the sky. The people said shortly after they saw these things people soon began to die. Was the black shadowy figures where we get the term "the grime reaper?" from. And did they cause the black death by UFO beings who we just read are demons from hell at the center of the earth coming up from there (the bottomless pit) just as the book of Revelation predicted. See my book *The experiment at Philadelphia* drawing 6 page 422 for a drawing of the bottomless pit.

Zechariah 9:14 predicts whirlwinds and arrows to hit the south in 2014. In chapter year codes of the Bible Zechariah chapter 9 is our year 2002 A.D. See Chapter 7: The Codes. Add 12 years of the Chinese cycle and it equals 2014 when great whirlwinds (=storms or hurricanes=plural) hit the south in the U.S. The "arrows" predicted in that same verse could mean an terrorist attacks, or bombs, missile or bullets hitting the southern U.S.. Or it could mean a school or public shooting in the south on a Thursday. Our day of Thursday is the blood covenant when Jesus died on the cross on that day as Zechariah 9:11, 14 predicts. Are those predictions near or on a new moon (trumpet of verse 14) and when earthquakes and tidal waves, wars, attacks, shootings and storms are about to happen in July-August of 2013-2014 and 2018? The ancient Jewish people sounded a trumpet at the new moon each month and at the time when war was about to happen. The storms or hurricanes and attacks, wars, terrorist attacks and shooting may happen near each other when these earthquake strikes or the other dates given in this book.

Nostradamus in quatrain C6:Q24 predicts a war when Mars (Leo-or Tuesday) and scepter (=Jupiter=Thursday) happens in Cancer. Leo could mean the Leo sign from

July 21-23 to August 22-23, plus a cusp of seven to August 28-30. It could also mean a U.S. President born in Leo as President Obama is. The Cancer sign starts on June 21 to July 21-23, 2014 and star time from July 21-23 to August 21-23, 2014, plus the cusp to August 28-30, 2014. In June of 2002 Pakistan and India were on the verge of war in that year, which is the same Chinese Year as 2014. Will we see them again on the verge of war then in 2014 or some other war or attack in July-August of 2013-2014? A strange thing is happening now (July 15, 2011) and that is India has just been attack by someone and they are already threatening to attack Pakistan if they were the attackers. And U.S. President Obama is reporting to make a deal with congress to raise taxes and wants the deal done by August 2, 2011. Add nine, the number of Mars, which we seen in that Nostradamus quatrain, to 2002, the year we seen connected to these ancient prophecies, and it equals 2011 in Leo sign or star time from July 21-September 23+7=30, 2011 or August 2, 19, 28-29, 2011. Is that when this plane crash could happen or the war between India and Pakistan happens? Is this what Daniel 11:19-20 was predicting as a vile man raising taxes and then takes a trip by plane (=eagle) around the world and it crashes into the ocean and his body is never found or hard to find? Both events are in the July-August-September-October time space a few years earlier than 2013-2014. Will they happen now or as Colossians 2:16-17 predicts are a sign of them happening in our future in 2013-2014, 2015, 2016-2018 in those same months, or March-April and in the same ways?

That same plane crash was predicted for President Clinton in April of 1996, but failed to happen. He was from Little Rock, which Obadiah 1-6 predicts a leader from a "small" (=little) and "rock" (=Edom) would fly like an eagle high in the sky (=airplane) and be brought down to the ground. Will this event happen to him sometime in the future or to another U.S. President in the future? Twelve years of Chinese cycles from 1996 equals 2008, plus six years as the polar opposite, equals 2014 when this plane crash with someone famous happens.

The ancient prophecies of that plane crash are predicted in Obadiah 1-6, Psalms chapter 99, Daniel 11:19-25, Zechariah chapter 11, Jeremiah 23:19-20 and 30:23-24 and Amos 2:14. Those predictions are that of an airplane crash with some leader on board and possibly in the ocean and his body never found or hard to find. This airplane crash maybe by accident caused by mechanical failure or by lightning or storm. These ancient prophecies predict an invention failure as Psalms 99:8 predicted for someone who sits between the Cherubs and is leader of a nation spiritually known as Babylon, which could be the U.S., Rome, Italy, Turkey or Iraq. He raises taxes and then takes a trip around the world and his plane goes down in the ocean on the way back. See Daniel 11:19-25. The Cherubs represents the sun that rule the double Pisces zones as the two longitude zones over the eastern U.S. where the White House is and in land. The middle of those zones (=sits between the Cherubs=sun) that go through almost exactly between New York City, Philadelphia and Washington, D.C.

These prophecies could also mean airplanes are again used in terrorists attacks on those cities or Chicago or Los Angeles or the White House. If President Obama is President in 2013 it maybe him at the White House whose attacked. He is born in the Leo sign that is ruled by the sun and Pisces, which rule the cities of Los Angeles, Chicago, Philadelphia, New York City and Washington, D.C. Twelve years added to 9-11-2001 when planes attacked buildings in New York City equals 2013 when they may again strike as Chinese cycles of 12 predicts. Or will this time they attack nuclear power plants or our electricity power source? If a woman is the U.S, President at this time it may be her that these ancient prophecies happen to. There are several prophecies of an end time woman leader of the U.S. See Revelation chapters 17-18; *Unusual prophecies being fulfilled* by Perry Stone page 67;and *The Book Of Angels* by Ruth Thompson, L.A. Williams, and Renae Taylor, pages 116-121. That woman President of the U.S. may come in 2012 or 2016 and be the U.S. President in 2013 and/or 2017 and rule until the end comes.

Note: This past chapter and that book predicted a Hanukah school shooting in December 2012 and great pestilence's (=diseases or epidemics) in 2014 compare with the swine flu like in 1918-1919, which in Chinese astrology equals our years 2014-2015 when Ebola broke out and might be followed by others like swine flu in fall and winter of 2015-2016. There is now a diseases effecting Children with coughing and causing lost of movements in their feet and arms effects of some. This note was written by October 15, 2014). The book was published on 11-11-11.

The Carving

The ancient Egyptian carving on the ceiling of the temple Hathor in Dendera, Egypt dated 100-300 B.C. or earlier might predict the events in this book. See my book entitled *The Experiment at Philadelphia* page 462 drawing 45 for a look at part of that ancient carving. In it you see a kneeling woman, near three stars, one star, a pig, seven stars, a raft with a goat's head on it and the sun or moon disk between its horns, one star again and a table with four snakes on it. Near that table is a kneeling woman. The woman represents Cancer the woman sign that runs from June 21 to July 21-23 and star time from July 21-23 to August 21-23. Add seven days (=the seven stars) to the August 21-23 and it equals August 28-30.

The pig seen on the carving is the Chinese Year of the Pig which 2007 A.D. is. Add seven years (the seven stars) to the year 2007 and it equals 2014 in June 21 to August 30, which we just seen the kneeling woman meant. Add the four snakes seen on the carving near the pig to 2014 and it equals 2018. The snakes can also mean the Chinese Year of the Snake, which is 2013, plus one star (one year) added to that, and four years more as the four snakes, and it equals 2013+1=2014+4=2018. The polar opposite of Snake in Chinese astrology is the Pig. And the kneeling woman in Chinese astrology equals our Cancer sign and July and is ruled by the Chinese Sheep or Goat, which head (goat's head on a raft=waters=Cancer sign) is seen next to the kneeling woman on that carving. From these calculations we can conclude that on June 21-August 30, 2013, 2014, 2015, 2016 and 2018 certain events may happen then as documented in this book.

The Trumpets and Sun

The word "trumpet" or "trumpets" are predicted six times in the book of Revelation. Could this have been a prediction of some event or events happening on a new moon in which we seen the ancient Jewish people would sound a trumpet at the sight of a new moon or right after it? The new moons in June 21-August 30, 2013, 2014 and 2018 are July 8, 2013 and August 6, 2013 and June 27, 2014, July 26, 2014, August 25, 2014, July 12-13, 2018 and August 11, 2018. May 28, 2014 is also a new moon as well as November 22, 2014. Are these dates when a great earthquake strikes San Francisco and/or Seattle with possible tidal waves or a great earthquake and tidal waves strike somewhere in the world?

Revelation chapter 5 predicts a small book with seven seals (=seven chapters) to be open by the "Lamb" from the tribe of Juda and root of David. The "Lamb" is a sheep or goat in which we seen Chinese astrology rules our Cancer sign and month of July. It also is the star time of Cancer when certain events may happen in from July 21-23 to August 21-23. The tribe of Juda the lion equals Leo the lion sign that runs from July 21- 23 to August 22-23, plus seven day cusp to August 28-30. Leo the lion is ruled by our sun, which rules the eastern U.S. and possibly the Sun tabloid and National Enquirer. The "root of David" is David's father Jesse who was born in the Cancer sign. Were these ancient prophecies predicting a seven chapter book to be open by David (Perel?) or Jesse, John or Ed in the Sun and/or National Enquirer tabloids on the dates mentioned in 2013, 2014 or 2018? Is the "lamb" that opens the seven chapter book might be born on April 6 or 9, the dates of Jesus's death and resurrection (the slain lamb in Revelation chapter 5)? Or is he born on June 24-25 (Jesus's birthday and December 21-25, 28-29 the birthday of John the Baptist and Bob), or on June 27, which is Jesse's birthday the father or root of David (=Ed?)? Or is it June 20 the birthday of John the Disciple of Jesus who wrote down the Bible's book of Revelation in heaven on June 12, 96 A.D., which was a Sunday the same as August 10, 2014. And David's birthday the father of Solomon was September 7-8, 19 or 26-27 and Solomon's birthday was October 15. July 19 is the ancient Egyptian New Year, which could be the birthday of this editor. The lion (Leo) from the tribe of Juda that Revelation 5:5 predicts could be the editor or leader of the Sun and/or National Enquirer birth sign or star sign of July 21-September 23, plus or minus the cusp of seven days to September 30 or July 14. Are any of these names and birthdays connected to the Sun or National Enquirer? Will one of them named above or born on the above dates help open or publish an excerpt of this seven chapter book (seven seals) in the seventh month (September-October) of 2013?

You may ask what in the world does a seven sealed book opened in heaven have to do with a seven chapter book opened on earth? Psalms 84:11 states God in heaven is a sun and the Sun tabloid on earth is not only in the sunshine state of Florida, but in the Pisces zone that rules the sun and the tabloid is called the Sun. And if they decide to publish an excerpt from this book of seven chapters (=seven seals) they would open (publish or go public) one or more seals from this book when no one else would just as Revelation chapter 5 predicts they would. Revelation 1-5 states that God and the lamb in heaven shine as the strength of the sun (=Sun tabloid). And Revelation chapter 5 predicts two sevens, which could mean twice is this book excerpt published in July-August or later in 2013 and in July-August or later in 2014. The seven churches that the book of Revelation was sent to long ago were in western Turkey which was the end of the Virgo zone and near the beginning of the Libra zone. The great pyramids below them are exactly on the Virgo-Libra zones. Is that when Revelation's small book is opened (published) in the Sun or National Enquirer? The end of Virgo and beginning of the Libra sign is from September 14-23, plus the cusp of seven days to September 30, or into Libra, which runs from September 23-October 22. The ancient Egyptian New Year where the great pyramids were built as a starting point began on July 19, which is when some of these events in this book may happen on.

The "little book" that Revelation chapters 4-5-10 predict could mean a small 5x8 paperback written on the front and back of each page with seven chapters as those prophecies predict in this book. In ancient times books were large and only written on one side and so these prophecies were predicting a modern day book.

Note that part of the book above was written by August 29, 2011 and published 11-11-11. The earthquakes failed to happen but the code is still true and may happen again in our future. The school shooting during Hanukah in

December 2012 equals our year 2013 when Sandy Hook school shooting occurred during Hanukah as predicted in that book. The pestilence's came true exactly in the fall of 2014 as predicted in that book with EBOLA outbreak. See "Predictions for 2013-2014" chapters 1, 2, 4.

In my book "Predictions for 2013-2014" has a chapter that predicts where this book excerpt will be published, which is the sun and time of the sun. My dream of the Chicago airport might just mean the newspaper Chicago Sun Times instead of the Sub tabloid if it is still around... Chicago is ruled by Leo the lion sign which rules the sun.

...In Revelation chapter 5 it predicts the root of David (=David's father Jesse) and the lion (=Leo sign) the tribe of Juda could mean Chicago Sun-Times will publish this book excerpt on the event or events predicted in this book...

"...Revelation chapter 5 predicts the little book (5x8) open in the end times is by the Root or offspring of or a man named David, Jesse (=David's father=root), Ed or Edward. John (These past two names were added to this prophecy by October 15, 2014 and Solomon (offspring) born on September 19, June 20-27 and October 15 as a man whose an editor or CEO of the Chicago Sun- Times..." See "The Seven Thunders" page 47.

Note: The following was written by February 14, 2012 in which serial killers were exposed and even the weather was predicted during that time.

The Four

Nostradamus in quatrain C6:Q35 predicted the Unabomber as living in Lincoln, Montana four hundred years before he was ever born. It also predicted the Zodiac's name and possibly the BTK killer's name and place. The five signs given in that quatrain are Aries, Taurus, Cancer, Leo and Virgo. Aries is the first sign or one and the number 9. Its cosign is Scorpio and 8, which rules the planet Saturn (=Saturday) and the sign of Aquarius (February 14). Taurus is the second sign or two. Cancer is given the number 2-7 or 2, 7, or 2x7=14 and 2+7=9. Leo is given the numbers 1-4 or 1, 14 and 4 with Aries symbol as a "Y". Virgo is given the number 5 and its cosign is Gemini that rules San Francisco. These numbers together spell out:

4=D
5=E
14=N
14=N
9=I
19=S

18=R
1=A
4=D
5=E
18=R

Nostradamus quatrain C6:Q35 predicts not only those five signs, but two-three planets or stars in the plains (Great

Plains) where two-three of these serial killers would be from and how many people they killed. The BTK killer lived and murdered in Kansas, which is the plains and killed 10 as the numbers of the planets or stars given shows. Those planets and stars are Jupiter, Mars and the sun. Jupiter is the number 3 and is Libra the seventh sign and given the number 6. Mars is given the number 9. The sun is the number 1 and rules Leo the fifth sign with the numbers 1-4. The Zodiac killed five people (the sun rules Leo and spells out his first name). The terrible Unabomber killed three (=Jupiter) and lived in Montana (the plains). The BTK killer Dennis Rader killed 10 (=9+1=10=Mars and sun) and lived in the plains. Charley Manson killed seven after Jupiter that rules Libra the seventh sign. Jack the Ripper killed six after Libra that is given the number 6. And O.J. Simpson killer two after Cancer (=one of five signs) ruled by the moon and is given the number 2. The ancient prophecies might identify two or three of these killers from the great plains cities as Quatrain C6:Q35 predicts when burning by the sun after Jupiter and Mars. Jack the Ripper was from Saint Louis as Francis Tumblety known by two authors as the first American serial killer. See the book titled *Jack the Ripper The first American Serial killer* by Stewart Evans and Paul Gainey. See my other book entitled *The Experiment at Philadelphia Appendix C and The Divine Code 2* chapter 5 for details of these serial killers. The BTK was living and murdered in Kansas (=the plains). Francis Tumblety was born in St. Louis, Missouri. And the Unabomber lived in Montana, which is the great plains. The two planets (Jupiter and Mars) and the sun in quatrain C6:Q35 predicts the names of five of these serial killers one called the BTK killer. His name Dennis is spelled out with the sun as Leo that is given the number 1-4 or 4 as "D", then Mars as Leo the fifth sign which is "E", then 1-4 together as 14 or double "N", then Mars as 9 equals "I" and finally 1 and 9 as 19 or "S" spelling out his exact name as one from or killed in the great plains that the fire burns their cities or towns. At the time of this writing in 2011 Texas as part of the plains had one of the hottest (burned by the sun) summers and droughts and many fires burned in it for many days destroying woods and towns (cities) as the quatrain predicted. Also many of the Northern great plains had great heat as well during the summer of 2011. This is when the final name was made known to me in this quatrain perfectly clear as for the Zodiac after the storm in August of 1992 that hit South Florida. You may say what does beasts (=cherubs, seraphims) have to do with great storms, wars, attacks, volcano eruptions, earthquakes and tidal waves, murders and other events? The word "beast or beasts" in the Bible are the exact same beings as Cherubims and seraphims, which some are lawful, some are lawless and some are neutral. The lawless ones literally cause volcano eruptions, earthquakes, storms, wars, attacks, tidal waves, murders and other events. Every time God's used the word Selah or Sela or rock or Edom or Esau (red=Mars) in the Bible He meant Him as the dunghill (=rock=pyramid) of hell. Every time He used the name Jacob or Israel He meant the Holy Rock and pyramid in heaven. One is a evil rock and one a Holy Rock as Deuteronomy 32:31 states. The same goes for Amen or beast or cherubs or seraphim. These names and places were signatures of God as those things like Alpha and Omega. One is hell as the ancient Egyptian Amen god and one is in heaven as the Bible's

Amen God that Revelation tells of and also as my book entitled *The experiment at Philadelphia* explained. They are joined together and is why one name can mean both good and evil. On the *History Channel* it noted that Cherubs were ancient symbols of Cupid and Saint Valentine's Day. The Cherubs or beasts run the sun which symbol is a circle with a dot in the middle. The sun rules Leo that rules the heart that is a symbol of a cross. Thus, the cross through the circle the Zodiac killer signed as his name to letters was telling when he was born and his first name. He was born on Saint Valentine's Day or Heart's Day and Cupid, which is the Aquarius sign the polar opposite of Leo that rules the sun and heart and are the numbers 1-4 that spell out his (Zodiac) name. From these cherubs and symbols is how we got the phrase "cross my heart and hope to die."

As for the word "woods" in the quatrain mentioned above it might have two meanings. They are that of the fire burning the woods as in the great plains of Texas, Oklahoma and other parts in 2011. And as Dennis Rader being a worker for the Park City's compliance supervisor in charge of a grass and property upkeep of the grass and trees (=park). The name "Park" in Park City is usually known as woods as the quatrain predicted for a serial killer in the Plains, which are known for their earth as growing of food and the dust bowl. This would make Dennis Rader a earth sign as we will see shortly connects to these prophecies.

Daniel chapter 7 predicts four kings, four winds and four serial killers with three coming from the fourth and counting the fourth. Daniel 7:1-8 predicts:

"In the first year of Belshazzar king of Babylon Daniel had a dream and visions of his head upon his bed: then he wrote the dream, and told the sum of the matters.

Daniel spake and said, I saw in my vision by night, and behold, the four winds of the heaven strove upon the great sea.

And four great beasts came up from the sea, diverse one from another.

The first was like a lion and had eagle's wings: I beheld till the wings thereof were plucked, and it was lifted up from the earth, and made stand upon the feet as a man, and a man's heart was given to it.

And behold another beast, a second, like to a bear, and it raised up itself on one side, and it had three ribs in the mouth of it between the teeth of it: and they said thus unto it, Arise, devour much flesh.

After this I beheld, and lo another, like a leopard, which had upon the back of it four wings of a fowl; the beast had also four heads; and dominion was given to it.

After this I saw in the night visions, and behold a fourth beast, dreadful and terrible, and strong exceedingly; and it had great iron teeth: it devoured and brake in pieces, and stamped the residue with the feet of it: and it was diverse from all the beasts that were before it; and it had ten horns.

I considered the horns, and, behold, there came up among them another little horn, before whom there were three of the first horns plucked up by the roots: and, behold, in this horn were eyes like the eyes of man, and a mouth speaking great things.

I beheld till the thrones were cast down, and the Ancient of days did sit, whose garment was white as snow, and the hair of his head like the pure wool; his throne was like the fiery flame, and his wheels as burning fire."

Daniel 7:1-9 (Old King James Version).

The four kings coming up out of the sea have one or two or more possibilities. One is this:

1.=Prince of Tyrus born Cancer sign=seas Ezekiel chapter 28
2.=Alexander the Great born July 1 or 22 Cancer sign=seas
3.=Julius Caesar born July 11-12 the Cancer sign=seas
4. President Bush Jr. born July 6, 1946 a Cancer sign=seas, or President Obama we read in my other books as coming up out of the sea. Mitt Romney born March 12, 1947, which is the date we seen in this book important for 2016-2018 and March 12 is the Pisces sign another water sign or king coming up out of the sea. There are three water signs. They are Cancer, Scorpio and Pisces. Any one can mean a fourth beast or king or serial killer or storm coming up out of the sea. If he (Romney) loses this election in 2012 will he win in 2016? Was Herman Cain born in a water sign making him to coming up from the sea? There could be another one who wins the U.S. President election in 2012 or 2016 and is one who comes up out of the sea being born in a water sign. Hillary Clinton born October 26, 1947 is a water sign too and born in the year 1947 as Mitt Romney and is the Chinese Year of the Pig the same as 2019 when the end may come. Will

she run for the office of the U.S. President in 2016? Or will some other woman born in the water sign run in 2012 as Vice President or in 2016 and win? Newt Gingrich was born June 17, 1943 the cusp of the Cancer sign a water sign or coming up out of the sea. His birth year in Chinese astrology is a Sheep which rules our Cancer sign. Sarah Palin was born February 11, 1964, which is the Aquarius sign known as the "water-bearer" or the beast coming up out of the sea. The other person born in the water sign or a symbol of coming up out of the sea was Hitler, which I shown in my other book as the fourth beast or king coming up out of the sea.

Herman Cain being born December 13, 1945 would make him a Chinese Rooster that Proverbs predicted and is our Virgo sign an earth sign as the second beast coming up out of the earth as Revelation chapter 13 predicted. Him being born December 13 would make him a Scorpio star time, which is a water sign and a beast coming up out of the sea as Revelation chapter 13 and Daniel chapter 7 predicts. His economic plan of 999 for all of America, if he was elected and it succeeded, all the world would like it, is an upside down 666 exactly as Revelation chapter 13 predicted the beast (=sea=Scorpio) and false prophet (=earth=Virgo) would enforce in the world for an economic plan for everyone. If he also became President of the U.S. he would be the leader of the nation called MYSTERY BABYLON THE GREAT MOTHER OF HARLOTS AND ABOMINATIONS OF THE EARTH as Revelation chapters 17-18 predict over a very prospering nation of the U.S. that is spiritually called

Babylon. It's interesting the word harlot is used in these prophecies, which are sex sins that caused Herman Cain to withdraw from the Presidential race in December of 2011. But the prophecies about him and 999 are very interesting. We may have dodged a bullet there.

In these prophecies you have four kings coming up out of the sea. As for the four winds that blow upon the sea as Daniel 7:1-3 predicts they are hurricanes Andrew, Opal, Charley and Frances after the four serial killers of the Zodiac, O.J. Simpson, Charley Manson and Francis Tumblety as Jack the Ripper. Jack the Ripper's name was a male name and he killed females who's name as his is Frances (=Francis). All four storms hit Florida hard where the fourth beast was born there or off the coast of Florida in the city of Atlantis. All four serial killers were coming up out of the sea as Daniel 7:1-4 and Revelation chapter 13 predicts with two coming up out of the earth. The Zodiac killer being born in the Aquarius sign known as the "water bearer" is coming up out of the sea. O.J. Simpson being born July 9 is the Cancer sign or water sign or coming up out of the sea. Charley Manson born the Scorpio sign is a water sign coming up out of the sea. And the fourth Francis Tumblety I don't know his birthday, but he killed in London, which is partly in the Cancer zone making him to be coming up out of the sea. The two others after him being Ted the Unabomber and the BTK killer may also be connected to the two beasts coming up out of the earth. Ted was born May 22, which is the cusp of the Taurus sign or the Taurus sign today and is an earth sign. The BTK serial killer Dennis Rader might of been born in an earth sign (Taurus, Virgo and Capricorn) making Revelation chapter

13 four beasts coming up out of the sea (Cancer, Scorpio, Pisces or Aquarius) with two coming up out of the earth. An additional 30 days to the three water signs or earth signs also equal a sea or water sign and a earth sign. I couldn't find Dennis Rader's birthday, but him being in Kansas in the Plains makes him a earth sign as noted earlier because the great plains are known for their earth for growing food and the dust (=earth) bowl.

Daniel 7:7-8 predicts three serial killers coming from one making two more after these as the BTK killer and the Unabomber with Francis Tumblety as the fourth and first of the three just like Hitler and Italy and Japan were allies of his Germany. And almost of all of the six serial killers were connected to San Francisco. The Zodiac killed in San Francisco. O.J. Simpson was born in San Francisco. Charley Manson spent time in San Francisco as well as Frances Tumblety. And the Unabomber taught college there, in or near, San Francisco before moving to the state of Montana.

Daniel 7:1-8 predicts a man given a heart (Saint Valentine's Day=Zodiac) and plucks up his wings (feathers), or his hair for a wig he wore when doing the murders. It mentions him as a lion (Leo) and being lifted up and fly like an eagle and a heart of a man is given it. Was this Saint Valentine's Day as heart's day and to be lifted up is to fly by airplane as a eagle like cupid flies to shoot arrows (bullets or knives) into the hearts of lovers in lovers lanes just as the Zodiac did? The heart in those verses could also mean Leo that rules the heart and is given the numbers 1-4, which spells out his name with a "Y" at the end as Mars rules Leo, but also Aries, which symbol is a "Y". Also Daniel chapter 7 predicts a serial killer between a bear's mouth and white and wool, which in the Greek dictionary can mean wolf or Wolf Creek. When pointing between Bearmouth and Wolf Creek, Montana you are pointing at Lincoln, Montana where the Uanbomber was living who killed three people as the three ribs in the mouth of the bear as Daniel 7:4-5 predicted. And the heart is ruled by Leo and is the fifth sign, which equals five people the Zodiac would kill who was born on Saint Valentine's Day and named Andy as the alphabet numbers of 1-4 of Leo with a upside down "Y", the symbol of Aries (=Mars=Leo), which symbol looks like a "Y".

The five Zodiac signs and two planets and sun might as well spell out all six serial killers just mentioned. We seen the spelling of the Zodiac and BTK serial killers and here's the rest:

O.J. Simpson:

O=15=Aries and Virgo=1-5=15=O
J=10=Jupiter=3 and 7 or 3+7=10=J

Charley Manson:

C=Jupiter=3=C
H=Aries=Scorpio=8=H
A=Aries=1=A
R=Aries-Scoprio=1-8=18=R
L=Mars and Jupiter=9+3=12=L
E=Leo=5=E
Y=Aries symbol=Y

Francis Tumblety:

F=Jupiter=Libra=6=F
R=Aries-Scorpio=1-8=18=R
A=Aries=1=A
N=Cancer=2-7=2x7=14=N
C=Jupiter=3=C
I=Mars=9=I
S=Aries=1-9=S

T=Cancer=2+0=20=T
U=Jupiter=3x7=21=U
M=Mars-Leo=9+4=13=M
B=Taurus=2=B
L=Aries and Jupiter=9+3=12=L
E=Leo=5=E
T=Cancer=2+0=20=T
Y=Aries symbol=Y

Ted Kaczynski-the Unanbomber

T=Cancer=2+0=20=T
E=Leo=5=E
D=Leo=1-4=4=D

Dennis Rader the BTK serial killer:

D=4
E=5
N=14
N=14

I=9
S=19

R=18
A=1
D=4
E=4
R=18

U.S.A.

One preacher on TV told of how Daniel 7:4 was predicting Britain as the lion and the eagle's wings plucked out of it as the birth of the U.S.A. on 7.4.1776 after Daniel 7:4 (7.4=July 4, 1776) when the U.S.A. was born. He claimed when he was in Britain or England he saw many statues of lions around it. And the U.S.A. with its dollar bill on its back cover has an eagle. Thus, having Britain as the lion with wings of an eagle plucked up or flown away from that nation to start a new nation with eagles as its national bird and on the back of dollar bills. See the book entitled *World Almanac and book of facts* under calendars for George Washington birthday and year.

The first United States President was George Washington born February 11, 1731 by the Old Julian calendar. That year is the Chinese Year of the Pig the same as 2019 is the Chinese Year of the Pig. Daniel 7:4 predicts a man's heart is given to it, the first beast, in this case a good beast or cherub, which was George Washington. February 11, 1731 is the Aquarius sign, which polar opposite it is the Leo sign that rules hearts. Was that what Daniel 7:4 mean by a man's heart was given to it? Or does it mean the first U.S. President would be born then and the last U.S. President would be born as a woman in the heart sign or polar opposite that sign in Leo or Aquarius? Or are they born in one of the water signs, which could mean Cancer, Scorpio, Pisces and Aquarius, which is the water-bearer? President Obama was born in the Leo sign of the heart and could be the last President killed in office near the end. George Washington had a vision or angel visitation from a woman showing him the entire U.S. history right before his great battle for freedom from Britain. She shown him at the end a great battle would destroy all the great cities of the U.S.A. Being a woman was it referring to a U.S. woman President at the time of the end of the U.S.A.?

Daniel chapter 7 prediction of three horns plucked up by the roots could be in WWII when the U.S.A. conquered Germany, Italy and Japan, winning the war. The other prophecies of Daniel chapter 7 noted in this book and my other books could also be true and this is not a contradiction because prophecies in the Bible have many different fulfillment's.

Daniel 7:1-4 predicts the winds upon the seas blows over from a lion (Britain) to an eagle (U.S.A.) and starts a new nation and king (President). England is partly in the Cancer zone, which is ruled by the moon that rules tides and seas as the first beast or king come up from. The U.S.A. was formed by British colonies sailing (winds upon the seas) in sail boats from England across the Atlantic Ocean (=seas) to the U.S.A. to start a new nation.

This same man on TV that told of July 4 as Daniel 7:4 also showed and told how a green (=pale) horseman was photograph right in the middle of a protest in the Middle East in 2011. He also said the fourth horseman of the apocalypse maybe Muslims that are over the fourth part of the earth or the fourth part of the population of the earth. He estimated the Muslim population as between 1.3-1.6 billion which is almost approximately a quarter of the earth's population.

Obadiah 1-6 predicts a rumor of war from the Lord when a ambassador (messengers=angels) appear at the name and place of Edom in the grape harvest (July-August). In Jeremiah 51:46 predicts a rumor of war for the U.S. and/or Israel one year and then the next year war happens. In my books I show how the Bible predicted angels to appear to certain people telling of them of these books in July-August of 2013. That year (2013) is the time of the rumor of wars against Edom (a type of Israel and U.S. and the twin brother of Jacob named Esau, who lived in Edom). Then the next year rumor and then war in 2014 in the grape harvest of July-August of 2014 (Amos 1:6). Edom being Esau and the twin brother of Jacob (=Israel) equals Gemini the twins. In Chinese astrology the Horse rules our Gemini sign and month of June. The year 2014 is the Chinese Year of the Horse. Song of Solomon 6:10, 13 predicts "four returns" at the time of "two armies" on a "full (=fair) moon and clear Sun" (=Sunday August 10, 2014.) Those two armies are ones that attacked and destroyed Jerusalem two times once in July-August of 585-586 B.C. and the other in July-August of 70 A.D. both on the exact same date to the Jewish calendar. Does the "four returns" mean the fourth year as 2014 ends in four? And does the "return" mean twins, or Gemini, that the Chinese Year of the Horse rules in

2014 when these wars and rumors happen? Will also the volcano off the West Coast of Africa erupt then causing a great tidal wave to hit Florida and the U.S. East Coast on August 10, 2014? Or is the rumor of war in 2011 at or near December 2011 and then the beginning of the next year rumor and then war in January 1-4, 14, 15-24 of 2012 or later in 2012-2013 on February 14, 26-29, March-April-12, 1, 6, 9, 10, 14-15, 20-21, 24-25, 19-20, May 9-10, 19-20, June 9-12, 20- 25, 29, July-August, August 9-10-11, 9ᵗʰ of Av, September 7-8, 19, 26-27, October 15, 22, 31, November 1-2, 11, 28, Thanksgiving, December 4-16, 20-22, 24-25 (Christmas Eve and Day), 31, or on Hanukah, Purim, Passover, Pentecost, Rosh Hashanah, Yom Kippur, Feast of Tabernacles when after another rumor that year or two in 2012-2013 is when war (on those dates or December 24-25, 2012-2013) happens between Iran and Israel and the U.S.? See my other book *2012* for more details of this. Or does these events of war with Iran and the other events predicted in this book and my other books happen on August 10, 2011-2019, or those other dates that were just mentioned in those years 2011- 2019? The "arrows" of Deuteronomy 32:22-23, Zechariah 9:14 and Isaiah 7:14, 24 predicts might be missiles or bombs or attacks on Iran and Israel and the U.S. on one of the above dates in the year 2012-2013. Isaiah 7:14 predicts Jesus' conception which would lead to His birth a year later are in the Chinese Years of the Dragon and Snake in 5-4 B.C. In that same chapter it predicts "arrows" or missiles or bombs. Was it predicting a Christmas or Hanukah or December or June 24-25 (=Jesus' real birthday) or the dates above for an attack by Israel and the U.S. on Iran or vice-versa in those same years of a Dragon and Snake, which are 2012 (=Dragon) and 2013 (=Snake)? Is it a time of a great earthquake, great volcano eruptions, tidal waves, famines, pestilence's, fearful and great signs from heaven and darkness at noon or all day? See Deuteronomy 32:22-23, Isaiah 7:14, 24, and 16:3, Amos 5:8, Revelation 16:10 and Luke 21:9-11. Will both places be left uninhabitable for years to come as Isaiah chapters 7 and 13 predicted with briers and thorns growing up among the empty or destroyed houses and buildings? If the Canary Islands volcano doesn't erupt and cause a tidal wave then or 2014-2016 then maybe the great Yellowstone or Mount Saint Helens volcano will erupt causing these same events and troubles for the U.S. in 2011-2019. Or does a EMP bomb explode over the United States knocking out all electronics and our electrical power causing great darkness, heat, famines, pestilence's and other problems on one of these dates and years mentioned above?

Amos 1:1 in the Bible predicts "herdmen" and a hill or mount "Tekoa two years before an earthquake" when trouble will come upon the U.S. and/or Israel. The "herdmen" are connected to Sheep in which the Chinese Year of the Sheep is 2015 A.D. With Amos chapter one being our year 1995 and you add 12 years to it that equals 2007 A.D. Add the polar opposite that of six years and it equals 2013 A.D. Then add the two year more to when a hill or mount (Tekoa) falls into the sea and causes a great tidal wave that hits the eastern U.S. destroying much and maybe killing 10 million Americans. Two years added to 2013 equals 2015 when this volcano erupts off the West Coast of Africa and part of the island slides into the sea and causes a great tidal wave (=whirlwind=Amos 1:14) to race across the Atlantic Ocean and destroy the Eastern Sea Coast of the U.S. from the

Coast to 20-40 miles or more in land. Add 12 years to 2007 A.D. and it equals 2019 when the Pig (=1995 and 2007) rules. In Bible chapter/year codes for Amos chapter 1 in the month and sign of the polar opposite of the Herdsmen, or Sheep, which is the Ox that rules our month and sign of January and Capricorn. That time is January of 2019 in the Capricorn sign or its star time or cusp. Amos 1:1, 14 predicts a day of battle and whirlwind and tempest or wind at this time in 2015. The elevation of Tekoa is 2700 feet according to *Halley's Bible Handbook* page 359. Could 2700 feet be an anagram for the year 2007, which is 12 years from 1995 in Bible chapter/year codes for Amos chapter 1? We seen that the polar opposite of that year (=2007) is the Chinese Year of 2013+2years=2015 when a volcano (Tekoa=mountain or mount) erupts and sends a tidal wave across the Atlantic to Florida and the U.S. East Coast. When that tidal wave hits there maybe war or attacks and/or storms or hurricanes hitting the U.S. at the same time or some other time that year fulfilling the "double" trouble predicted in Isaiah 40:2. It could mean double trouble for two nations in two times and ways in two years. Those two nations would be the U.S. and Israel. Isaiah 40:2 is our year 1940 the Chinese Year of the Dragon, which 2012 is also the Chinese Year of the Dragon. Will in 2011-2012-2013 we see these double trouble for the U.S. and Israel? Is the "double" those two nations and/or two types of troubles for those two nations in attacks, tidal waves, storms and great earthquakes on the dates given above for the years of 2011-2012-2013 or 2014-2016? Are the two troubles (double=Daniel 10:19=two be strongs) and possibly three or four troubles as Haggai (=three be strongs) and Amos (3-4 transgressions) predict in the Bible as the number or years of events of trouble for the U.S. and Israel? Amos chapters 1-2 repeat eight times "for three transgressions and for four." Eight times four is 32 the number of the Song of Moses in Deuteronomy chapter 32 and Revelation chapter 15. And we seen in my book how in 1981 me and my mom and dad came south to Florida 27 years (=2700 feet elevation of Tekoa of Amos 1:1) after my birth (=1954=27=1981) when I was born in a storm (=whirlwind=tidal wave). My first name Kurt has a "K" as the first letter that means hand which has 27 bones in it which equals 27 years from my birth. Add 32 (=4x8=32 transgressions of Amos chapter 1-2) to 1981 and it equals 2013. Add the two years to the earthquake or volcano eruption in the Canary Islands that causes a great tidal wave to hit Florida and you have 2015. That is when the grape or wine harvest of July- August is and these events happen as Amos chapter 1 and Obadiah 1-6 predicts. The name Edom in Amos 1:6, 9 is Esau who is Jacob's twin (=2=2 events and 2 years=double) brother born September 19, which is the Virgo sign. The Virgo sign is ruled by the Chinese Rooster, which 1981 was, plus the 32 years and two years added to it equals the great earthquake in 2015 (=herdmen=Sheep=2015=Sheep Year). That year is when a volcano erupts and a earthquake causing a great tidal wave (=whirlwind= tempest=tidal wave=battle and/or hurricane and attacks) as Amos 1:14 predicts. The rumor of war may happen in 2013 or 2014 with messengers sent out in 2013 (=two years before the earthquake and volcano eruption). But no war happens then. But in 2015, two years later, another rumor of war and messengers are sent out to tell of these books. Then war and tidal waves happen near or when this earthquake and volcano erupts just as Obadiah 1-6 predicts, which tells of Edom and the grape harvest of July-August of 2015. Amos 3:12 predicts this time after the 32 times (4x8) of three or four transgressions repeated eight times in Amos chapters 1-2, as a time of the two paws of a lion. This is seen on the ancient carving from the temple Hathor as mentioned in my books and seen in a picture in them. Two paws times five equals 10 in the lion sign of Leo which is the fifth sign (=2x5-10). July 10 is the Cancer sign and September 10 is the Virgo sign, only August 10, 2015 is the Leo the lion sign in the fifth month of the Bible's calendar and the year ending in five (=2015). In year/chapter codes Amos chapter 3 would be our 1997, which is the Chinese Year of the Ox, which polar opposite is the Chinese Year of the Sheep in 2015 on exactly August 10 (=Leo the lion two front paws as Amos 3:12 and the ancient Egyptian carving shows). See my book *The Experiment at Philadelphia* drawing 47 page 464. That drawing shows the lion with its two front paws on a box (=coffin=death) with three wavy lines in it. Was that carving predicting three events over three years from August 10, 2013, August 10, 2014 and August 10, 2015? The volcano island in the Canary Islands off the West Coast of Africa erupted in 1949 and caused a great crack in the island. If another eruption and earthquake happens the whole side of the volcano or mountain will slide into the ocean causing a great tidal wave to head for Florida and the East Coast of the U.S. People studying this island said the crack has been slowly sliding down toward the ocean ever since the 1949 eruption. The year 1949 in Chinese astrology is the Year of the Ox, which polar opposite is the Chinese Year of the Sheep in 2015 on August

10. Are the double blessings and double troubles for the U.S. and/or Israel on or near Hanukah and/or the grape or wine harvest of July-August of 2013 and 2015? Hanukah in 2012 is from December 9-16 and in 2015 is December 7-8-15-16 and is November 28-December 5, 2013. Are any of those dates when Israel and the U.S. attack Iran or Iran attacks them causing a great response from Israel and the U.S. back? If Rick Santorum is elected in 2012 as the U.S. President he was born May 10, 1958 and has said that he would bomb Iran. May 10 is the Taurus sign and the President of Iran now (January 2012) if still in office then was born October 28, which is the Scorpio sign. The one star chart I show in my book *The Experiment at Philadelphia* drawing 25 page 441 shows the Milky Way going from Scorpio to Taurus not seen. Was that star chart predicting many missiles and bombs being sent out between Israel (=Taurus=born May 14-15) and the United States (Santorum=Taurus) to Iran (President at this time is Scorpio born) on the dates of this book or my others in 2012, 2013, 2014, 2015 or 2016? Or is the Milky Way (missiles) on that star chart Sagittarius the archer of arrows (missiles) shooting at Scorpio (D.C.). Iran is partly in the Sagittarius zone and Washington, D.C. is ruled by Scorpio just like that star chart shows? Will Israel and the U.S. attack Iran and Iran attack back or first on one or two of those dates given in this book for 2012-2013 or later?

In this book I tell how Mount Sinai, the Canary Islands and Florida are all near the same latitude of where these events all happen. Edom is also near that same exact latitude. Revelation chapter 15 that predicts the Song of Moses again is in chapter/year codes is 1995. Adding 12 years to that equals 2007. The polar opposite of that equals

2013+2 years that Amos 1:1 predicts to when this great earthquake and volcano eruption and tidal is to hit Florida in 2015. See also Jeremiah 51:46. Revelation being the 27th book of the New Testament may also relate to that number added to my birth in 1954 to the first chapter of Revelation in chapter/year codes as 1981. Then adding 32 years plus two years to 1981 equals 2015 when these events happen on a Sunday-Monday on August 9-10, 2015. That is when Revelation chapter 12 predicts a baby born in a storm (=flood=whirlwind=hurricane) for satan to try again to kill that person in Florida by a tidal wave that the land (=earth) swallows up as it moves inland just as predicted. The "sun" and "moon" mentioned in Revelation chapter 12 might mean a Sunday-Monday, which August 9-10, 2015 is. The "red dragon" of Revelation chapter 12 could mean the Aries sign that the Chinese Dragon rules, which is a ram connected to Sheep or the Chinese Year of the Sheep in 2015. The "red" part of this prophecies would be the red planet Mars that is Leo the lion, which sign rules on August 10, 2015, plus or minus three days, and is a Sunday-Monday August 9-10, 2015 when a storm or tidal wave hits Florida and the East Coast of the U.S.

In 2011 I became aware of the serial killer's name who murdered in San Francisco in 1968-1969 by a storm's name in 1992. At that time in 2011 the prophecy of a whirlwind (=hurricane or tidal wave) hitting the wicked (Bahamas-South Florida) became perfectly clear to me at that time. These prophecies tell of these things exactly:

"Behold, a whirlwind of the Lord is gone forth in fury, even a grievous whirlwind: it shall fall grievously upon the head of the wicked.

The anger of the Lord shall not return, until he have executed, and till he have performed the thoughts of his heart: in the latter days ye shall consider it perfectly."

Jeremiah 23:19-20 (Old King James Version).

"Behold, the whirlwind of the Lord goeth forth with fury, a continuing whirlwind: it shall fall with pain upon the head of the wicked.

The fierce anger of the Lord shall not return until he have done it, and until he have performed the intents of his heart: in the latter days ye shall consider it."

Jeremiah 30:23-24 (Old King James Version).

"And woe unto them that are with child, and to them that give suck in those days!

But pray ye that your flight be not in the winter, neither on the sabbath day."

Matthew 24:19-20 (Old King James Version).

"And take heed to yourselves, lest at any time your hearts be overcharged with surfeiting, and drunkenness, and cares of this life, and so that day come upon you unaware.

For as a snare shall it come on all them that dwell on the face of the whole earth."

Luke 21:34-35 (Old King James Version).

"Let no man therefore judge you in eat, or in drink, or in respect of an holyday, or of the new moon, or of the sabbath day:

Which are a shadow of things to come; but the body is of Christ."

Colossians 2:16-17 (Old King James Version)

"In the day of prosperity be joyful, but in the day of adversity consider: God also hath set the one over against the other, to the end that man should find nothing after him." Ecclesiastes 7:14 (Old King James Version).

"And from the days of John the Baptist until now the kingdom of heaven suffereth violence and the violent take it by force."

Matthew 11:12 (Old King James Version).

"And they that dwell upon the earth shall rejoice over them, and, make merry, and shall send gifts one to another;..."

Revelation 11:10 (Old King James Version).

"And when he had taken the book, the four beasts and four and twenty elders..." Revelation 5:8 (Old King James Version).

Nostradamus in quatrain C6:Q35 predicted the Zodiac's name and also predicts the plains, cities and woods burning. The summer of 2011 saw Texas and Oklahoma, both plain states, have great drought, heat and wild fires in their woods and houses. This too became perfectly clear at this time when I was working on finishing my 14 books by February 14, 2012 on the intents and thoughts of God's heart as we read in the book of Jeremiah. Is the "heart" in those verses Saint Valentine's Day and/or the Leo sign that rules the heart and is in July-August when Texas saw such great heat, drought and wild fires as Nostradamus also predicted?

Several of those 14 books of mine showed predicted events for 2013-2019 and beyond. But Psalms 90:14 predicted to satisfy early God's servant by an earlier fulfillment of the predicted events of several of his books for 2013-2019 and beyond before another great hurricane (whirlwind or tidal wave) hits South Florida and the U.S. East Coast. The "return not until" that Jeremiah predicted from one whirlwind to another as Psalms 90:14 predicts shall not come until these wars and attacks happen in Israel, Iran and the U.S. Then another great hurricane and/or tidal wave (whirlwinds) can hit Florida and the Eastern U.S. Coast line as my book *Predictions for 2015* predicted for that year or 2014-2016 caused by an earthquake, volcano eruption and tidal waves. Psalms 90:14 to "satisfy early" may mean that the tidal wave doesn't strike in 2015, but in 2014 making this book and my others sell well and have great success. Psalms chapter 90 is the Chinese Year of the Horse the same as 2014 when that tidal wave strikes and this book and others sell very well earlier than 2015. If that tidal wave strikes August 10, 2014, plus or minus three days, or July- August of 2014, the world wide popularity of this book and the others would be known and many would want to be read them. That would be satisfying God's servant early. It would make his days of evil and shame for two years in 2001+2=2003 come good (glad) days in two years from 2013-2014 with great rewards of the works of his hands (=books) just as Psalms 90:14-15-16- 17 predicted. On December 25, 2000 I saw what I believe were two angels on Christmas Day. If Psalms 90:14-17 predicts an early success on that Day of Christmas in 2011+2 years of being glad and again another success on December 7, 2013, as we read or will read in my books, it would fulfill these prophecies perfectly. Could two sets of angels one set coming on December 24-25, 2011. And then again on August 10, 2013 to tell people of where to buy my books making the servant of God to be satisfied early and for two years more from December 2011+2= 2013? I had a dream December 21-22, 2011 of me putting on pink pants. *The Dreamer's Dictionary* under colors says the color pink means "predicts unusual great success." My books up to this point showed no interest or success, but maybe these things will come true. Song of Solomon 8:11-14 predicts 1000 people to bring a 1000 pieces of silver as Isaiah chapter 7 and Deuteronomy 32:30 predicts. A 1000 pieces of silver is approximately 610-620 dollars. The books I have published at this time times ten the royalty rate equals almost exactly 610- 620 dollar. If each of the 1000 people bought ten copies of each of my books at this time in December of 2011 it would equals 610-620 dollars each. Then on August 10, 2013 angels the second time, the two angels seen on Christmas Day in 2000, will tell 10,000 or 20,000 people where to buy a copy of each of my 14 books just as Psalms 68:17 predicted. These ancient prophecies could also mean two or three times publicity is shown my books for their predictions of several earthquakes, attacks, storms, volcano eruption and tidal waves in 2013-2015- 2016 just as the ancient prophecies predicted. The angel (spirit) you see at this time if chosen will be a bluish-white light that sparkles and makes you smile ear to ear and will speak to you. Do what ever he tells you to. See Revelation 2:29.

Or does Psalms 90:14-17 "satisfy us early" mean the events of Iran and Israel and the U.S. attacking each other happens in 2012 or 2013 as my book *2012* predicted a war between those nations in those years earlier then 2014-2016 as this book and some of my other books predict. And one or two years after that (=2012-2013) comes the great tidal wave, volcano eruption, earthquakes, and storms in 2014-2016 on the exact date of August 10 making the prophecy perfectly clear of a whirlwind (=tidal wave and/or hurricane) happening then. See Jeremiah 23:19-20 and 30:23-24. The word "early" in Psalms 90:14-17 are the wars that come early, but the other events come on the times predicted in these books. The wars could come in 2012- 2013 and the volcano eruption, earthquake, tidal waves and storms could come in 2014-2015-2016. If the wars come in December of 2012 on the 24-25th day it would fulfill many prophecies. One is that of Revelation chapter 12 (=2012) where it predicts a woman clothed with the sun and the moon under her feet and a great red dragon that pulls down a third of the stars (=missiles-bombs). December 24-25, 2012 is a Monday (=moon) Tuesday, which Tuesday is Latin for Mars. The planet Mars is called the red planet and rules Leo and the sun. Thus, the woman clothed in the sun (=Tuesday) and the moon under her feet might mean the day of Monday is ending and going into the day of Tuesday. The red dragon is the Chinese Year of the Dragon in 2012. Revelation chapter 12's red dragon is not only the Chinese Year of the Dragon in 2012, but chapter number 12 equals the year ending in 12

(=2012) and in the 12 month of December and on the date 21, which is reverse of 12, thus the exact date of December 21, 2012. The Mayan prophecies, along with II Peter 3:1-7 and Luke 21:34-36, may predict December 21, 2012 is when the Mayan calendar ends on and many people think something will happen then, but nothing does. So they mock God, Christians and the Bible for those prophecies and go about celebrating Christmas Eve and Day by partying with much food, drinks and giving of gifts then sudden destruction comes. See Luke 21:34-36 and Revelation 11:10 for these times of giving gifts one to another all over the world, which we do exactly on Christmas Eve and Day and all the partying (=drunkenness) we do in celebrating that day. Mars (=Tuesday=Leo) also is known as the "god of war," which may happen on Christmas Eve and Day of December 24-25, 2012. This maybe what Ecclesiastes 7:14 in the Bible predicts as the day of prosperity (=Christmas Day) is the same day as adversity (war). II Peter 3:2-7 prediction may mean that Israel is destroyed in this war as their fathers fell asleep (died) and Jesus did not come back to save them and many will say and mock "where is the promise of his coming for since the fathers fell asleep things continue as they were since the beginning." See II Peter 3:2-7 and my book *2012*.

Another interpretation of these ancient prophecies could be fulfilled in August 10, 2013 by angels (spirits) are sent to 20,000 people telling them to buy a copy each of my 14 books at that time. Then two years (double) later on August 10, 2015 angels are sent out to 20,000 other people (double) telling them where to buy a copy each of my 14 books. See Isaiah 61:1- 7 and Zechariah 9:1-14. The latter date is when the tidal wave strikes after an earthquake and volcano eruption as predicted in Psalms 68:8, 17. At that time is when many people travel (to and fro) by cars (chariots) on summer vacations. See Daniel 12:4 and Psalms 68:17. Mount Sinai in Psalms 68:8, 17 is connected to a volcano off the West Coast of Africa. That volcano eruption and earthquake causes a great tidal wave that hits Florida and the East Coast of the U.S. Mount Sinai is also connected to Passover in the year 1484 B.C. That year is the Chinese Year of the Ox, which polar opposite equals the Sheep Year or our 2015 A.D. on August 10, plus or minus three days. We seen these dates to be connected to Revelation chapter 12 as a time in the Leo sign and on a Sunday-Monday.

Still another possible interpretation is 20,000 people (=Psalms 68:17) are told of these books on August 10, 2013 and then 100 million more are told of them on August 10, 2015, plus or minus three days or July-August of 2013 and 2015. See Revelation 5:11 and Daniel 7:10. The "thousands of thousands" and "ten thousand times ten thousands" in those verses means 20,000 and 100 million. The thousands of thousands is also mentioned in Psalms 68:17 which we seen connects to these dates and places and events in 2013 and 2014 when double blessings and double trouble happens in those two years and two troubles in August 10, 2015 when a tidal wave and a attack happens. Revelation chapter 5 tells of a book unsealed in God's hand taken by the Lamb who is from the tribe of Juda the lion (=9=Leo). The "Lamb" is Aries the Ram or Sheep year of 2015 when in August 10, plus or minus three days these events happen in which is the Leo sign of the lion (=tribe of Juda-the lion). Aries is given the number 9 as is Mars that rules Leo the lion on August 10, 2015. Revelation chapter 5 could be the fifth sign of Leo (=chapter 5) when these events happen in the year ending in 5 (=chapter 5), or August 10, 2015. In year/chapter codes Revelation chapter 5 equals the year 1985, which is the Chinese year of the Ox, which we seen is the polar opposite of the Sheep Year of 2015 when on August 10 these events happen. Two years of sadness and shame for me in 2001-2003 and two years or double blessings in 2013-2015 with the sales of these books just as Psalms 90:14-17 and Haggai predicted. Two in the summer vacations of 2013 and 2015 and the two blessing from those events at that time equals Hanukah or Christmas in December of 2013-2015 just as predicted. The latter trouble in 2015 could be a double trouble and double blessing (=10,000 double equals 10,000 x 10,000=100 million) when on August 10, 2015 two trouble occurs in the forms of great tidal waves and attacks and/or storms or earthquakes. See Isaiah 40:2, 61:1-7 and Zechariah 9:10-14. Revelation chapter 5 also predicts that book in the right hand of the Lamb to have seven seals that are seven eyes and seven horns that go around the world. Are they these 14 books, which equals 7+7=14, that go around the world in sales on the world wide web or WWW.Authorhouse.Com or Amazon.Com or Barnes&Noble.Com?

In August 10, 2014 after a second earthquake on that same date a year earlier will a rumor come of an attack on the U.S. and/or Israel, then a year later a rumor and then war, king against king, just as Jeremiah 51:16, Isaiah 40:2 and Obadiah 1-6 predicted. "Edom" in Obadiah 1-6 equals Gemini. The Gemini sign is the Chinese Year of the Horse or our year 2014. Is that when the first rumor comes as Luke 21:9 predicts as "by and by" or two years from when these events predicted start happening in 2013-2014 till the great tidal wave and attack in 2015 happens two years later, but that is not the end? The Cancer sign mentioned above as Passover, Sinai, Lamb and book has its star time from July 21-23 to August 21-23, which puts Cancer star time right in August 10, 2015, plus or minus three days, or July-August of that year. The Ox Year is the polar opposite of the Sheep Year of 2015 and rules Cancer, which star time is that time just mentioned putting the exact date of August 10, 2015.

These prophecies of God's wrath shall not return until he performs or tells the thoughts or intents of his heart might mean that another great hurricane and a tidal wave will not hit Florida until after February 14, 2012 when my 14 books are finished and the Zodiac killer is identified. Those same prophecies could also mean that the great hurricane that revealed the Zodiac killer that hit south Florida in 1992 won't return and a tidal won't hit there until or before two completed Chinese Yearly cycles are finished from 1992. The year 1992 plus 12+12=2016. Between now (February 14, 2012= heart's day), when I have completed the 14 books of God's heart, and the Zodiac killer identified, will there be another great hurricane and tidal wave that returns to hit Florida with God's wrath between those years of 2011 to 2016 exactly as this book and my other books predicted? See Jeremiah 23:19-20 and 30:23-24.

Will Israel attack Iran's nuclear factories on December 23- 24-25, 2011? December 24, 2011 is a new moon, a Sabbath Day (=Saturday=Jewish Sabbath) and a holyday or holiday. That date is Christmas Eve and Day. It is also winter time when people all over the whole world give gifts to one another. This is just as all those verses above predicted for a time of great prosperity (Christmas Eve and Day=Sabbath Days=Saturday-Sunday) and is the same time as the time of great adversity (=trouble= attacks). People will be partying and celebrating hard the Christmas Holidays (=holyday) and over eating and drinking with the cares of this life just as Luke 21:34-35, Matthew 24:19-20, Colossians 2:16-17, Revelation 5:8, 11:10 and Ecclesiastes 7:14 predicted when these attacks happen. Or does the attack happen on Hanukah or near it and/or on Christmas in December of 2012, 2013, 2014, 2015 and 2016 or in that month or the other dates given in these years just given?

The "four beasts and twenty four elders" of Revelation 5:8 are dates of the fourth month (=four beasts) and 24th day (=24 elders). When they are calculated to the Jewish Civil calendar translated to ours equals December 24, 2011-2013, or December 23-24-25, 2011-2013. At that time is when these events of attacks and wars happen between Israel, Iran and the U.S. The Jewish Sabbath starts Friday evening and ends Saturday evening, which are December 23-24, 2011. And Sunday December 25, 2011 is the Christian Sabbath, which is Christmas Day the time of giving of gifts or prosperity and a holyday. The song Silent Night proclaims this day as a holynight or holyday Christmas Eve and Day. See the quotes above for documentation for these events in Colossian 2:16-17, Matthew 24:19-20, Revelation 11:10 and Ecclesiastes 7:14.

Matthew 11:12 tells of John the Baptist's birthday and how on that day the kingdom of heaven is greatly shaken or taken by violence and by the violent. Was this referring to a bomb over Iran that causes all the electronics to fail? Or is it missiles and bombs from the heavens that shake the ground and skies (=heavens) over Iran and Israel in 2011 and 2012-2013? John the Baptist was born on December 24 in the Chinese Year of the Dragon, which 2012 is. See my other book *The experiment at Philadelphia* for details.

These events happen earlier then expected as Psalms 90:14 predicts and before the return of the fierce anger of the Lord by another whirlwind (=hurricane) and/or tidal wave hits from Florida to Boston in 2013-2014 as this book and my other books *Predictions for 2013-2014, Predictions for 2015, and The Divine Code 3* predicted for 2013-2019. The intents or thoughts of Gods heart are finished and revealed at this time in 2011-2012. His thoughts or heart reveal the great hurricane Andrew (as the identifying factor for the exact name for the Zodiac killer). That hurricane hit South Florida in 1992. After these times is when the return of God's wrath falls again there at the place where the wicked antichrist was born in the Bahamas or South Florida with another whirlwind (=hurricane) or tidal wave. This other great hurricane and tidal wave would be after the years 2011-2012-2013. This is when these attacks or wars with Iran, Israel and the U.S. happen in December 23-24-25, 2011-2013. That is earlier then what those books predicted for 2013-2019 for those wars making the prophecies perfectly clear as the Nostradamus and the Bible predicted. See Psalms 90:14; C6:Q35.

Did Daniel chapter 10 in the Bible predict Israel's attack on Iran (Persia) then 21 days or three weeks later Iran attacks Israel and Israel returns to attack Iran again? Is this what Obadiah 1-6 and Jeremiah 51:46 meant by rumor in one year then the next year rumor and war? The rumor of war for December 23- 25, 2011 is the one year, then 21 days later is the next year, starting in January 2012 and then another rumor and then king against king as Jeremiah 51:46 predicted. Or is it one rumor of 2013 then in 2014 rumor and war and king against king in the grape harvest of July-August (August 10?) as Obadiah 1-6 and Jeremiah 51:46 predicted? Will a great earthquake, volcano eruption and tidal wave also hit then in 2014 instead of 2015- 2016? Is that the time to flee Florida and the East Coast of the U.S.? Revelation chapter 11 predicts trouble for Israel or Jerusalem in a three and a half day period. Will Israel attack Iran on December 23-25, 2011-2013 then three and a half days later on December 27-29, 2011-2013 Israel is attack and/or an earthquake happens in Jerusalem? Or are the dates of December 31, 2012-2013 and January 1, 2012-2013 important for these events when people are celebrating New Year's Eve and Day all over the world? Do we flee then from the tidal wave to come upon Florida and the East Coast of the U.S. in January of 2012, or the other dates that year or those dates in the years 2011- 2019? The latest report out of Israel is a leader said that Israel will not attack Iran at this time (=December of 2011). But Hal Lindsey on his TV show said attacks may be weeks away. He said that on December 9, 2011. What will happen is not known right now.

If the tidal waves hit Florida and the U.S. East Coast on August 10, 2014-2016 then those on the East Coast of the U.S. and Florida are to flee inland to about 50 miles. This, as Revelation chapter 12 predicts, will save you from the flood (=tidal wave) if it doesn't go inland farther. The land will eventually swallow up the water and tidal wave as it moves inland exactly as Revelation 12:16 saving the woman (May 19) and other women and men (=10,000 women and 10,000 men=Song of Solomon 5:10) in Florida and/or the East Coast of the U.S. It may be wise to move inland before these dates so you can save all your belongings. An angel may warn you of this event. He or someone maybe on the rooftop one day near August 10, 2014- 2016 which is a symbol to flee inland. He maybe an angel or the angel appears at night as a bluish-white light that sparkles and makes you smile ear to ear. He may warn you to flee inland or wherever. Do as he says and don't say this author was in error or insane. It may not be smart to move or travel inland from the East Coast of Florida at these times because after the tidal wave, even if it doesn't reach you 50 miles inland, 20-40 miles inland from Florida East Coast will be destroyed followed by famines, pestilence's and power outages. And if the volcano ash blows over into Florida you may not be safe even 50 miles inland and it too could cause famines and other problems. Flee inland and up I-75 into Georgia and then Road 24 and 65 into Indiana might be the best thing to do.

Hanukah this year of 2011 begins on December 20-21, which is the ninth month and 24-25th days as the book of Haggai predicts a great blessing on and a time to be strong. Is that date when Israel attacks Iran and then three and a half days later Iran attacks Israel on December 23-25, 2011? See Revelation 11. December 8-16, 2012 is Hanukah in 2012. Will we see these events then or on December 20-21-22, 2012 as the ancient Mayans believed or in December or the other dates given in this chapter in 2012-2013?

The "by and by" "wars and rumors of wars then earthquakes, famines and pestilence's" of Matthew 24:6-8 and Luke 21:9-11 might just mean these rumors of wars (2011-2012) and wars with Iran by 2012-2013, along with the two wars with Iraq (1991 and 2003) that have already happened years ago and the one in Afghanistan that is still happening now (2012). Then the "by and by" or two years later a great earthquake and volcano eruption that causes a great tidal wave, famines and great pestilence's (2015) that causes many deaths and many to think the end has come, but the end is not yet at that time two years from 2013 (=2013+2=2015). Then years (2016-2018-2019 or later) after that people will begin to think and mock and scoff God, Christians and the Bible of all those things that happened and no Rapture, Second Coming, the end, or the Kingdom of God has come after all those people died (fathers fell asleep) in the wars and by the tidal waves. See II Peter 3:2-7.

Proverbs 30:30-31 predicts a lion that no one can stand up against and a greyhound (=dog) and he-goat in the Old King James Version as Years and times of predicted end time events. In the NIV version it translated "greyhound" as "rooster." Was this a prediction of a lion a Leo born President of the U.S. kills Bin Laden who was reported to be born in 1957, which is the Chinese Year of the Rooster? President Obama was born August 4 making him a Leo sign born the sign of the lion. As for the "greyhound and he-goat" in those verses it could of given important years for the U.S. and President Obama or someone else. Those years would be 2018-2019 the Chinese Year of the Dog (=greyhound) and its polar opposite the Dragon in 2012 and the he-goat as the Chinese Year of the Sheep in 2015 on August 10 (=Leo the lion sign). President Obama born in the lion sign in 1961 is the Chinese Year of the Ox which is a bull or Taurus the bull sign in which sign Bin Laden (=Rooster=1957= Rabbit=2011 polar opposite) was killed on May 1-2, 2011 the Chinese Rabbit and Taurus the bull sign (=May 1-2).

Matthew 24:37-39 predicts the end times to be as "the days of Noah" when people went about the cares of life and suddenly the flood (=tidal wave and/or hurricane) came and took them all away. On August 10, 2015 people will be on summer vacations enjoying the beach and the cares of this life when the tidal wave strikes the Eastern U.S. sea board and Florida from Miami to Boston and takes them all away. I don't know if we have tidal wave warnings in the eastern U.S., but even if we do they still would be caught in massive traffic jams trying to get away. If the tidal wave strikes at night or early morning then all might be swept away by it suddenly and unaware as they sleep just as predicted a thief in the night.

In January of 2012 there were solar storms and flares on the sun that caused great Northern lights seen on NBC evening news for several nights. Will seven years later (2012+7=2019) in January we see again these same events and the sun becoming seven times brighter along with the moon and stars as the books of Isaiah and Revelation predicted? Will there also be other strange events in the skies as Luke 21:25 predicted and a solar and lunar eclipses then (=January of 2019) as Revelation 6:12- 13 predicted? And/or will strange darkness come in the heavens and/or by volcano eruptions off the west coast of Africa and/or the U.S. in Yellowstone or Mount Saint Helens right after the tidal waves and/or storms (seas and waves roaring) in 2015 or January of 2019 as Revelation and Isaiah also predicted?

Luke 21:25-26 predictions of signs in the sun, moon and stars and seas and waves roaring and men's hearts failing them for fear maybe because of these events mentioned above. And nations in distress could mean tidal waves, Nor'Easters, storms and hurricanes hitting the Northeast U.S. and/or the United States Southeast or out in the Atlantic Ocean in January of 2019 when the above events are happening and then the sun goes into a supernova shaking the powers of the heavens as Luke 21:26 predicted. It could also mean these events of storms and tidal waves (=seas and waves roaring) in 2012-2015 along with these signs in the sun, moon and stars with wars and attacks happening. Or they all happen in January of 2019. Here are these predictions:

"And there shall be signs in the sun, and in the moon, and in the stars; and upon the earth distress of nations, with perplexity; the sea and the waves roaring;

Men's hearts failing them for fear, and for looking after those things, which are coming on the earth; for the powers of heaven shall be shaken." Luke 21:25-26 (Old King James Version).

I once watch a network two hour documentary in the 1990's about ancient prophecies. They had a American Indian on it who made predictions. She predicted in the end that the seasons would be all mixed up. Hal Lindsey in one of his books in the 1970's said there would be strange weather conditions in the end times. In June of 2010 or 2011 the people in the Northeast U.S. called it June-u-ary after June and January because June of that year was so cold like January, but it was June the beginning of summer. In January of 2012 NBC evening news mentioned again June-u-ary because most of the whole country was warm like summer in June when it was winter in January. Over 2800 records were broken. The seasons were all mixed up exactly as the American Indian predicted.

On another show recently they discovered that an American Indian prophecy of a "web" happening in the end times. They claim this could be WWW as the world wide web that connects the whole world to the internet.

Note: The parts written above from my book "Predictions for 2011-2019" is also interesting showing names of serial killers that Nostradamus and the Bible predicted exactly along with great heat, drought and hail in the mid-west (=Plains) and the West Coast.

This is a book excerpt from the book "The Boy Who Could Predict Earthquakes" by Kurt B. Bakley available at this web site: WWW.Authorhouse.Com. It was written by February 14, 2010.

Introduction

This book is about the predictions of earthquakes over the next five years from 2010 to 2015. The places and times are given by code from the Bible, Nostradamus and other sources. The dates could be plus or minus 21 days as Daniel 10:13 states. The times may not be the exact times. They also maybe where the writer was writing them from, for example, me in the eastern U.S. making the times eastern standard time or eastern daylight time. They also could be from Israel, France and England where the Bible was written and Nostradamus wrote from and Universal time starts at in England. It is also possible the times are in the places where the quakes strike.

Where I got the exact times for some of these earthquakes is from the Bible, dreams, visions and angel visitations. They are 12:18 or 1:18 a.m. according to Matthew 25:1-13, 3 p.m. the ninth hour when Christ died on the cross, see Matthew 27:46, 51, 12 midnight according to Acts 16:25-26, 12 noon as predicted in Psalms 37:6 and Isaiah 16:3, Isaiah 59:10, 7:18 p.m. and 6:38 p.m. by angel visitation on January 4, 1983 see chapter 6, _2:43 p.m. see the movie Psycho_, morning see Isaiah 58:8 and Amos 5:8, 8:11 p.m. my birth time, 8:08 p.m. a dream time I had, 11:10-11:11 a.m. when my dad died and times of new moons, first quarters-last quarters and full moons at Universal time or eastern time or some other time zone. And the polar opposites of each those times from a.m. to p.m. and p.m. to a.m. are also possible and also polar opposite of say 1:18 is 1:48. And each Chinese Year from 2010-2015 are given two hour time periods different in each year when these quakes and other events could happen.

Earthquakes in the Greek dictionary of the Strong's Concordance of the Bible can mean "tempest" and "commotion" and "air or gale of wind". This could mean that there are not only these earthquakes, but also storms, attacks, wars, volcano eruptions, flooding, drought, heat, cold, wild fires, hail, tidal waves, plane crashes, inventions failing, strange events in the skies, like comets, asteroids, nova's and signs in the sun, moon and stars, and strange events with electricity and any other man made or natural destruction during these years as a woman in labor pains as Matthew 24:7-8 predicted causing the earth and air (heavens) to shake. The word "sorrows" in verse 8 of Matthew chapter 24 means "labor pains" of a woman. In our astrology the woman is Virgo the Virgin who is given the number 5 in numerology and is ruled by Mercury that is Latin for our day of Wednesday. And the moon in the Greek dictionary for earthquakes or commotions is Latin for our day of Monday. Revelation 6:12-13, Joel and Acts chapters 2 predict end time events as happening when the sun and moon are darkened. This could be caused by fires caused by the earthquakes, attacks, wars or what ever. And that these events happen on a new moon or full moon on a Wednesdays or Mondays during the years of 2010-2015. Solar and lunar eclipses could be what darken the sun and moon or the earthquakes and/or other events darkens the sun, moon and stars. See Deuteronomy 32:22-23, Luke

21:9-11, 25, Joel and Acts chapters 2, Haggai 2:17, Isaiah 42:25, Psalms 99:8, Daniel 11:19-21, Daniel 2:19-21, Daniel 7:25, Mark 13:5- 37, Revelation 8:10-13, 11:13, 19, 16:8-10, 18-19, 21, and Ecclesiastes 12:2-7.

The 10 virgins with five wise and five foolish could mean ten as the last two digits of our year 2010 plus five years (five wise virgins) till 2015. The five wise and five foolish virgins could also mean polar opposites of those years in May and November of 2010-2015 when predicted events happen. Wise is polar opposite of foolish as our month of May is polar opposite our month of November.

The book of Habakkuk in the Bible predicts "in the midst of the years" and a certain time from attacking the Chaldeans or the Iraqis (Babylon.) The year 2015 is in the midst of that decade. And when you add Daniel 12:11-12 days of 1290 and 1335 days together it equals 2625 days from when Iraq (Chaldeans) was attacked by ground forces on March 20-21, 2003 till events on May 29-30, 2010. Those days don't count leap year days. See Habakkuk 1:6, 2:1-4, 3:2.

The famines and pestilence's predicted Matthew 24:7-8 maybe caused by the earthquakes or other events just mentioned. They also could be new diseases caused by animals or insects at this time as Revelation 6:8 predicts. Plagues of insects and animals that hurt or kill could also come during these years. And murder trials of great notice can take place with a verdict and storm hitting a certain place with the first letter of the first name of the murderer as the storm's first letter of their first name. The storm, could hit at the time or near the time of the verdict. See Jeremiah 30:11, 23-24? Will we see a storm hit Central

Florida named after "C" after the trial and verdict is given in the Casey Anthony trial? And will we see a "T" named storm in 2015 named after Ted the Unabomber happen then? That would finish the prophecy of four named serial killers and the storms connected to them. The exact words "measure" and "whirlwind" in Jeremiah 30:11, 23-24 means "verdict," guilty or not, and hurricane in Hebrew.

Chinese astrology has 12 signs to it that rule the whole year and not just a month. They repeat every 12 years and are connected to predicted events that happen in the past in that same Chinese Year sign. That's why I mentioned them because they predict future events according to the Chinese sign of that year and years past in that same sign today. For example, the San Francisco earthquake in 1906 was the Chinese Year of the Horse, the same as 2014 is the Chinese Year of the Horse when another great San Francisco earthquake may happen.

Chinese astrology also rules hours. Each of its 12 signs rule a two hour period over a 24 hour day (2x12=24). This too relates to future events by a Chinese year being ruled by those two hour periods. For example, the Chinese Horse rules the hours of 11 a.m. to 1 p.m. Is that when the San Francisco earthquake happens in 2014?

The years 2010-2015 rules in Chinese astrology the Years 1999-2003. Psalms 99:8 equals our year 1999 when Nostradamus predicted something falling from the sky in the seventh month. Add 12 years to that and it equals 2011-2012 when there could be an air plane crash, helicopter crash, comet or asteroid crash here or on other planets and moons and some kind of invention failure that could pollute the waters. A nuclear power plant melt down? See Revelation chapters 8-9, Psalms 99:8, Daniel 11:19-21, Amos 2:14, Zechariah chapter 11, Obadiah 1-6, Revelation chapter 8-9 and 12, and Nostradamus C10:Q72. The seventh months in Nostradamus' quatrain C10:Q72 being plural could mean July or <u>March-April</u> and/or September-October to our calendar or the Bible or Jewish civil calendars. Are the dates July 16-17 and/or August 28-29, 2011-2012 when these events happen? Or September 27, October 15 and March 20-26 and April 6, 10-16? If the plane crash is that of someone famous and is over the ocean their bodies may never be found and it is an accident by lightning, electricity or some mechanical failure, but is not caused by war or anger. See Daniel 11:19- 22.

The year 2000 plus 12 years equals 2012 when electronics and electricity may see failure or troubles around the turn of the century in December of 2011 or 2012. Hosea 6:2 predicts a time when the second millennium passes and the third begins which is December into January 1999-2000-2001 plus 12 equals 2011-2012=2013. It is also a time of the resurrection of someone in December-January of 2011-2012-2013 as Matthew 12:39- 45, Daniel chapter 7 and Revelation chapter 13 predicts.

The year 2001 plus 12 equals 2013 when strange events are seen in the sky. It could be comets, asteroids, sun flares or some strange sun disturbances, a strange darkness, strange lights, seasons all mixed up, time and calendar changes, star nova's seen in night and day and any other signs in the sun, moon and stars as Luke 21:25 predicted with trouble on earth d stormy seas. Amos 8:1-6 predicted this in June of 2013 as when there is a new moon, Sabbath Day (Saturday or Sunday) and summer begins and the scales are part of the prophecy. The scales are Libra that rules in September-October-November and could mean those months and/or a Libra zone or city ruled place where these events happen. The polar opposite Libra is Aries that rule from March 21 to April 19 and begins with spring when the leaves of the trees form. See Matthew 24:32 and Luke 21:29-32. The Libra time in Chinese astrology is 7-9 p.m.

The year 2002 plus 12 years equals our year 2014 when trouble in Asia happens in June as Nostradamus predicted in C6:Q24 predicted for June 21, 2002 (+12=June 21, 2014).

The last year was 2003 plus 12 equals 2015 when in late September troubles could occur. September 27, 2003 was a time of a new moon, Jewish Sabbath (Saturday) and the Jewish New Year Rosh Hashanah. Nothing happened then but it may just be a "shadow of things to come" as Colossians 2:16-17 predicts for September 27, 2015 or on Rosh Hashanah of that year.

The 12 years added to each of those years is after the 12 year cycle of Chinese astrology signs that repeat every 12 years and marks when future events may happen in those coming years.

In several of Nostradamus quatrains he mentions "milk" when predicting disasters or trouble. See C2:Q46. I often wondered what in the world did he mean by "milk?" Then when putting together Appendix A: The Codes I found that each full Moon of each month every year are given certain names. The full Moon of May is called "The full Milk Moon." Was he predicting these earthquakes and other events happening in May or its polar opposite month of November from 2010-2015? May is our fifth month making milk the number 5 and five years of trouble from 2010 to 2015 in the months of May or November.

Nine years (=27-2+7=9=Moon=Cancer sign) after the Moon or a Cancer born U.S. President (Bush born July 6, the Cancer sign= moon) the cycle is over and the Sun (=Leo=President Obama) takes over and the antichrist (Bin Laden) destroys three (Obama, Biden, Hillary) nine years after September 11, 2001 when President Bush started the war on terror trouble will ccur in 2010 (2001+9=2010.) Then a new leader will arise different then the first or is a woman being Nancy Pelosi or Sarah Palin or some one else, man or woman. See Nostradamus C8:Q77 and C1:Q48, Daniel chapter 7 and Zechariah 11:8-17.

Nostradamus also predicted in these quatrains C2:Q5 and C2:Q41 may predict an earthquake and/or a terrorist attack by submarine with a nuclear missile on Rome, Italy or Washington, D.C. The star burning for seven days and the sun double when a large Dog (mastiff) is seen the Pope or U.S. leader changes his abode (dies) could refer to the seven stars of Taurus that are seen in April-May of 2010-2012. The double sun could mean two times 12 or 24 years from when Halley's comet was seen as a double sun or near the sun in 1986. Twenty four years added to 1986 equals 2010-2011. Why two times 12 are used is because "double" equals two and the sun equals Pisces, which is the number 12 as 2x12=24. See Appendix A. The large dog mention in C2:Q41 would be between March-August as Canis (dog=mastiff) Major (Large) just as quatrain predicts. The documents in C2:Q5 with people going under the sea to the Italian shore to make war may mean a book predicts this. Is March 23 the date of this event? Remember Italy and Rome are a spiritual Babylon and can mean the U.S. as well as Rome and Iraq. The dog mentioned in this quatrain may mean the Chinese Dog time of 7-9 p.m. or a.m. and/or a place ruled by Libra or Aries in our astrology or the astrology zones.

There may be other great earthquakes besides the ones we read about in this book. Already there was a great earthquake in Haiti on January 12, 2010 and there possibly will be others in different places in the years 2010-2015 besides the ones predicted in this book just as Matthew 24:7-8 predicted there would be earthquakes in divers (different) places increasing in numbers and size as a woman in labor pains for five years from 2010-2015.

Kurt B. Bakley

February 14, 2010. Note see my book "The Seven Thunders" pages 21, 25, 60, 72-73, 87 for more documentation of this plane crash that went missing at 1:19 a.m. local time I was a minute off at 1:18 a.m. See my book "End Time Signs II" for where I got that exact time. And see the introduction of my book entitled "The boy who could predict earthquakes" (seen above) and "The Seven Thunders" for more details and documentation. As for the Japan earthquake it in the movie *Psycho* was a Friday the 11th at 2:43 p.m. as to the time the movie starts. This introduction predicts earthquakes that cause nuclear melt downs. March 11, 2011 was a Friday and at 2:46 p.m. a great earthquake and tidal wave hits Japan and causes nuclear power plants melt down exactly as predicted. I was three minutes off. The above also predicted the oilrig fire and disaster in the Gulf or Mexico that happened on April 20, 2010. I predicted several dates in April but when I was about to type in April 20 a agent's voice kept saying you give to many ways and possibilities and did not write April 20. Later that year on April 20, 2010 the Oilrig broke and man's invention failed as predicted. As to me giving to many possibilities and dates that's the way prophecy is written some words come true and some words fail and some words fail now but later come true on those many different dates. See Colossians 2:16-17 and I Corinthians chapter 13. No one can be a 100 per cent true in prophecy. My friend said Nostradamus was estimated to be 50 percent which is high if correct. I estimate my predictions coming true up to now at about 25 percent. These different dates and events I write about are like Matthew chapter 24 where Jesus predicts the end and His Second Coming. In that chapter spring, summer, winter and fall are all mentioned as the one time event. It also gives many different events as well as those many dates for one event. That is fact not theory. The ignorant must learn that!

My book "The Seven Thunders" written by February 14, 2010 predicted that a plane accident or some event like the oilrig leak would happen on April 20, 2010 (=the oilrig leak) and March 8, 2014 as to when flight 370 went missing. Here are those predictions from that book:

"…March 7-8-21, April 19-20…2014…These dates are also dates of these events and the other great events predicted in this book and in my other books…A lightning strike may hit his plane or some type of mechanical failure happens, but it is not in war or anger that the prophecy tells 9of… March 6-7-8…2014- 2015…March 6-7-8, 2014-2017…"

See my book "The Seven Thunders" pages 25, 72, 87 for the documentation of these predicted events of the Oilrig leakage on April 20, 2010 and flight 370 went missing on March 8, 2014. I also predict in one of my books how July 16-17 is a time of bad omens in the sky. TWA flight 800, the comet that hit Jupiter on July 17, JFK, Jr. July 16-17 and now flight 17 shot out of the air over Ukraine the same as its flight number and date July 17, 2014.

About the Author

Kurt Brian Bakley was born 8:11 p.m., Friday evening, October 15, 1954, at Cooper Hospital in Camden, New Jersey, across the river from Philadelphia during Hurricane Hazel. He grew up hating books, reading, and writing because of his eye problems and learning disabilities and dropped out of high school. Then one Saturday night when he was twenty-one years old, after partying that night, he woke up early Sunday morning with a massive amount of knowledge and yearning to read, write, and research all kinds of knowledge. He went out first thing that Sunday morning to the mall and waited till noon for the bookstore to open. He immediately went in and bought several books and began his reading, writing, and researching to this day. That was on August 29 of 1976, and today (2014), he is still reading, writing, and researching information on prophecy and Christianity. His twenty books from 2001 that he's written are all available by September 27, 2015. All twenty books are available at this web site: www.authorhouse.com.